BOOKS BY MARIO PUZO

FICTION

The Dark Arena

The Fortunate Pilgrim

The Godfather

Fools Die

The Sicilian

The Fourth K

The Last Don

NONFICTION

The Godfather Papers

Inside Las Vegas

CHILDREN'S BOOK

The Runaway Summer of Davie Shaw

THE FORTUNATE PILGRIM

MARIO PUZO

THE FORTUNATE PILGRIM

Fawcett Columbine
The Ballantine Publishing Group • New York

A Fawcett Columbine Book
Published by The Ballantine Publishing Group

Copyright © 1964, 1992, 1997 by Mario Puzo

This work was originally published in 1964 by Atheneum Books, a division of Simon & Schuster, Inc. This edition is published by arrangement with the author and Random House, Inc.

http://www.randomhouse.com

Library of Congress Catalog Card Number: 98-96096

ISBN: 0-449-00358-2

Typographic title design by S. Neil Fujita
Cover photo: UPI/Corbis-Betmann

Manufactured in the United States of America

First Ballantine Books Edition: August 1998

10 9 8 7 6 5

For my Family and Norman

At the bottom of the heart of every human being from earliest infancy until the tomb there is something that goes on indomitably expecting—in the teeth of all crimes committed, suffered, and witnessed—that good and not evil will be done to him. It is this above all that is sacred in every human being.

—Simone Weil

PREFACE

I CONSIDER MY second book, *The Fortunate Pilgrim,* my best novel and my most personal one. It proved also to be my most interesting book because it was full of surprises.

When I began, the plan was to make myself the hero. It was supposed to be the story of a struggling writer, poorest of the poor, whose mother, sister, and brothers were enemies of his art, and how, in the end, he succeeded in spite of them. It was written to show my rejection of my Italian heritage and my callow disdain of those illiterate peasants from which I sprang.

But what a surprise it was when I discovered that my mother turned out to be the hero of the book. And that my sister was more honest, trustworthy, and braver than me. Through the writing, those immigrant Italians who worked twelve hours a day in gray, sweat-soaked fedoras, wearing great handlebar mustaches, had the dignity of heroes. How it happened, I never knew.

All young writers dream of immortality—that hundreds of years in the future the new generations will read their books and find their lives changed, as my life was after reading *The Brothers Karamazov* at the age of fifteen. I vowed I would never write a word that was not absolutely true to myself. And I felt I had achieved that in *The Fortunate Pilgrim.* I assumed that such a writer would automatically become rich and famous.

I received marvelous reviews. But then came the next surprise: Nothing happened. I didn't become rich and famous. In fact, I was poorer than before; I had to work two jobs instead of one.

I was furious, but only at myself. I rethought my whole life. Why should the public care that I put so much of myself into that book, so much care into each sentence? Why should my family care about my writing when it didn't earn my daily bread? Why should they indulge my eccentricity? And the public, why should they care about tragedies that didn't reflect their own experience? I concluded that I had worked ten years of my life in sheer self-indulgence. I thought myself that most despised figure in Italian culture, a "chooch"—that is, a man who could not earn a living for himself or his family.

But then came another surprise. In reaction to my disappointment, and to feed my family, I decided to write a bestseller. And to use some stories that my mother—who is *Pilgrim*'s heroine, Lucia Santa—told us as we were growing up. That book was *The Godfather*. It took me four years to write, still working two jobs. But it accomplished my aim. It was a bestseller, and this time I became rich and famous. I had done the right thing.

But there were more surprises to come. Whenever the Godfather opened his mouth, in my own mind I heard the voice of my mother. I heard her wisdom, her ruthlessness, and her unconquerable love for her family and for life itself, qualities not valued in women at the time. The Don's courage and loyalty came from her; his humanity came from her. Through my characters, I heard the voices of my sisters and brothers, with their tolerance of human frailty. And so, I know now, without Lucia Santa, I could not have written *The Godfather*.

It is thirty years since I wrote *The Fortunate Pilgrim*. The changes in the culture, and the change in women's roles, as well as the growing interest in ethnic subjects, have made this book in many ways contemporary. The human experience, I hope, is timeless.

I am immensely flattered that Random House is republishing it after all this time. That it still holds its power, maybe more now than then.

I've reread the book and I still love it, and most of all I love my mother and hold her in true reverence. She lived a life of tragedy and still embraced life. She is, I can see from this vantage point, in every one of the books I have written. And I know now I am not the hero of my life, she is. All these years later, her tragedies still make me weep. And the book cries out, "Behold how she was wronged."

—Mario Puzo
November 1996

PART
ONE

L ARRY ANGELUZZI SPURRED his jet-black horse
proudly through a canyon formed by two great walls of
tenements, and at the foot of each wall, marooned on their
separate blue-slate sidewalks, little children stopped their
games to watch him with silent admiration. He swung his red
lantern in a great arc; sparks flew from the iron hoofs of his
horse as they rang on railroad tracks, set flush in the stones of
Tenth Avenue, and slowly following horse, rider and lantern
came the long freight train, inching its way north from St.
John's Park terminal on Hudson Street.

In 1928 the New York Central Railroad used the streets of
the city to shuttle trains north and south, sending scouts on
horseback to warn traffic. In a few more years this would end,
an overhead pass built. But Larry Angeluzzi, not knowing he
was the last of the "dummy boys," that he would soon be a tiny
scrap of urban history, rode as straight and arrogantly as any
western cowboy. His spurs were white, heavy sneakers, his
sombrero a peaked cap studded with union buttons. His blue

4 • MARIO PUZO

dungarees were fastened at the ankle with shiny, plated bicycle clips.

He cantered through the hot summer night, his desert a city of stone. Women gossiped on wooden boxes, men puffed cigars of the De Nobili while standing on street corners, children risked their lives in dangerous play, leaving their blue-slate islands to climb on the moving freight train. All moved in the smoky yellow light of lamp posts and the naked white-hot bulbs of candy-store windows. At every intersection a fresh breeze from Twelfth Avenue, concrete bank of the Hudson River, refreshed horse and rider, cooled the hot black engine that gave warning hoots behind them.

At 27th Street the wall on Larry Angeluzzi's right fell away for a whole block. In the cleared space was Chelsea Park placed with dark squatting shapes, kids sitting on the ground to watch the free outdoor movies shown by Hudson Guild Settlement House. On the distant giant white screen, Larry Angeluzzi saw a monstrous horse and rider, bathed in false sunlight, thundering down upon him, felt his own horse rise in alarm as its tossing head caught sight of those great ghosts; and then they were past the intersection of 28th Street, and the wall had sprung up again.

Larry was nearly home. There was the pedestrian bridge that spanned Tenth Avenue on 30th Street; when he passed beneath that bridge he would be home, his work done. He set his cap at a jauntier angle, rode straight in the saddle. All the people sitting on the sidewalk from 30th to 31st Streets were relatives and friends. Larry made his horse gallop.

He passed swiftly beneath the bridge, waved to the children leaning on its rails above his head. He made his horse rear up for the people on the sidewalk on his right, then turned the animal left into the open railroad yards that formed a great spark-filled plain of steel down to the Hudson River.

Behind him the huge black engine chugged white clouds of steam, and as if by magic, the bridge and its children vanished, leaving behind them thin beautiful screams of delight rising to the pale, almost invisible stars. The freight train curved into the yards, the bridge reappeared, and scores of damp children hurtled down the stairways to run along the Avenue.

Larry tied his horse to the hitching post by the switchman's shanty and sat on the bench against the shanty wall. On the other side of the Avenue, painted on a flat screen, the familiar world he loved came alive inch by inch.

The brightly lit bakery was near the corner of 30th Street, its festooned lemon-ice stand surrounded by children. The *Panettiere* himself filled white-ridged paper cups with cherry-red, pale-yellow and glittering-white crystals of ice. He scooped generous portions, for he was rich and even went to race tracks to squander his money.

Next to the bakery, toward 31st Street, was the grocery, its windows filled with yellow logs of provolone in shiny, waxy skins and prosciutto hams, meaty triangles hanging in gaily colored paper. Then there was the barber shop closed for business but open for card playing, the jealous barber even now alert for any freshly cut heads that did not bear the mark of his scissors. Children covered the pavement, busy as ants, women, almost invisible in black, made little dark mounds before each tenement door. From each mound a buzzing hum of angry gossip rose to the summer, starry sky.

The dwarf-like switchman came from the tracks and said, "No more trains tonight, kid." Larry unhitched his horse, mounted, then made the animal turn and rear up.

As the horse rose in the air, the row of tenements, the western wall of the great city, billowed, tilted toward Larry like some fragile canvas. In the open window of his own home, on the top floor of the tenement directly opposite, Larry saw the dark shape of what must be his little brother Vincent. Larry waved but there was no answering motion until he waved again. In the wall there were only a few scattered panes of yellow light. Everyone was down on the street, everyone was

watching him. He struck his horse across the neck and galloped up the cobblestones of Tenth Avenue to the stable on
35th Street.

Earlier that evening, in twilight, when Larry Angeluzzi
saddled his horse in St. John's Park, his mother, Lucia Santa
Angeluzzi-Corbo, also mother of Octavia and Vincenzo Angeluzzi, widow of Anthony Angeluzzi, now wife of Frank
Corbo and mother of his three children, by name Gino, Salvatore and Aileen, prepared to leave her empty flat, escape the
choking summer heat, spend her evening with neighbors in
quarreling gossip and, most of all, to guard her children playing in the darkness of the city streets.

Lucia Santa was at ease tonight, for summer was the good
time—the children never ill with colds or fevers, no worries
about warm coats, gloves, boots for the winter snow and extra
money for school supplies. Everyone rushed through supper to
escape the airless rooms and move with the tide of life in the
streets; there were no evening quarrels. The house was easily
kept clean since it was always empty. But, best of all for Lucia
Santa, her own evenings were free; the street was a meeting
place and summer was a time when neighbors became friends.
So now, heavy jet-black hair combed into a bun, wearing a
clean black dress, she picked up the backless kitchen chair and
went down the four flights of stairs to sit on the Avenue.

EACH TENEMENT WAS a village square; each had its
group of women, all in black, sitting on stools and boxes and
doing more than gossip. They recalled ancient history, argued
morals and social law, always taking their precedents from the
mountain village in southern Italy they had escaped, fled from
many years ago. And with what relish their favorite imagin-
ings! Now: What if their stern fathers were transported by
some miracle to face the problems *they* faced every day? Or
their mothers of the quick and heavy hands? What shrieks if
they as daughters had dared as these American children dared?
If *they* had presumed.

The women talked of their children as they would of strangers. It was a favorite topic, the corruption of the innocent by the new land. Now: Felicia, who lived around the corner of 31st Street. What type of daughter was she who did not cut short her honeymoon on news of her godmother's illness, the summons issued by her own mother? A real whore. No no, they did not mince words. Felicia's mother herself told the story. And a son, poor man, who could not wait another year to marry when his father so commanded? Ahhh, the disrespect. *Figlio disgraziato.* Never could this pass in Italy. The father would kill his arrogant son; yes, kill him. And the daughter? In Italy—Felicia's mother swore in a voice still trembling with passion, though this had all happened three years ago, the godmother recovered, the grandchildren the light of her life—ah, in Italy the mother would pull the whore out of her bridal chamber, drag her to the hospital bed by the hair of her head. Ah, Italia, Italia; how the world changed and for the worse. What madness was it that made them leave such a land? Where fathers commanded and mothers were treated with respect by their children.

Each in turn told a story of insolence and defiance, themselves heroic, long-suffering, the children spitting Lucifers saved by an application of Italian discipline—the razor strop or the *Tackeril.* And at the end of each story each woman recited her requiem. *Mannaggia America!*—Damn America. But in the hot summer night their voices were filled with hope, with a vigor never sounded in their homeland. Here now was money in the bank, children who could read and write, grandchildren who would be professors if all went well. They spoke with guilty loyalty of customs they had themselves trampled into dust.

The truth: These country women from the mountain farms of Italy, whose fathers and grandfathers had died in the same rooms in which they were born, these women loved the clashing steel and stone of the great city, the thunder of trains in the railroad yards across the street, the lights above the Palisades far across the Hudson. As children they had lived in solitude, on land so poor that people scattered themselves singly along the mountain slopes to search out a living.

Audacity had liberated them. They were pioneers, though they never walked an American plain and never felt real soil beneath their feet. They moved in a sadder wilderness, where the language was strange, where their children became members of a different race. It was a price that must be paid.

In all this Lucia Santa was silent. She waited for her friend and ally, Zia Louche. She rested, gathering up her strength for the long hours of happy quarreling that lay ahead. It was still early evening, and they would not return to their homes before midnight. The rooms would not be cool before then. She folded her hands in her lap and turned her face to the gentle breeze that blew from the river below Twelfth Avenue.

A small, round, handsome woman, Lucia Santa stood at the height of her powers in health, mental and physical; courageous and without fear of life and its dangers. But not foolhardy, not reckless. She was strong, experienced, wary and alert, well-equipped for the great responsibility of bringing a large family to adulthood and freedom. Her only weakness was a lack of that natural cunning and shrewdness which does so much more for people than virtue.

When she was only seventeen, over twenty years ago, Lucia Santa had left her home in Italy. She traveled the three thousand miles of dark ocean to a strange country and a strange people and began a life with a man she had known only when they had played together as innocent children.

Shaking her head at her own madness, yet with pride, she often told the story.

There had come a time when her father, with stern pity, told her, his favorite daughter, that she could not hope for bridal linen. The farm was too poor. There were debts. Life promised to be even harder. There it was. There could be found only a husband witless with love.

In that moment she had lost all respect for her father, for

her home, for her country. A bride without linen was shame-ful, shameful as a bride rising from an unbloodied nuptial bed; worse, for there could be no recourse to slyness, no timing of the bridal night near the period of flood. And even that men had forgiven. But what man would take a woman with the stigma of hopeless poverty?

Only the poor can understand the shame of poverty, greater than the shame of the greatest sinner. For the sinner, vanquished by his own other self, is in one sense the victor. But the poor are truly vanquished: by their world, by their *padrones,* by fortune and by time. They are beggars always in need of charity. To the poor who have been poor for centuries, the nobility of honest toil is a legend. Their virtues lead them to humiliation and shame.

But Lucia Santa was helpless, though her sulky, adolescent rage endured. Then a letter from America; a boy from the neighboring farm, her companion when they were both little children, wrote and asked her to join him in a new land. It was all done correctly through both fathers. Lucia Santa tried to remember the boy's face.

And so one sunny Italian day Lucia Santa and two other village maidens were escorted to the town hall and then to the church by their weeping parents, aunts, and sisters. The three girls went on board ship, brides by proxy, sailing from Naples to New York, by law Americans.

IN A DREAM Lucia Santa entered a land of stone and steel, bedded that same night with a stranger who was her legal husband, bore that stranger two children, and was pregnant with the third when he carelessly let himself be killed in one of those accidents that were part of the building of the new con-tinent. She accepted all this without self-pity. She lamented, true, but that was not the same thing; she only begged fate for mercy.

So then, a pregnant widow, still young, with no one to turn to, she never succumbed to terror, despair. She had an enormous strength, not unusual in women, to bear adversity. But she was not a stone. Fate did not make her bitter; that was left to friends and neighbors—these very neighbors who so intimately shared the summer night.

Ahh, the young wives, the young mothers, all the other young Italian women in a strange land. What cronies they were. How they ran to each other's apartments, up and down the stairs, into the adjoining tenements. "*Cara* Lucia Santa, taste this special dish"—a platter of new sausage, Easter pie with wheat germ and clotted cheese and a crust glazed with eggs, or plump ravioli for a family saint's day, with a special meat and tomato sauce. What flutters, what compliments and cups of coffee and confidences and promises to be godmother to the yet-to-be-born infant. But after the tragedy, after the initial pity and condolences, the true face of the world showed itself to Lucia Santa.

Greetings were cold, doors were shut, prospective godmothers disappeared. Who wished to be friendly with a young, full-blooded widow? Husbands were weak, there would be calls for assistance. In the tenements life was close; a young woman without a man was dangerous. She could draw off money and goods as the leech draws blood. They were not malicious, they showed only the prudence of the poor, so easy to mock when there is no understanding of the fear which is its root.

One friend stood fast, Zia Louche, an old, childless widow, who came to help, stood godmother when the fatherless Vincenzo was born and bought her godson a beautiful gold watch when he was confirmed so that Lucia Santa could hold up her head! for such a magnificent present was a mark of respect and faith. But Zia Louche was the only one, and when mourning time had passed Lucia Santa saw the world with new and wiser eyes.

Time healed the wounds and now they were all friends again. Perhaps—who knows?—the young widow had been too harsh in her judgment, for these same neighbors, true, in their own self-interest, helped her find a second husband who would feed and clothe her children. There was a marriage in church. These same neighbors gave her a glorious wedding-night feast. But Lucia Santa never let the world deceive her again.

AND SO ON this heavy summer night, with her first batch of children grown and safe, her second batch of children no longer infants except for Lena, and with some money in the post office; now, after twenty years of struggle and a fair share of suffering, Lucia Santa Angeluzzi-Corbo stood on that little knoll of prosperity that the poor reach, reach with such effort that they believe the struggle is won and that with ordinary care their lives are safe. She had already lived a lifetime; the story was over.

ENOUGH. HERE CAME Zia Louche, completing the circle. Lucia Santa paid attention, prepared to enter the torrent of gossip. But she saw her daughter Octavia coming from the corner of 30th Street, past the *Panettiere* and his red glass box of pizza and pale tin cans of lemon ice. Then Lucia Santa lost sight of her daughter; for one blinding moment her eyes were filled by the *Panettiere*'s wooden tub, brimming with red coppers and gleaming silver fishes of dimes and nickels. She felt a quick, hot surge of passionate anger that she could never possess such treasure and that the ugly baker should find fortune so kind. Then she saw the *Panettiere*'s wife—old, mustached, no longer able to bear children—guarding that wooden tub of copper and silver, her wrinkled shell-lidded dragon eyes flashing fire in the summer light.

Lucia Santa felt Octavia sitting beside her on the backless chair; their hips and thighs touched. This always irritated the mother, but her daughter would be offended if she moved, so she accepted it. Seeing her daughter so oddly handsome, dressed in the American style, she gave the old crony Zia Louche a smile that showed both her pride and a hint of derisive irony. Octavia, dutifully silent and attentive, saw that smile and understood it, yet she was bewildered once again by her mother's nature.

As if her mother could understand that Octavia wanted to be everything these women were not! With the foolish and transparent cleverness of the young, she wore a powder-blue suit that hid her bust and squared the roundness of her hips. She wore white gloves, as her high school teacher had done. Her eyebrows were heavy and black, honestly unplucked. Hopelessly she compressed the full red lips to an imaginary sternness, her eyes quietly grave—and all to hide the drowning sensuality that had been the undoing of the women around her. For Octavia reasoned that satisfying the terrible dark need stilled all other needs and she felt a frightened pity for these women enchanted into dreamless slavery by children and the unknown pleasures of a marriage bed.

This would not be *her* fate. She sat with bowed head, listening, Judas-like; pretending to be one of the faithful, she planned treason and escape.

Now with only women around her, Octavia took off her jacket; the white blouse with its tiny red-ribboned tie was more seductive than she could ever know. No disguise could hide the full roundness of her bust. The sensual face, crown of blue-black curls and ringlets, great liquid eyes, all mocked the staidness of her dress. With malice she could not have made herself more provocative than she did in her innocence.

Lucia Santa took the jacket and folded it over her arm, an act of love that was maternal, that meant possession and dominance. But above all an act of reconciliation, for earler that evening mother and daughter had quarreled.

Octavia wanted to go to night school, study to become a teacher. Lucia Santa refused permission. No; she would become ill working and going to school. "Why? Why?" the mother asked. "You, such a beautiful dressmaker, you earn good money." The mother objected out of superstition. This course was known. Life was unlucky, you followed a new path at your peril. You put yourself at the mercy of fate. Her daughter was too young to understand.

Unexpectedly, shamefacedly, Octavia had said, "I want to be happy," and the older woman became a raging fury, contemptuous—the mother, who had always defended her daughter's toity ways, her reading of books, her tailored suits that were as affected as a lorgnette. The mother had mimicked Octavia in the perfect English of a shallow girl, *"You want to be happy."* And then in Italian, with deadly seriousness, "Thank God you are alive."

IN THE COOL evening air Octavia accepted her mother's act of peace, sat gracefully, hands folded in her lap. Remembering the quarrel, she mused on the mystery of her mother's speaking perfect English when mimicking her children. Out of the corner of her eye Octavia saw Guido, the dark son of the *Panettiere,* wavering through the warm summer night toward the light of her white blouse. In his dark, strong hand he bore a tall paper cup of fruit ice, lemon and orange, which he gave her, almost bowing, whispering hurriedly something that sounded like "Don't spoil your shirt," and then hurrying back to the stand to help his father. Octavia smiled, took a few mouthfuls out of politeness, and passed the cup to her mother, who had a passion for ices and sucked on the cup, greedy as a child. The buzz of the old women's voices went on.

Her stepfather turned the corner of 31st Street and entered the Avenue, wheeling the baby carriage before him. Octavia watched him go from 31st Street to 30th and back again. And as her mother's irony bewildered her, this tenderness of the stepfather confused her emotions. For she hated him as someone cruel, villainous, evil. She had seen him give blows to her mother, act the tyrant to his stepchildren. In the faded memories of Octavia's childhood his courting of her mother followed too swiftly the day of her real father's death.

She wanted to look at the sleeping baby, the little sister she loved passionately, though she was her stepfather's child. But she could not bear speaking to the man, looking into his cold blue eyes and harsh angular face. She knew her stepfather hated her as she hated him and that each feared the other. He had never dared strike her as he sometimes struck Vinnie. And she would not have minded his blows to his stepson if he had been paternal in other ways. But he brought presents for Gino and Sal and Aileen and never for Vincent, though Vincent was a child still. She hated him because he never took Vincent for walks or haircuts with his natural children. She feared him because he was strange—the evil mysterious stranger of story books, the blue-eyed Italian with the Mephistophelean face; and yet she knew that really he was an illiterate peasant, a poor, contemptible immigrant who gave himself airs. One day she had seen him on the subway pretending to read a newspaper. She had rushed to tell her mother, laughing, contemptuous. Her mother had only given her a curious smile and said nothing.

BUT NOW ONE of the black-clad women was telling a story about a villainous young Italian girl (born in America, naturally). Octavia attended. "Yes, yes," the woman said. "They were married for a month, they had finished with their honeymoon. Oh, she loved him. She sat on his lap in his mother's home. When they visited she played with his hand. Like this—" two gnarled hands with warty fingers linked themselves lovingly, obscenely, in the storyteller's lap—"and then they went to dance, in the church. The foolishness of those young priests who do not even speak Italian! Her husband won a prize for entering the door. He took the prize and dropped to the earth, dead. His poor heart, he was always sickly. His mother had always warned him, cared for him. But now. The young bride, dancing with another man, is told. Does she rush to the side of her beloved? She shrieks. She cried, 'No, no. I cannot.' She fears death like a child, not a woman. The loved one lies in his own piss alone, but *she* no longer loved him. She cries out, 'No, I will not look at it.' "

Slyly Zia Louche, her tongue rolling up both meanings, said, "Ah! You may be sure she looked at It when It was alive." A great burst of coarse laughter from all the women filled the Avenue, drawing jealous looks from other circles of women. Octavia was disgusted, angry that even her mother was smiling with delight.

To more serious things. Lucia Santa and Zia Louche stood fast against the rest of the circle on a point of ancient history, the exact details of a scandal twenty years ago across the sea in Italy. It amused Octavia to see her mother defer to Zia Louche and the old crone valiantly do battle for her mother, each of them treating the other like a duchess. Her mother turning to Zia Louche and asking respectfully, *"E vero, Comare?"* And Zia Louche always answering imperiously, *"Sì, Signora,"* showing no callow familiarity before the others. Octavia knew the relationship behind this, her mother's gratitude for that valuable alliance in the hour of her most terrible misfortune.

But the quarrel was too finely drawn and Octavia became bored. She got up to look at her baby half sister, staring down at the carriage, not greeting her stepfather. She gazed down at the baby girl with an overwhelming tenderness, an emotion she did not even feel for Vincent. Then she walked toward the corner of 31st Street to look for Gino, saw him playing, saw little Sal sitting on the curb. She took Sal back to his mother. Vinnie was missing. Looking up, she saw him far above her, sitting on the window sill of the apartment, dark, motionless, guarding them all.

Frank Corbo, somber, watched his big stepdaughter lean over his baby. Strange with blue eyes, object of amusement (what Italian male wheeled his baby in the summer night?), illiterate, his mind mute, he saw the beauty of the stone city in darkness, felt the hatred of his stepdaughter without returning hatred. The harsh thin face concealed a wordless and consuming anguish. His life was a dream of beauty felt and not understood, of love twisted into cruelty. Countless treasures went by like shadows, the world was locked away. In search of deliverance, he would leave the city tonight and desert his family. In the early morning hours, while it was still dark, he would meet a farm truck and disappear without a word, without quarreling or giving blows. He would work in the brown and green fields of summer, gain peace from love, restore his strength.

He suffered. He suffered as a deaf-mute suffers who would sing seeing beauty, who cannot cry out in pain. He felt love and could not give caresses. There were too many people sleeping in the rooms around him, too many beings walked the streets around him. He dreamed terrible dreams. Tapestried on black, his wife and children circled him round, and from their foreheads each drew a dagger. He had cried out.

It was late, late; the children should be in bed, but it was still too hot. Frank Corbo watched his son Gino run crazily in some sort of tagging game incomprehensible to the father, as was the child's American speech, as were the books and newspapers, the colors of the night sky, the beauty of the summer night and all the joys of the world he felt cut off from, all colored with pain. The world was a great mystery. Vast dangers that others could guard their children against would bring him and his loved ones into the dust. They would teach his children to hate him.

But still, the father, never knowing he would be saved, wheeled the carriage back and forth. Not knowing that deep down in his blood, in the tiny mysterious cells of his brain, a new world was forming. Slowly, day by day, pain by pain, beauty by lost beauty, the walls of the world he feared so much were crumbling in the timelessness of his mind, and in a year a new fantastic world would spring up, himself the god and king, his enemies startled and afraid, his loved ones forever lost and yet that loss of love not felt or mourned. A world of such chaotic pain that he would be drowned in ecstasy, mystery and fear banished. He would be free.

But it was like magic, and no hint or warning could come beforehand. Now, this night, he put his trust in one summer of tilling the earth, as he had done so long ago, a boy in Italy.

THE WORLD HAS a special light for children, and sounds are magical. Gino Corbo moved through the clang of engines, circles of mellow lamp-post lights, heard young girls laughing, and played his game so intently that his head ached. He ran back and forth across 31st Street, trying to capture other children or surround them. But someone always backed against a wall, hand outstretched. Once Gino was trapped, but a taxi cut his opponents off and he ran back to his own sidewalk. He saw his father watching and ran to him shouting, "Gimme a penny for lemon ice." Snatching the coin, he ran along Tenth Avenue and planned a beautiful trick. He tried to run past his mother and her friends. Zia Louche grabbed his arm and pulled him off his feet, her bony fingers a trap of steel.

His dazed, impatient eyes saw a circle of old women's faces, some hairy and mustached. Frantic to be away, afraid the game would end, Gino tried to run. Zia Louche held him like a fly, saying, "Rest—sit with your mother and rest. You'll be sick tomorrow. Feel how your heart is beating." And she put her withered claw upon his chest. He pulled violently. The old crone held him and said with ferocious love, *"Eh, come è faccia brutta."* He understood she was calling him ugly, and that made him still. He stared at the circle of women. They were laughing but Gino did not know they laughed with delight at his fierce desire, his blazing eyes.

He spat at Zia Louche, the fake spit of Italian women that shows contempt in a quarrel. It got him free, and he was so quick that his mother hit his face only a glancing blow as he sped away. Around the corner, along 30th Street to Ninth Avenue, up the Avenue to 31st Street, and then through 31st

Street to Tenth Avenue he would go; having traveled the four sides of the city block, he would swoop into the game out of the darkness and with one masterly stroke shatter the enemy.

But as he ran full speed toward Ninth Avenue, a line of alien boys formed a wall against him. Gino pumped his legs higher and faster and burst through, shattered them. Clutching hands tore his shirt, the wind rushed against his face. On Ninth Avenue the boys came after him, but when he turned into the darkness at the top of 31st Street they did not dare to follow. Gino stopped running and walked softly along the stoops. He was on the final side of the square and below him, at the foot of the street, near Tenth Avenue, painted into the dim yellow cones of light cast by lamp posts, his friends scurried to and fro like little black rats, still playing. He was in time.

He rested in darkness and then went very softly, slowly, down the street. In a basement room he saw a little girl leaning against a wall half white, half electric blue. She rested her head against her arm upon the wall, hiding her eyes from the cold, artificial light of the room, empty, deserted behind her. Gino knew she was playing hide and seek, not crying, and that if he waited, the deserted room would come magically alive with shrieking girls. But he did not stop, not knowing he would always remember the girl alone, hiding her eyes against a blue and white wall; desolate, never changing, as if by not stopping he left her there forever, enchanted. He went on.

A dim patch of light made him pause. He shivered. Sitting at the window, leaning out of her street-level flat, an old Irish crone rested her head on a furry pillow and watched him move past her down the empty silent street. In that weak yellow light her head was bony with age, her thin, whiskered mouth bloody with the light of a holy red candle. Behind that feral face, faintly visible in the shadows of her room, a vase, a lamp, and a graven image gleamed like old bones. Gino stared at her. The teeth bared in greeting. Gino ran.

Now he could hear the shouts of his friends; he was near the circles of light on Tenth Avenue. He crouched on the steps of a cellar, hidden, powerful, ready to strike. He never thought to be afraid of the dark basement below or of the night. He forgot his mother's anger. He existed only for this moment and the moment he would enter the pool of light and shatter it.

High over Tenth Avenue, Gino Corbo's half brother, Vincenzo Angeluzzi, thirteen years old, brooded to the softened, whispery sound of the summer night that floated up to him. He brooded on his window sill, the long line of rooms behind him dark and empty, the door from the hall to the kitchen securely locked. He was self-exiled.

The dream of summer, freedom, and play had been taken from him. His mother had informed him that in the morning he would start working for the *Panettiere,* and work until school started in the fall. He would carry heavy baskets of bread in the hot sun while other boys swam in the river, played stickball and "Johnny Ride the Pony," and hitched onto the backs of trolley cars to see the city. There would be no sitting in the shade eating lemon ice or reading by the wall of Runkel's factory or playing "Bankers and Brokers" and "Seven-and-a-half" for pennies.

A watcher on the western wall of the city, everything weighed down his soul and spirit, the wasteland of railroad yards, steel tracks, deserted box cars, engines giving off dirty red sparks and low hoots of warning. The Hudson was a black ribbon beneath the cragged Jersey shore.

He dozed on his window sill, and the babel of voices rose like a faint shout. Far down the Avenue he saw the red lantern of a dummy boy leading his freight train from St. John's Park. The children below him played on, and Vincent waited with gloomy satisfaction for their shouts of joy, savoring his bitterness at not sharing their pleasure. And then the children were screaming and scrambling up the steps of the bridge to wait for the damp cloud of steam that would make them invisible.

Vincent was too young to know that he was melancholy by nature, that this distressed his sister Octavia so that she brought him presents and candy. When he was a toddling infant Octavia used to take him into her bed, tell him stories, and sing songs so that he would go to sleep with a remembrance of smiles. But nothing could change his nature.

Below, he could hear Zia Louche quarreling shrilly and his mother's strong voice supporting her. The resentment came that this old crone was his godmother and that the five-dollar gold piece she gave him every birthday must be paid for with a kiss—a kiss he gave only to make his mother happy. He thought his mother beautiful, though she was fat and always dressed in black, and he always obeyed her.

But Zia Louche, ever since he could remember, had made him hate her. Long ago when he played on the kitchen floor between his mother's feet, Zia Louche would study him. The two women would be talking violently, without their public formality, recalling with gusto their misfortunes through the years. There would be a silence. The two women would look at him thoughtfully, sipping coffee. Then Zia Louche would sigh through age-browned teeth and say with hopeless, angry pity to the little boy, "Ah, *miserabile, miserabile*. Your father died before you were born."

That was the climax; the old crone went on to other things, leaving him bewildered and watching his mother's face go pale and her eyes turn red. She would reach down to touch him, but she never spoke.

Down in the street Vincent saw his sister Octavia get up to look at the baby. He hated her, too. She had betrayed him. She had not protested their mother's sending him to work. Then the dummy boy rode under the bridge, and Vincent saw his brother Larry riding like a real cowboy on a black horse.

Even from so far up he could hear a loud clatter of hoofs on cobblestones. The children disappeared and the bridge vanished in a cloud of steam from the engine. With a great shower of sparks, the train slid into the railroad yards.

It was late. The night air had cooled the city. His mother and the other women picked up their stools and crates, called to husbands and children. His stepfather wheeled the baby to the tenement door. It was time to get ready for bed.

Vincent left his window sill and went back through the bedrooms to the kitchen. He unlocked the door to the hallway, opening the house for his family. Then he took the thigh-sized loaf of Italian bread and sliced off three thick, crusty chunks. Over these he poured red wine vinegar, then thick, yellow-green olive oil. He stood back and scattered salt over all three, inspecting them with a satisfied air. The coarse bread was a lovely red dotted with blots of greasy green. Gino and Sal would be delighted with this bedtime snack. They would all eat together. He waited. From the street, through windows still open and coming down the corridor of rooms between, he heard Gino's voice in a loud continuous scream.

That scream froze Lucia Santa with the baby in her arms. Octavia, on the corner of 30th Street, turned toward 31st. Across the Avenue Larry wheeled around on his horse. The father, his temples bursting with fear, started to run and curse. But the child's scream was one of hysterical triumph. Gino had shot out of the darkness and circled his enemies and was screaming, "Burn the city, burn the city." So ending the game, he could not stop screaming the magic words or stop running. He aimed himself at his mother's enormous menacing figure with great leaps into the air, remembered his insult to Zia Louche, and swerved away, through the door and up the stairs.

Lucia Santa, with every intention of striking him to the ground, stood overwhelmed by a fierce pride and tenderness at her child's wild joy, the spirit that she must someday break. She let him pass unharmed.

The Neapolitan Italians dissolved from the dark streets and left the city to the clatter of hoofs on cobblestones as Larry Angeluzzi galloped his horse to the stable on 35th Street.

2

THE ANGELUZZI-CORBO family lived in the best tenement on Tenth Avenue. There was only one apartment to each of the four flights so windows opened to the west on Tenth Avenue and to the east on the backyards, giving cross-ventilation. The Angeluzzi-Corbos, by having the whole floor—and the top floor at that—were able to use the back of the hallway for extra storage space. The icebox, a bureau, countless cans of tomato paste, and boxes of macaroni were stacked against the wall, for though the apartment consisted of six rooms, they were crowded for space.

The apartment was shaped like a long *E* with the middle prong missing. The kitchen formed the lower shelf; then the dining room, the bedrooms and the living room, with its windows facing on Tenth Avenue, made the long vertical line; and Octavia's small, doored bedroom off the living room was the top prong of the *E*. Gino, Vinnie, and Sal slept in the living room on a bed that folded up into an upright dolly. This was put in a corner during the day and covered with a made-over drapery. The parents slept in the bedroom first on the line, and Larry in the next one. Then came the dining room, which was called the kitchen—it had a great wooden table, for eating and living—and at right angles to that was the real kitchen, with its boiler, sink, and stove. By the standards of the neighborhood, the apartment was wastefully commodious, and an example of Lucia Santa's unthriftiness.

OCTAVIA PUT BABY Aileen on her mother's bed and went into her own room to change into a house dress. When she came out the three boys were already sound asleep, their great bed having been unfolded onto the middle of the living room floor. She went down the corridor of rooms to the kitchen to wash her face. Her mother sat in the dining room, waiting, sipping a small glass of wine. Octavia knew her mother would stay up to finish their quarrel and that afterward, like conspirators, they would make plans together for the family's fortune—a house on Long Island, college for the brightest child.

Lucia Santa began with intended conciliation, saying in Italian, "The baker's son, he has his eye on you. Does he give you ices to make sure you won't speak to him?" She enjoyed her irony, but paused to listen intently at a sound from the bedroom. She asked worriedly, "Did you put Lena in the middle of the bed? She won't roll off?"

Octavia was furious. She could forgive the deliberate teasing, though her mother knew her aversion to the young men of the neighborhood. But she herself had given her little half sister the name Aileen. After long consideration Lucia Santa had consented. It was time to be American. But the name could not be said by an Italian tongue. Impossible. And so it had been shortened to the familiar Lena. Lucia Santa, after some valiant tries to please her daughter, one day lost her temper and shouted in Italian, "That is not even American." And so the baby was Lena to everyone except the other children of the family. Octavia's hand was in their face when they took such liberties.

Mother and daughter prepared for battle. Octavia patted her curls, then took her fingernail kit from a shelf in the kitchen. She said in meticulous, contemptuous English, "I'll never marry one of these guineas. They just want a woman they can treat like a dog. I don't want what you had in your life." She began an elaborate operation on her nails. She would paint them tonight. It would annoy her mother.

Lucia Santa watched her daughter with exaggerated operatic calm, letting her breath go short and heavy. They resembled each other very much in anger—black liquid eyes flashing; full, sensuous features deadened with rage and sullenness. But when the mother spoke, her voice was reasonable.

"Ah," she said. "This is how a daughter speaks to her mother in America? *Brava.* You would make a fine schoolteacher." She bowed her head coolly to her daughter. "*Mi, mi dispiace.* I, I don't care for it." And the young girl knew that another such insolence would bring her mother upon her like a cat, hand open in her face. Octavia was not afraid, but she was dutiful within reason; and she knew that her mother, the family chief, leaned heavily on her, respected her, would never side with the outside world against her. She felt guilt at her disloyalty because she thought her mother's life a waste.

Octavia smiled to make her words less cruel. She said, "I just meant I don't want to get married or have children if I do. I don't want to give up my whole life just for *that.*" In the last word she expressed her contempt and also her hidden fear of what she did not know. Lucia Santa looked her American daughter up and down. "Ah," she said, "poor child of mine." Octavia grew hot with a rush of blood and was silent. The mother thought of something else, rose, went into the bedroom, and returned with two five-dollar bills in the postal savings book. "Here, quick—put it in your dress before your father and brother come. Bring it to the post office tomorrow at work."

Octavia said casually but with venom, "He's not my father."

Not the words but the quiet hatred behind them brought quick and passionate tears to the mother's eyes. For only the two of them could remember Lucia Santa's first husband; only the two of them had really shared that first life, suffered together. He was the father of three children, but only this child could hold his memory between them. To make it worse, Octavia had loved her father with passion, and his death had affected her greatly. The mother knew all this; she knew that the second marriage had destroyed some feeling in her daughter for herself.

The older woman said in a low voice, "You're a young girl, you don't understand the world. Frank married a widow desolate with three small children. He gave us our bread. He protected us all when no one except Zia Louche would even spit on our doorstep. Your own father was not as beautiful as you think. Ah, I could tell you stories—but he's your father." The tears were gone now and Lucia Santa wore the familiar mask of remembered sorrows, a mask of pain and rage which always distressed the young girl.

They had this quarrel many times and found the wound always fresh.

"He won't help," Octavia said. She was young, pitiless. "You make the poor kid, Vinnie, work for that lousy baker. He won't have any fun this summer. And meanwhile, your beautiful husband, all he can do is be a janitor for free work. Why can't he find work? Why is he so goddamn proud? Who the hell does he think he is? My father worked. He died working, for Chrissakes." She paused to hold back her tears.

Then she went on quietly, as if she believed she could really convince her mother, "But him, he lost his job on the railroad just to be smart. The boss tells him, 'Don't take all day to get a pail of water,' and so he took the pail and never went back. He thought that was so funny, he was really proud of that. And you never said a word. Not a goddamn word. I would have locked him out, I'd never let him in the house. And I god-damn sure hell wouldn't let him give me another baby." She said this scornfully, with a look meaning she would never let him commit a dark act of communion and domination that filled the night. But now her mother had lost patience.

"Talk about something you understand," Lucia Santa said. "You are a young, stupid girl and you will be old and stupid. Christ give me patience." She finished her wine in one swallow, and sighed wearily. "I'm going to bed. Leave the door open for your brother. And my husband."

"Don't worry about our beautiful Lorenzo," Octavia said. She dabbed paint on her nails. The mother stared with distaste at the bright redness, came back into the room.

"What is it now with Lorenzo?" she asked. "He stops work midnight. Why shouldn't he be home? All the girls are off the street except those little Irish tramps on Ninth Avenue." She added with mock fervor, "Thank Jesus Christ he only ruins good, decent Italian girls." She smiled with a touch of pride.

Octavia said coolly, "Larry might stay at the Le Cinglatas'. Mr. Le Cinglata is in jail again."

The mother understood immediately. The Le Cinglatas made their own wine and sold it by the glass in their own home. In short, they were bootleggers violating the Prohibition laws. Only last week the Le Cinglata woman had sent Lucia Santa three great flagons, supposedly because Lorenzo had helped unload a wagon of grapes. And Signora Le Cinglata had been one of the three married in church by proxy those long years ago in Italy. The shyest, the coyest of them all. Good. There was nothing to be done tonight. The mother shrugged and went to bed.

But first she went into the living room and covered the three boys with a sheet. Then she looked out the open window, down into the dark street, and saw her husband still pacing up and down Tenth Avenue. She called softly, "Frank, don't stay too late." He did not look up at her or see the sky.

Finally she was in bed. And now she was reluctant to go to sleep, for it seemed to her that as long as she was awake she controlled, in some measure, the actions of her husband and son. She felt annoyance, a real displeasure, that she could not make them leave the world and enter their home, sleep when she slept.

She reached out. The infant was safely trapped against the wall. She called out, "Octavia, sleep, go to bed, it's late. You work tomorrow." But really because she could not sleep when anyone in the house was still awake. And then her daughter passed through the room without a word, rebellious.

In the heavy summer darkness sighing with the breath of sleeping children, Lucia Santa pondered over her life. Marrying a second husband, she had brought sorrow to her first child. She knew Octavia held her guilty of not showing proper grief. But you could not explain to a young virginal daughter that her father, the husband whose bed you shared, whom you were prepared to live with the rest of your life, was a man you did not really like.

He had been the master, but a chief without foresight, criminal in his lack of ambition for his family, content to live the rest of his life in the slum tenements a few short blocks from the docks where he worked. Oh, he had made her shed many tears. The money for food he had always given, but the rest of his pay, savings-to-be, he spent on wine and gambling with his friends. Never a penny for herself. He had committed such an act of generosity in bringing Lucia Santa to the new country and his bed, beggar that she was without linen, that he had no need to be generous again. One deed served a lifetime.

Lucia Santa remembered all this with a vague resentment, knowing it was not all truth. His daughter had loved him. He had been a handsome man. His beautiful white teeth chewed sunflower seeds and the little Octavia would accept them from his mouth as she never did from her mother. He had loved his daughter.

The truth was simple. He had been a kind, hard-working, ignorant, pleasure-loving man. Her feeling had been the feeling of millions of women toward improvident husbands. That men should control the money in the house, have the power to make decisions that decided the fate of infants—what folly! Men were not competent. More—they were not serious. And she had already begun the struggle to usurp his power, as all women do, when one terrible day he was killed.

But she had wept. Oh, how she had wept. A grief compounded with terror. Not grief for departed lips, eyes, hands, but a wail for her shield against this foreign world, a cry for the bringer of her children's bread, the protector of the infant in her womb. These widows tear their hair and gash their cheeks, scream insane laments, do violence, and wear mourning for the world to see. These are the real mourners, for true grief is thick with terror. They are *bereaved.* Lovers will love again.

His death was comically grotesque. While a ship was being unloaded, the gangplank had given way high above the water, plunging five men and untold tons of bananas down into the river mud. Human limbs and banana stalks buried together. Never rising once.

She dared herself to think it: he had given them more dead than alive. In the darkness, now, years later, in mockery of her younger self, she smiled grimly. At what her younger self would think of such thoughts. But the court had awarded each of the children a thousand dollars—even Vincent not yet born but only too visible to the world. The money in trust, because here in America there was wisdom; not even parents were given charge of their children's monies. She herself had received three thousand dollars that no one on the Avenue knew about except Zia Louche and Octavia. So it was not all in vain.

Not to be spoken of, not to be thought of even now, were those months with the child in her belly. A child whose father had died before he was born, like the child of a demon. Even now she was struck with a terrible superstitious fear; even now, thirteen years later, tears sprang beneath her eyelids. She wept for herself as she was then, and for the unborn child, but not for the death of her husband. Her daughter Octavia could never know or understand.

And then the most shameful: only a year after her husband's death, only six months after the birth of that dead husband's son, she—a grown woman—had for the first time in her life become passionate about a man, the man who was to become her second husband. In love. Not the spiritual love of young girls or priests; not the emotion for heroes in romances that could be told to a young girl. No; love was the word for the hot flesh, the burning loins, feverish eyes and cheeks. Love was the feel of turgid, spongy flesh. Ah, what madness, what foolishness for the mother of children. Thank Jesus Christ in heaven she was beyond that now.

And for what? Frank Corbo was thirty-five, never married; slender, wiry, and with blue eyes; considered odd for being unwedded at that age, odd also in his reticence, his silent nature and lonely pride—that pride so ludicrous in those who are helpless before society and fate. The neighbors, searching for a widow's mate and feeder of four hungry mouths, thought him capable of any foolishness and a fine candidate. He worked steadily on the early morning shifts of the railroad gangs, and his afternoons were free for courting. There would be no scandal.

So the neighbors, out of kindness and self-preservation, brought them together, with conscience clear that both would make a good bargain.

The courtship was surprisingly young and innocent. Frank Corbo knew only the quick, cold whore's flesh; he would come to a marriage bed fresh with love, with a boy's eagerness. He pursued the mother of the three children as he would a young girl, making himself even more ridiculous in the eyes of the world. In the late afternoons he visited her as she sat before the tenement, guarding her playing and sleeping children. Sometimes he would take supper with them and leave before the children were put to bed. Finally one day he asked Lucia Santa to marry him.

She gave him an arch look, treating him like a young boy. She said, "Aren't you ashamed to ask me, with a baby still in the carriage from my first husband?" And for the first time she saw that dark look of hate. He stammered out that he loved her children as he loved her. That even if she did not marry him he would give her money for the children. In fact, he made good money on the railroad and always brought the children ices and toys. He had sometimes even given her money to buy the children clothing. At first she had tried to refuse, but he had become angry and said, "What is it, you don't wish to be friends with me? You think I'm like other men? I don't care for money—" and started to tear up the dirty green bills. For some reason this had brought tears to her eyes. She had taken the money from him, and he had never presumed on his gifts. It was she who became impatient.

ONE SUNDAY IN spring, invited, Frank Corbo came to the midday meal, the feast of the week for Italian families. He brought with him a gallon of biting homemade Italian wine and a box of cream pastries, *gnole* and *soffiati.* He wore a shirt, a tie, a many-buttoned suit. He sat at table with children about him: shy, awkward, more timid than they.

The spaghetti was coated with Lucia Santa's finest tomato sauce, the meatballs were beautifully round and peppered with garlic and fresh parsley. There was the dark green lettuce with olive oil and red wine vinegar, and then walnuts to eat with the wine. Everything had a bite to it of herbs and garlic and strong black pepper. They all stuffed themselves. Finally the children went down to the street to play. Lucia Santa should have kept them with her in the house to avoid scandal, but she did not.

And so in the golden afternoon with sunlight streaming

through the long railroad flat, with the poor infant Vincenzo's eyes shielded from sin by a conveniently placed pillow, they sealed their fate on the living room couch, the mother only slightly distracted by her children's voices rising sweetly from the street below.

Ah, delight, delight, the taste of love. After so long an abstinence the animal odor was an aphrodisiac, a bell to ring in the coming joy; even now, so many years later, the memory was fresh. And in that act of love she had been the master.

The man so harsh, so strong against the world, had wept on her breast, and in the fast-fading sunlight she understood that in all his thirty-five years of life he had never received a caress with real tenderness. It was too much for him. He had changed afterwards. He had come too late to love, and he despised his weakness. But for that one afternoon she forgave him many things, not everything; and cared for him as she had never cared for her first husband.

There was very little trouble until his first child was born. His natural love for Gino became cancerous, murdering his love for wife and stepchildren, and he became evil.

But in the first year of marriage, in the trust of love, he told her of his childhood in Italy as the son of a poor tenant farmer. He had often been hungry, often cold, but what he could never forget was that his parents made him wear cast-off shoes which were too small. His feet became horribly deformed, as if every bone had been broken and then bound together in one grotesque lump. He showed her his feet as if to say, "I keep nothing from you; you needn't marry a man with such feet." She had laughed. But she did not laugh when she learned that he always bought twenty-dollar shoes, beautiful brown-grained leather. The act of a true madman.

His parents were a rarity in Italy, drunken peasants. They relied on him to work the farm and give them their bread. When he fell in love with a young girl of the village, the marriage was forbidden. He ran away and lived in the woods for a week. When they found him, he was little more than an animal. He was in shock and was committed to a mental institution. After a few months he was released, but he refused to return to his home. He emgirated to America, where in the densest city in the world he lived a life of the most extreme loneliness.

He took care of himself; he never became ill again. In his life of solitude and hard work he found safety. As long as he did not become emotionally entangled with other human beings, he was safe, as something immobile is to some degree safe from the dangers of motion. But this love which brought him back to life brought him back to danger, and perhaps it was this knowledge, animal-like, felt rather than known, that had made him so weak that Sunday afternoon.

Now, after twelve years of life together, the husband was as secretive with her as he had always been with other people.

SOMEONE HAD COME in the door. Someone was moving in the kitchen. But the footsteps went out again and down the stairs. For his own mysterious reasons, her husband had gone back into the street.

Night. Night. She wanted her husband in her bed. She wanted her older son in the house. She wanted everyone asleep in this safe tenement castle four stories above the ground, sealed against the world by brick and concrete and iron. She wanted everyone asleep, asleep in darkness, safe from life, so that she need no longer stand guard, could deliver herself up to oblivion.

She sighed. There was no recourse. Tomorrow she must quarrel with Frank to keep the janitor's job. She must settle the Le Cinglata hash, the children's clothes, the stove to boil the laundry soap. She listened to the breath of the sleeping children all around her—Lena in her bed, the three boys in the room separated from hers only by an archway, Octavia in the bedroom with its door open for air. She made her breath fall into their great rising and falling sighs, and then she was asleep.

OCTAVIA STRETCHED OUT on her narrow bed. She wore her rayon slip as a nightdress. The room was too small for any additional furniture except a tiny table and a chair, but it had a door she could close.

She was too hot and too young to sleep. She dreamed. She dreamed of her real father.

Oh, how she had loved him, and how angry she had been that he let himself be killed, left her alone with no one to love. At the end of each day she had met him in front of the tenement and kissed his dirty bearded face, its black stubble so hard it bruised her lips. She carried his empty lunch pail up the stairs and sometimes cajoled from him the wicked steel clawed baling hook of the longshoreman.

And then in the house she set his plate for dinner, jealously placing the fork with the straight tines, the sharpest knife, his small wineglass polished and flashing like a diamond. Fussing until the exasperated Lucia Santa smacked her away from the table so that food could be served. And Larry, sitting in his high chair, could never interfere.

Even now, so many years later, waiting for sleep, the thought like a cry, "Why weren't you more careful?" Reproaching him for his sinful death, echoing her mother, who sometimes said, "He didn't take care of his family. He didn't take care of his money. He didn't take care of his life. He was careless in everything."

Her father's death had brought the thin blue-eyed stranger with his slanting, uneven face. The second husband, the stepfather. Even as a child she had never liked him, accepted his gifts distrustfully, stood with Larry in hand, holding him, hiding behind the mother's back, until he patiently found her. Once he had made a gesture of affection and she shrank away from his hand like an animal. Larry was the favorite until his own children came. He never liked Vincent for some reason, the lousy bastard—hateful, hateful.

But even now she could not blame her mother for marrying, could not hate her mother for bringing so much sorrow. She knew why her mother married this evil man. She knew.

IT WAS ONE of the most terrible times of Lucia Santa's life, and much of the distress that followed her husband's death was the fault of friends, relatives, and neighbors.

They had, every one, kept after Lucia Santa to let the newborn infant, Vincent, be taken care of by a rich cousin, Filomena, in New Jersey. Just for a little while, until the mother regained her strength. "What a boon to that childless couple. And she can be trusted, Filomena, your own first cousin from Italy. The child would be safe. And the rich Filomena's husband would then certainly consent to be godfather and assure the child's future." And how they had spoken in tones of most sorrowful pity, so tenderly, "And you, Lucia Santa, everyone worries about you. How meager you are. Not yet recovered from the birth. Still grieving over your beloved husband and torn to rags by lawyers over the settlement. You need a rest from care. Treat yourself well for your children's sake. What if you should die?" Oh, no threat was too much for them. "Your children would perish or go into a home. They could not be sent to the grandparents in Italy. Guard your life, your children's only shield." And they went on and on. And the child would be back in a few months, no, a month, perhaps a few weeks. Who could tell? And Filomena would come Sundays, her husband drove a *Forda*. They would bring her to their beautiful home in Jersey to visit the baby Vincenzo. She would be an honored guest. Her other children would have a day in the country, in the fresh air. *La la la la.*

Now. How could she deny them or herself or her children? Even Zia Louche nodded her warty head in agreement.

Only little Octavia began to weep, saying over and over again with childish despair, "They won't give him back."

Everyone laughed at her fear. Her mother smiled and patted Octavia's short black curls, ashamed now of her own reluctance.

"Only until I am well," she told the little girl. "Then Vincenzo will come home."

Later the mother was not able to understand how she had come to let the child go. True, the shock of her husband's death and a midwife's harshness at Vincenzo's birth had left her weak. But this never excused her in her own mind. It was an act that gave her so much shame, made her despise herself so much that whenever she had a difficult decision to make, she recalled that one act, to make sure she would not be cowardly again.

And so little Vincent had gone away. The strange Aunt Filomena had come one noon when Octavia was in school, and when Octavia came home the crib was empty.

She had wept and screamed, and Lucia Santa had given *one* the left hand, *two* the right hand, fine, heavy slaps across the face, making her little daughter's ears ring, saying, "Now, there is something to make you cry." Her mother was glad to get rid of the baby. Octavia hated her. She was evil, like a stepmother.

But then came that terrible beautiful day that had made her love and trust her mother. Part of it she saw herself as a little girl, but the story had been told innumerable times, so that now it seemed to Octavia as if she had seen everything. For naturally it was told; it became a legend of the family, mentioned in an evening of gossip, spread out at the Christmas table over walnuts and wine.

The trouble started after only a week. Filomena did not come that first Sunday, there was no automobile to take Lucia Santa to visit her infant son. Only a telephone message to the candy store. Filomena would come the following week, and to show her good heart and regret there would be a money order for five dollars in the mail, a small peace offering.

Lucia Santa brooded that dark Sunday. She went to take

counsel with her neighbors on the floors below. They reassured her, urged her not to think foolish things. But as the day wore on she became more and more somber.

Early Monday morning she said to Octavia, "Run. Go to 31st Street and get Zia Louche." Octavia wailed, "I'll be late for school." Her mother replied, "Today you are not going to your beautiful school"—saying it with such menace that the girl flew from the house.

Zia Louche came, a shawl around her head, a blue wool-knitted jacket reaching to her knees. Lucia Santa served the ceremonial coffee, then said, "Zia Louche, I am going to see the little one. Care for the girl and Lorenzo. Do me this favor." She paused. "Filomena did not come yesterday. Do you think I should go?"

In later years Lucia Santa always insisted that if Zia Louche had reassured her she would not have gone that day, and that for the honest answer she would always remain in the old woman's debt. For Zia Louche, nodding her old crone's head like a repentant witch, said, "I gave you bad advice, Signora. People are saying things I don't like." Lucia Santa begged her to speak out, but Zia Louche would not, because it was all gossip, nothing to be repeated to an anxious mother. One thing could be noted, though: the promise to send five dollars. The poor did well not to trust such charity. Best to go, set everyone's mind at rest.

In the gay light of winter, the mother walked to the Weehawken Ferry at 42nd Street, and for the first time since coming from Italy, she rode water again. In Jersey, finding a streetcar, she showed a slip of paper with the address on it, and then walked many blocks until a friendly woman took her by the hand and guided her to the dwelling of Filomena.

Ah, what a pretty house it was for the devil to live in. It had a pointed roof, like nothing she had ever seen in Italy, as if it were a plaything, not to be used for people full grown. It was white and clean, with blue shutters and a closed-in porch. Lucia Santa was suddenly timid. People so well off would never practice treachery on a poor woman like herself. The breaking of the Sunday promise could be explained in many ways. Still, she knocked on the side of the porch. She went through the screen door and knocked on the door of the house. She knocked again and again.

The stillness was frightening; as if the house were deserted. Lucia Santa went weak with fear. Then, inside the house, her baby began to wail, and she was ashamed of her terrible, ridiculous suspicion. Patience. The baby's wailing turned to shrieks of terror. Her mind went blank. She pushed against the door and went into the hallway and up the stairs, tracing those shrieks to a bedroom.

How pretty the room was; the prettiest room Vincenzo would ever have. It was all in blue, with blue curtains, a blue crib, a white stuffed toy horse standing on a little blue bureau. And in that beautiful room her son lay in his own piss. No one to change him, no one to quiet his shrieks of terror.

Lucia Santa took him in her arms. When she felt the lump of flesh warm and soaked in its own urine, when she saw the wrinkled rose face and the jet-black infant hair, she was filled with a savage, exultant joy, a knowledge that only her death could loosen this child from her. She stared around the pretty room with the dumb anger of an animal, noting all its assurances of permanency. Then she opened a bureau drawer and found some clothing to dress the baby. As she did so, Filomena came bursting into the room.

Then, then what a drama was played. Lucia Santa accused the other of heartlessness. To leave an infant alone! Filomena protested. She had only gone to help her husband open the grocery store. She had been gone fifteen minutes—no, ten. What a terrible, unlucky chance. But had not Lucia Santa herself sometimes left her infant alone? Poor people could not be as careful as they wished (how Lucia Santa sneered when Filomena included herself among the poor); their babies must be left to cry.

The mother was blind to reason, blind with an agonizing,

hopeless rage, and could not say what she felt. When her child was left crying at home, it was flesh and blood of its own that came to the rescue. But what could a baby think if left alone and only a strange face appeared? But Lucia Santa said simply, "No, it's easy to see that since this is not your own blood you don't care to put yourself out. Go help in the store. I will bring my baby home."

Filomena lost her temper. Shrew that she was, she shouted, "What of our bargain, then? How would I appear to my friends, that I can't be trusted with your child? And what of all this I have bought, money thrown into air?" Then, slyly, "And we both know, more was meant than said."

"What? What?" Lucia Santa demanded. Then it all came out.

There had been a cruel plot to do a kindness. The neighbors had all assured Filomena that, given time, the helpless widow, forced to work for her children's bread, would gradually relinquish all claims to her infant son and let Filomena adopt the baby. They were deviously cautious, but made it understood that Lucia Santa even hoped for such good fortune. Nothing could be said outright, of course. There were delicate feelings to consider. Lucia Santa cut all this short with wild laughter.

Filomena played another tune. Look at the new clothes, this pretty room. He would be the only child. He would have everything, a happy childhood, the university, become a lawyer, a doctor, even a professor. Things that Lucia Santa could never hope to give. What was she? She had no money. She would eat dirt with her bread her whole life long.

Lucia Santa listened, stunned, horrified. When Filomena said, "Come, you understood why I would send you money every week," the mother drew back her head like a snake and spat with full force into the older woman's face. Then, child in her arms, she fled from the house. Filomena ran after her, screaming curses.

That was the end of the story as it was told—with laughter, now. But Octavia always remembered more clearly the part never told: her mother's arriving home with the baby Vincent in her arms.

She entered the house feverish with cold, her coat wrapped around the sleeping infant, her sallow skin black with the blood of anger, rage, despair. She was trembling. Zia Louche said, "Come. Coffee waits. Sit down. Octavia, the cups."

Baby Vincent began to cry. Lucia Santa tried to soothe him, but his shrieks grew greater and greater. The mother, furious with guilt, made a dramatic gesture, as if to hurl the infant away; then she said to Zia Louche, "Here, take him." The old crone began to coo to the baby in a cracked voice.

The mother sat at the round kitchen table. She rested her head on her hand, hiding her face. When Octavia came with the cups she said, still shielding her face, "See. A little girl knows the truth and we laugh." She caressed her daughter, her fingers full of hatred, hurting the tender flesh. "Listen to the children in the future. We old people are animals. Animals."

"Ah," Zia Louche crooned, "coffee. Hot coffee. Calm yourself." The baby continued to wail.

The mother sat still. Octavia saw that a terrible rage at the world, at fate, made her unable to speak. Lucia Santa, her sallow skin darkening, held back her tears by pressing her fingers in her eyes.

Zia Louche, too frightened to speak to the mother, scolded the infant. "Come, weep," she said. "Ah, how good it feels. How easy it is, eh? You have the right. Ah, how fine. Louder. Louder." But then the child became still, laughing at that toothless, wrinkled face mirrored from the other side of time.

The old crone shouted in mock anger, "Finished so soon? Come. Weep." She shook the baby gently, but Vincent laughed, his toothless gums a mockery of hers.

Then the old woman said slowly, in a sad, singsong voice, "*Miserabile, miserabile.* Your father died before you were born."

At these words the mother's control broke. She pressed her

nails tightly into the flesh of her face, and the great streaming tears mingled with the blood of the two long gashes she made in her cheeks. The old crone chirped, "Come, Lucia, some coffee now." There was no answer. After a long time the mother lifted her dark face. She raised her black-clad arm to the stained ceiling and said in a deadly earnest voice filled with venom and hate, "I curse God."

Caught in that moment of satanic pride, Octavia loved her mother. But even now, so many years later, she remembered with shame the scene that followed. Lucia Santa had lost all dignity. She cursed. Zia Louche said, "Shh—shh—think of the little girl who listens." But the mother rushed out of the apartment and down the four flights of stairs, screaming obscenities at the kind neighbors, who immediately locked the doors she pounded on.

She screamed in Italian, "Fiends. Whores. Murderers of children." She ran up and down the stairs, and out of her mouth came a filth she had never known she knew, that the invisible listeners would eat the tripe of their parents, that they committed the foulest acts of animals. She raved. Zia Louche gave baby Vincent into Octavia's arms and went down the stairs. She grabbed Lucia Santa by her long black hair and dragged her back to her home. And though the younger woman was much stronger, she let herself descend into howls of pain, collapsing helplessly by the table.

Soon enough she took coffee; soon enough she calmed and composed herself. There was too much work to do. She caressed Octavia, murmuring, "But how did you know, a child to understand such evil?"

Yet when Octavia had told her not to marry again, saying, "Remember I was right about Filomena stealing Vinnie," her mother only laughed. Then she stopped laughing and said, "Don't fear. I'm your mother. No one can harm my children. Not while I live."

Her mother held the scales of power and justice; the family could never be corrupted. Safe, invulnerable, Octavia fell asleep, the last image flickering: her mother, baby Vincent in her arms returning from Filomena's, raging, triumphant, yet showing guilty shame for ever having let him go.

LARRY ANGELUZZI (ONLY his mother called him Lorenzo) thought of himself as a full-grown man at seventeen. And with justice. He was very broad of shoulder, medium tall, and had great brawny forearms.

At thirteen he had quit school to drive a horse and wagon for the West Side Wet Wash. He had complete responsibility for the collection of money, the care of the horse, and the good will of the customers. He carried the heavy sacks of wash up four flights of stairs without loss of breath. Everyone thought him at least sixteen. And the married women whose husbands had already gone to work were delighted with him.

He lost his virginity on one of these deliveries, cheerfully, with good will, friendly as always, thinking nothing of it; another little detail of the job, like greasing the wagon wheels, half duty, half pleasure, since the women were not young.

The job of dummy boy, riding a horse and leading a train through the city streets, appealed to his heroic sense; and the money was good, the work easy, and advancement to brakeman or switchman possible—these were excellent jobs for a lifetime. Larry was ambitious; he wanted to be a boss.

Already he had the mature charm of the natural-born ladykiller. His teeth flashed pearly white when he smiled. He had strong, heavy, regular features, jet-black hair, and long black eyebrows and eyelashes. He was naturally friendly, always assuming that everyone thought well of him.

A good son, he always gave his mother the pay he earned. True, he now kept some money for himself, stashed it; but after all, he was seventeen and a young man in America, not Italy.

He was not vain, but he loved riding up Tenth Avenue on

his black horse, with the freight train coiling slowly behind him while he swung a red lantern to warn the world of danger. There was always a surge of joy when he rode under the iron and wooden bridge at 30th Street and entered his own neighborhood village, making his horse prance for the children who waited for him and for the engine with its white cloud of steam. Sometimes he would halt his horse near the curb and the young people would gather round, begging for a ride, especially the girls. His brother Gino always looked up like a connoisseur admiring a picture—not too near, one foot in front of the other, head slightly back, leaning away, admiration shining in his eyes; he was so worshipful of his brother riding a horse that he never even spoke.

And yet, though Larry was hard-working, quite responsible for such a young man, he had one fault. He took advantage of the young girls. They were too easy for him. Angry mothers brought daughters to Lucia Santa and made ugly scenes, shouting that he kept the girls out too late, that he had promised to marry them. *La la.* Famous for his conquests, he was the neighborhood Romeo, yet popular with all the old ladies of the Avenue. For he had Respect. He was like a young man brought up in Italy. His good manners, which were as natural as his pleasantness, made him always ready to help in the countless mild distresses of the poor: he would borrow a truck to help someone move to a new tenement, visit for a few moments when an elderly aunt was in Bellevue Hospital. But most important of all, he took part with a real zest in all the events of communal life—marriages, funerals, christenings, death watches, Communions and Confirmations; those sacred tribal customs sneered at by young Americans. The old women of Tenth Avenue gave him their highest praise; they said of him that he always knew which things were really important. In fact, he had been offered an honor that no Italian could remember being given to so young a man before. He was asked to stand godfather to the son of the Guargios, distant cousins.

Lucia Santa forbade it. He was too young for such a responsibility; the honor would turn his head.

LARRY HEARD GINO screaming "Burn the city," watched him run, saw the people disappear from the street into the tenements. He trotted his horse up the Avenue to the stable on 35th Street, then galloped, catching in his ears the rushing wind, the great clatter of hoofs on cobblestones. The stableman was asleep, so Larry took care of the horse and then he was free.

He went directly to the Le Cinglata home, a short block away on 36th Street. Signora Le Cinglata served the anisette and wine in her kitchen, charging by the glass and doling out her wit to the customers who drank the most. There were never more than five or six of these at a time; they were always Italian laborers, and bachelors or men whose wives had never joined them from Italy.

Mr. Le Cinglata was finishing up one of those thirty-day sentences that were a risk of his trade. "Ah, the police," Signora Le Cinglata always said on these occasions. "They have put my husband on the cross." She was religious.

When Larry entered the apartment there were only three men. One of them, a dark Sicilian, encouraged by the knowledge that her husband was in jail, badgered the signora, holding her skirt as she went by, singing suggestive Italian songs. There was in his actions only the innocent lechery, the childish malice, of a primitive man. Larry sat down at their table. He enjoyed a chat in Italian with older men. He returned the signora's smile of welcome, and his ready assumption of equality offended the Sicilian.

Raising his great, heavy brows in mock astonishment, he shouted in Italian, "Signora Le Cinglata, do you serve children here? Must I drink my glass of wine with suckling infants?" The woman put down a cherry soda for Larry and the Sicilian gave all a look of excruciating slyness. "Oh, excuse me," he said in a deferential, broken English. "Itsa your son? Youra nepha-ew? He protecta you when youra husband is ina his little hideout. Oh, excusa me." He roared until he choked.

The signora, plump, handsome, and tough, was not amused. "Enough," she said. "Cease or find another place to drink. And pray I do not tell my husband of your pretty behavior."

The Sicilian said with abrupt seriousness, "Thank God if nobody tells your husband of your pretty behavior. Why don't you try a man instead of a child?" And he struck his chest with both hands, like a singer at the opera.

Signora Le Cinglata, in no way shamed but out of patience, said curtly, "Lorenzo, throw him down the stairs."

The phrase was extravagant and meant only that the man should be persuaded to leave, as they all knew. Larry started to say something conciliatory, a friendly smile on his face. But the Sicilian, his honor affronted, stood up and roared in broken English, "You little shitta American cockasickle. *You* throw *me* down the stairs? I eat you up whole anda whole."

The man's broad, bearded face was lined with authoritative rage. Larry felt a quick surge of childish terror, as if it would be parricidal to strike this man. The Sicilian loomed, and Larry threw a straight right into that huge dark face. The Sicilian fell to the kitchen floor. Suddenly Larry's fear was gone and he felt only pity and guilt for the man's humiliation.

For the man could not use his hands and had not meant him real harm. He had come like a hugging bear to chastise a child, grotesque, human without being cruel. Larry helped him to a chair, gave him a glass of anisette to drink, murmured words of conciliation. The man struck the glass out of his hand and walked out of the flat.

THE NIGHT WORE on. Men came in, others left. Some played Brisk with an old dirty deck of cards, a convenience of the establishment.

Larry sat in the corner, subdued by his adventure. Then his

feelings changed. He felt pride. People would think of him with respect, as a man to be wary of, yet not mean or vicious. He was the hero in the cowboy pictures, like Ken Maynard, who never struck a man on the floor. He grew drowsy, blissful, and then Signora Le Cinglata was talking to him in her strange, flirting way, in Italian, and his blood leaped awake. The time had come.

Signora Le Cinglata excused herself, saying she must fetch another gallon of wine and another bottle of anisette. She went out of the kitchen, through the rooms of the long railroad flat, and to the farthest bedroom. She had a door there. Larry followed her, mumbling that he would help her carry the bottles, as if she would be surprised or angry at his youthful presumption. But when she heard him lock the door behind them, she bent over to take a huge purple-colored gallon jug from among the many standing against the wall. As she did so, Larry gathered up her dress and petticoats in both his hands. She turned in her enormous pink bloomers, her belly bare, and gave a laughing protest: *"Eh, giovanetto."* The large cloth buttons of her dress slipped from their holes and she lay on her back on the bed, the long, sloping, big-nippled breasts hanging out, the loose bloomers pulled aside. In a few great blind savage strokes Larry finished and lay on the bed, lighting a cigarette. The signora, buttoned up and respectable, took the purple jug in one hand and the clear, slender bottle of anisette in the other and together they returned to the customers.

In the kitchen, Signora Le Cinglata poured wine and touched glasses with the same hands that had fondled him. She brought Larry a fresh glass of cherry soda, but finicky that she had not washed, he would not drink.

Larry got ready to leave. Signora Le Cinglata followed him to the door and whispered, "Stay, stay for the night." He gave her his big smile and whispered back, "Hey, my mother would ask for stories." He played this role, the helpless dutiful son, when it pleased him to escape.

He did not go home. He went around the corner and back

to the stable. He made his bed on straw and a horse blanket, using his saddle for a pillow. The restless moving of the horses in their stalls was soothing to him; the horses could not disorient his dreams.

Lying so, he reviewed his future, as he did many nights, as all young men do. He felt a great power. He felt himself, knew himself, as one destined for success and glory. In the world he lived in he was the strongest of the boys his age, the handsomest, the most successful with girls. Even a grown woman was his slave. And tonight he had beaten a grown man. He was only seventeen, and in his youthful mind the world would remain static. He would not become weaker, or the world stronger.

He would be powerful. He would make his family rich. He dreamed of wealthy young American girls with automobiles and large houses who married him and loved his family. Tomorrow before work he would go up to Central Park on his horse and ride along the bridle paths.

He saw himself coming down Tenth Avenue, a rich girl on his arm and everyone looking at him with admiration. The girl would love his family. He was not snobbish. He never thought they could be looked down upon, his family, his mother and sister, his friends. For he considered them all extraordinary, since they were really part of him. He had a truly innocent mind, and, sleeping in the smelly stable, cowboylike on a prairie of stone, fresh from his conquests of man and woman, Larry Angeluzzi never doubted his happy destiny. He slept in peace.

IN THE ANGELUZZI-Corbo family only the children— Vincent, Gino, and Sal, tangled together in the one bed— dreamed real dreams.

3

IN THE MORNING Octavia rose as the last freshness of the night air burned away before the rising August sun. She washed in the kitchen sink, and, walking back through the corridor of rooms, saw that her stepfather was not in bed. But he slept little and was an early riser. The other empty bedroom proved she had been right; Larry had not come home at all. Sal and Gino were uncovered, their sexual parts showing through the BVD underwear. Octavia covered them with the rumpled bed sheet.

Dressing for work, she felt the familiar despair and hopelessness. She choked on the warm summer air, on the closeness of the sweet warm odor of sleeping bodies. The morning light too clearly showed the cheap battered furniture, the faded wallpaper, the linoleum with black patches where its colored skin had worn through.

At such times she felt doomed: she was afraid that one day she would wake on a warm summer morning as old as her mother, in a bed and home like this, her children living in squalor, unending days of laundry, cooking, dishwashing before her. Octavia suffered. She suffered because life was not elegant, human beings not completely separate. And it sprang from a few dark moments in a marriage bed. She shook her head angrily, yet fearfully, knowing how vulnerable she was, knowing that one day she *must* lie on that bed.

CURLY BLACK HAIR combed, wearing a cheap blue and white frock, Octavia left the tenement and stepped onto the blue-slate sidewalk of Tenth Avenue. She walked the already burning pavement to her dressmaking shop on Seventh Avenue and 36th Street, going past the Le Cinglatas' out of curiosity perhaps to see her brother.

Lucia Santa woke shortly afterward, and her first realization was that her husband had not come home. She rose instantly and checked the closet. His twenty-dollar shoes were there. He would be back.

She went through the other bedroom to the kitchen. *Bravo.* Lorenzo had not come home. Lucia Santa's face was grim. She made coffee and her plans for the day. Vincenzo started to work in the bakery, good. Gino would have to help her with the janitor work, good. A punishment for his father, who shirked. She went to the hall and picked up the bottles of milk and the great loaf of Italian bread thick as her thigh, tall as a child. She sliced off heavy chunks and spread one with butter for herself. She let the children sleep.

It was another time of day she loved. The morning still fresh, the children about to waken and everyone else out of the house, herself strong for the duties of living.

"QUE BELLA INSALATA" — what beautiful salad — the words rose up to the sleeping children at their moment of awakening. They all sprang out of bed, and Gino looked out the window. Below was the hawker, standing on the seat of his wagon as he held up to the sky and the watching windows a pearly green lettuce in each outstretched hand. *"Que bella in-*

salata," he said again, not asking anyone to buy, only asking the world to look at beauty. Pride, not cajolement, in his voice, he repeated his cry each time his horse took a mincing step along the Avenue. In his wagon were boxes of onions dazzling white, great brown potatoes, bushels of apples, bouquets of scallions, leeks, and parsley sprigs. His voice rose rich with helpless admiration, disinterested, a call to lovers. "What beautiful salad."

At breakfast Lucia Santa instructed her children. "Listen," she said, "your father has gone away for a little time. Until he comes back you must help. Vincenzo works in the *panetteria*. So you, Gino, will help me wash the stairs of the building today. Get me the clean pails of water, and wring the mop, and sweep if you prove not to be stupid. Salvatore, you can dust the bannisters, and Lena also." She smiled at the two little children.

Vincenzo hung his head, sullen. But Gino looked at her with cool, speculative defiance. "I'm busy today, Ma," he said.

Lucia Santa bowed her head to him politely. "Ah," she said, "you are busy every day. But I'm busy too." She was amused.

Gino pressed his advantage. He became very earnest. "Ma, I gotta get ice from the railroad today, I promised Joey Bianco. I'll give you free ice before selling." Then, with a stroke of genius, he added, "And Zia Louche too."

Lucia Santa regarded him with an affection that made Vinnie jealous. Then she said, "Good, but remember my icebox must be filled—mine first of all."

Vincent flung down his slice of bread and she gave him a menacing look. Then she said to Gino, "But this afternoon be home and help, or you will feel the *Tackeril.*" Her heart was not in it. He would not have much longer to play.

GINO CORBO, LIKE any ten-year-old general, had made great plans, not all of which he had told his mother. Looking out the window of the front room, he saw the railroad yards across the street chock full of helpless freight cars. Beyond them the Hudson River sparkled blue. To his child's vision the air was marvelously pure. He ran through the apartment and out the door, down the stairs and into the August sun.

It was burning hot, the pavement warm beneath his sneakered feet. His faded blue denims and laddered rayon polo shirt fluttered in the breeze, then stuck to his body. He looked around for his friend and partner, Joey Bianco.

Joey was twelve, but shorter than Gino. He was the richest boy on Tenth Avenue and had over two hundred dollars in the bank. In winter he sold coal, now in summer he sold ice, and both he stole from the railroad cars. He also sold paper shopping bags in Paddy's Market, which stretched along the streets on Ninth Avenue.

Here he came, dragging his great wooden box of a wagon behind him. It was the best wagon on Tenth Avenue. It was the only six-wheeled wagon Gino had ever seen, and the box could hold a dollar's worth of ice or pull three kids riding. The small, stout wheels had heavy rubber tires; a long tongue of wood steered the two front wheels, and there were four other wheels for the box of the wagon itself. Joey even had clothesline instead of ordinary rope for his steering reins.

They had a ceremonial cup of lemon ice together to start the day. The *Panettiere* himself served them, so delighted by their industry he put an extra pat on each cup.

Joey Bianco was happy when Gino came. Gino let him collect and count the money. And Gino went on top of the cars. Joey liked to go up on the cars, but hated to leave his wagon alone. Now Gino said to Joey, "Come on, get in and I'll give you a ride." Joey held the steering line, sitting proudly in the box, and Gino pushed the wagon across the Avenue, past the switchman's shanty, onto the gravel between the tracks. When they were hidden from view by the towering freight cars scattered around the yard, they stopped. Joey spotted an open hatch and took the ice tongs from his wagon.

Gino said commandingly, "Gimme those tongs." He ran to the freight car and climbed its iron ladder to the open hatch on top.

Standing on that car roof, high above the ground, he felt free. Far off he saw the window of his front room bedroom and the whole wall of tenements. There were stores and people and horses and wagons and trucks. Gino seemed to sail by on an ocean of freight cars—brown, black, yellow, with strange names like Union Pacific, Santa Fe, Pennsylvania. Some empty cattle cars scented the air. Turning, he saw the cliffs of the Jersey Palisades patched with green, and blue water below. Through the hundreds of immobile freight cars a few black round engines chugged quietly, their white smoke adding a fresh burning smell pleasant in the morning summer.

Joey shouted up to him, "Come on, Gino, throw down the ice before the Bull comes."

Gino took the shiny steel tongs and grappled blocks of ice out of the hatch. It was piled to the top and easy to drag out in one heave. He pushed each block over the car edge, watched it fall to the gravel. Great silvery chips broke off and flew back up at him. Joey put his arms around each crystal block and hugged it into the wagon. In no time it was full. Gino climbed down and pushed, while Joey pulled from the front and steered.

Gino had meant to fill up his mother's icebox, but the *Panettiere* caught them as they came across the Avenue and bought the whole first load for a dollar. Then they went back for another. This time the grocer intercepted them and bought the whole load for a dollar, plus soda and sandwich.

Drunk with wealth, they decided to let their mothers wait, the family iceboxes remain empty. The third load went to the people living on the first floor. It was nearly noon. On the fourth load they ran into trouble.

The railroad cop had spotted them earlier, as they moved deeper and deeper into the yard, opening up fresh ice cars so they would not have to take ice from a depleted source. They foraged like an animal that kills three or four victims and takes a bite from the best part of each. So the cop waited and then walked toward them from the Tenth Avenue side, cutting off their retreat.

Joey saw him first and hollered up to Gino, "*Butzo,* it's Charlie Chaplin." Gino watched from his perch as the bandy-legged Bull grabbed Joey by the shirt and cuffed his face lightly.

Still holding Joey fast, the Bull called up to Gino, "O.K., kid, get down here or I come up and break your ass."

Gino looked down, his face grave, as if he were really considering the offer, but scheming. The sun was very hot and warmed his blood, giving the world a special, fearless light. Gino quivered with excitement, but he felt no fear. He knew he was safe. The Bull would kick Joey out of the yard and break the wagon. But Gino had read a story about mother birds, and from it he made a plan as he looked down at the Bull: he would save Joey and the wagon.

Deliberately, he leaned his dark angular almost-man's face over the car and hollered down, "Ha, ha. Charlie Chaplin can't catch flies." Then he ducked away and started down the ladder on the freight car's other side. But took just a few steps and waited.

The Bull said ferociously to Joey, "You stay here." Then ducked under the car to intercept Gino. He was just in time to see Gino scramble back up the ladder. The Bull crawled back to guard Joey.

Gino jumped up and down on top of the box car, chanting, "Charlie Chaplin can't catch candy."

The Bull made his face mean, his voice menacing. "Kid," he said, "I'm warning you. Get down off that car, or when I get you I kick the shit outa you."

That seemed to sober Gino and he stared down gravely. He thumbed his nose at the Bull and ran slowly, awkwardly, along the top of the freight car, jumped, teetered to the next car. On the ground the Bull kept pace easily, glancing back with a threatening face so that Joey would not try to escape with his wagon. The string of cars was only ten or eleven long.

Gino jumped a few cars, then pretended to climb down the other side. The Bull ducked underneath. He could not keep track of Joey if he did this, but he didn't care. He had made up his mind the kid on top of the cars was going to get his ass broke.

Beckoning with his small hopping form, Gino ran along the car tops deeper into the yard, and then waited for the Bull to catch up, staring down at him. Then, raising his head, he could see Joey running and pulling the wagon toward freedom across the Avenue.

"Kid, you better come down," the Bull said. "You make me chase you and you'll get this." He waved his club. He thought of drawing his gun as a bluff, but Italian laborers on one of the yard gangs might see him and he would be a marked man. He ducked back underneath the railroad car just in time to see Joey and the wagon cross safely over the Avenue. He became so angry that he shouted up to Gino, "You little black guinea bastard, you don't come down and I'll break your hump."

Gratified, he saw the threat working; the kid was walking back the car tops to stand directly over him. But then that dark, grave child's face leaned out above him. He heard the little boy shout in sudden angry contempt that assumed equality of strength, "Fuck you, Charlie Chaplin." A great dazzling white rock of ice went whizzing past the Bull's head and the boy teetered clumsily along the car tops deeper into the maze of the yard.

The Bull, really angry now, but confident, ran hard to keep pace alongside, his head tilted upward comically. The kid was trapping himself. He was angry not at the curse, but at being called Charlie Chaplin. He was vain, and his bowed legs made him sensitive.

Suddenly Gino disappeared. The Bull ducked quickly under the freight car to catch him coming down the ladder on the opposite side. He tripped on the rails and lost a precious second. When he got to the other side, he saw no sign of his prey. He backed up to enlarge his field of vision.

He saw Gino almost literally flying along the top of the box cars, soaring from one to the other with no teetering awkwardness, up toward Tenth Avenue, and then disappearing over the side of the car away from the Bull. The Bull sprinted but was only in time to see the boy cross Tenth Avenue to the safe shade of the tenement wall, where, without a backward glance, Gino stopped to rest and get a lemon ice. There was no sign of the other kid.

The Bull had to laugh, he couldn't help it. The balls on the kid, a little shit like that. But just the same, his day would come; he'd be Charlie Chaplin, O.K.; he'd make 'em scream, but not laughing.

GINO DID NOT bother to look back once he had crossed the Avenue. He wanted to find Joey Bianco and the ice money. He heard his mother yelling from the fourth-floor window, "Gino, *bestia,* where is the ice? Come, eat."

Gino looked up, and above his mother he saw the blue sky. "I'll be up in two minutes," he shouted. He ran around the corner to 30th Street. Sure enough he saw Joey sitting on a stoop, his wagon tied to the iron railing of the basement.

Joey was brooding, almost in tears, but when he saw Gino he jumped in the air. He said excitedly, "I was gonna tell your mother—gee, I didn't know what to do."

Thirtieth Street was dusty and full of sun. Gino got into the wagon and steered, with Joey pushing him. On Ninth Avenue they bought hero salami sandwiches and Pepsis. Then they went on to 31st Street, where it was shady, and sat with their backs against the wall of Runkel's chocolate factory.

They ate their sandwiches with the contentment and good

appetite of men who have had a completely satisfying day: hard work, adventure, and their bread sweet with their own sweat. Joey was admiring and kept saying, "Boy, you sure saved me, Gino. You sure outfoxed that Bull." Gino was modest, because he knew he had learned the trick from a book about birds, but he didn't tell Joey.

The summer sun vanished. There were quick dark clouds. The dusty, heated air and the smell of hot stone pavements and melting tar were swept away by a rushing sheet of rain released by great claps of thunder; faintly, there was an elusive ghost and smell of something green. Joey and Gino crept under the loading platform. The rain pelted down, some of it coming through cracks in the platform floor, and they turned their faces up to the cool drops.

In the shaded, cellar-like darkness there was just enough light to play cards. Joey took the greasy pack out of his trousers pocket. Gino hated to play because Joey won a lot. They played Seven-and-a-half and Gino lost the fifty cents ice money. It was still raining.

Joey, stuttering a little, said, "Gino, here, here's your fifty cents back for saving me from the Bull."

Gino was offended. Heroes never took pay.

"Come on," Joey said more firmly. "You saved my wagon, too. You gotta let me give the fifty cents back."

Gino really didn't want the money. It would spoil the adventure if Joey paid him to do a job. But Joey was nearly in tears, and Gino saw that for some reason he had to take the money. "O.K.," Gino said. Joey handed it over.

Still it rained. They waited quietly while Joey restlessly riffled the cards. The rain kept coming down. Gino spun the half dollar on the pavement.

Joey kept watching the coin. Gino put it in his pocket.

"You wanta play Seven-and-a-half again double stakes?" Joey asked.

"Nope," Gino said.

Finally the rain stopped and the sun came out and so did they, crawling like moles from beneath the platform. The washed sun was far in the west, over the Hudson River. Joey said, "Jesus, it's getting late. I gotta go home. You comin', Gino?"

"Ha, ha," Gino said. "Not me." He watched Joey pull his wagon toward Tenth Avenue.

The late shift came out of Runkel's factory. The men smelled of the chocolate they made and the smell was sweet and sticky like flowers, heavy on the rain-freshened air. Gino sat on the platform and waited until no one came out.

He was deeply pleased with everything he saw—the tenement bricks dyed deep red by the ripening sun, the children coming out again to play in the streets, the few horses and wagons slowly wending toward the Avenue, one leaving a spotted trail of grainy, gold-flecked manure balls. Women came to opened windows; pillows appeared on ledges; women's faces, sallow, framed in black bonnets of hair, hung over the street like gargoyles along a castle wall. Finally Gino's eyes were caught by the swiftly flowing stream of rain water in the flooded gutters. He picked up a small flat piece of wood, took out his half dollar, balanced it on the wood, and watched it sail down toward the Avenue. Then he ran after it, saw he was nearing Tenth, picked up the wood and coin and walked back up toward Ninth Avenue.

On the way, passing a row of empty houses, he noticed a bunch of boys as big as Larry swinging on a rope hung from the roof four stories above them. They jumped from the ledge of the second-story window and swung high over 31st Street, riding through the air like Tarzan to the window of an empty house farther up the street.

A blond kid in a red shirt soared in his great half-circle, missed the window, pushed against the wall he hit with his feet and, twisting, soared back the way he had come. For a moment he gave the illusion of really flying. Gino watched with burning envy. But it was no use. They wouldn't let him do it. He was too small. He went on.

On the corner of Ninth and 31st, in the light-shot oblong shadow of the El, Gino put his stick of wood with its rider coin back in the gutter and watched it sail down to 30th Street; bobbing, riding little wavelets, snagged by soggy bits of newspaper, fruit skins and cores, eroded smooth remains of animal turds, scraping the shining blue-black tarred street bottom beneath the water. The wooden stick turned the corner and started down 30th Street to Tenth Avenue without losing the coin. Gino trotted watchfully beside it, keeping an eye sideways for the kids who had chased him the night before. His boat sailed around tin cans, whirled around piles of refuse, but always fought free to sail finally through a succession of tiny gutter rainbows. Then Gino grabbed his half-dollar piece as the boat sailed down through the grates of the sewer beneath the bridge on Tenth Avenue. Thoughtfully he walked around the corner onto the Avenue and was hit in the stomach by little Sal, who, head down, was running away from a game of "Kick the Can." Sal shouted excitedly, "Ma's lookin' for you. We already ate and you're gonna get killed."

Gino turned around and went back toward Ninth, searching for rainbows in the gutter. He backtracked to the empty houses, and found the rope dangling alone. Gino went to the basement and entered the house, climbing crumbling steps to the second floor. The house was gutted, the plumbing stolen for lead, the lighting fixtures gone. The floor was treacherous under a shale of plaster. Everything was still and dangerous as he tiptoed through the ghostly rooms and through doorless doorways. Finally he reached the window and could see the street. The square frame for the windows was only an empty stone socket. Gino stepped onto the ledge, leaned out, and grabbed the rope.

He pushed away from the ledge, and for one glorious moment he had the sensation of really flying of his own will. He soared through the air, out over the street, and, completing the arc, landed on the ledge of a window three buildings up the block. He pushed and sailed back, pushed and sailed out again—faster and faster, soaring back and forth, hitting the window ledges and the wall, then thrusting back out with his feet as if they were his wings, until his arms could no longer sustain him and he slid down the rope in midsail, burning his hands as he braked himself to the pavement and landed in a running movement toward Tenth Avenue, specially timed.

It was twilight. Gino was surprised, and purposeful with the knowledge that he was now in trouble, he trotted down 31st Street to Tenth Avenue, trying hard to keep the look of surprise on his face. But no one in his family was among the people already sitting before the tenements, not even Sal. He ran up the four flights of stairs.

Passing the second floor, he heard Octavia and his mother screaming at each other. Worried, he slowed down. When he came into the apartment he saw them both nose to nose, red spots on their sallow cheeks, eyes flashing black. They both turned to him, quiet, menacing. But Gino, fascinated, had eyes only for his brother Vinnie, already seated at table. Vinnie's face was powdered dead white with flour, his clothes were caked with it. He looked very tired, his eyes enormous and dark in that floury face.

"Ah. You're home," his mother was saying. *"Bravo."* Gino, noting that the two women were looking at him like judges, hurried to sit at the table so they would bring him food. He was starving. A stunning blow on the side of his head made him see stars, and through the dizziness his mother was shouting, "Sonamabitch. You escape the whole day. What did you do? And then the signor sits at table to eat without washing. Go. *Figlio de puttana. Bestia.* Vincenzo, wash also, you'll feel better." The two boys went to the kitchen sink to wash and came back to the table.

Tears were in Gino's eyes—not because of the slap, but because of the terrible end to such a beautiful day. First a hero, then his mother and sister angry as if they hated him. He hung his head, shamed as any villain, not even hungry until his mother put a platter of sausages and peppers under his nose.

Octavia gave Gino one burning look and said to Lucia Santa, "He has to do his share. Why the hell should Vinnie work for him when his own father doesn't give a damn? If he doesn't work Vinnie quits the bakery. Vinnie's going to have fun on his summer vacation, too."

Without jealousy, Gino noticed that Octavia and his mother watched Vinnie with pity and love as he ate tiredly, listlessly. He could see that his sister was close to tears for some reason. He watched the two women fussing over Vinnie, serving him as if he were a grown man.

Gino put his hand in his pocket and took out the fifty cents and gave it to his mother. "I made this selling ice," he said. "You can have it. I can bring home fifty cents every day."

"You better make him stop stealing ice from the yards," Octavia said.

Lucia Santa was impatient. "Eh, the railroad doesn't care about children taking a little ice." She looked at Gino, a curious warm smile on her face. "Bring your brother to the movies Sunday with the money," she said. And she buttered a big piece of bread for him.

Vinnie's face was still white, even with the flour gone. The strange lines of fatigue and tension, always obscene on the face of a child, made Octavia put her arm around him and say worriedly, "What did they make you do, Vinnie? Is the work too hard?"

Vinnie shrugged. "It's O.K. It's just so hot." Then he added reluctantly, "I got dirty carrying sacks of flour from the cellar."

Octavia understood. "The lousy bastards," she spat out. To her mother she said, "Your dirty guinea *paesan' Panettiere* making a kid like Vin carry those heavy sacks. When that son of his asks me for a date, I'll spit in his face right in the street."

Vinnie watched them hopefully. Octavia, so angry, might

make him quit the job. Then he felt ashamed because his mother needed the money.

Lucia Santa shrugged and said, "Five dollars a week and our bread free as extra, a courtesy. Then free lemon ice when Vincenzo serves, and that's money saved in summer. With their father gone—"

Octavia flared up. Her mother's calm acceptance of the father's desertion made her furious. "That's just it," she said. "His father left. He doesn't give a shit." Even through her anger she was amused at the look the two small boys gave her—a girl using a dirty word like that. But her mother was not amused and Octavia said in a reasonable tone, "It's not fair. It's just not fair to Vinnie."

The mother spoke in grim Italian, asking, "Who are you to be a schoolteacher when you have the mouth of a whore?" She paused for an answer. But she had upset Octavia's vision of herself. The mother continued, "If you want a house to give orders in, get married, have children, scream when they come out of your belly. *Then* you can beat them, then you can decide when they will work and how, and who works." She looked at her daughter, coldly, as at a deadly rival. "Enough. *Bastanza,*" she said.

She turned on Gino. "You, *giovanetto.* From morning to night I don't see you. You could be run over. You could be kidnaped. That's one thing. Now. Your father has gone away for a time and so everyone must help. Tomorrow if you disappear I'll give you this." She went to the cupboard and took out the skinny wooden club used for rolling dough for the holiday ravioli, "The *Tackeril.*" Her voice became hoarse, more angry. "By Jesus Christ, I'll make you visible. I'll make you so black and blue that if you were the Holy Ghost you could not vanish. Now, eat. After, wash the dishes, clean the table, and sweep the floor. And don't let me see you come down the stairs this night."

Gino was impressed. Though unafraid, he had been alert

and tense through the whole uproar. Out of such noise some-times would come a wild swing which it was permissible to evade. But nothing happened. The two women went down-stairs and Gino relaxed and ate, the fatty sausage, the oily pulpy peppers blending together deliciously on his hungry palate. The storm was over, there were no hard feelings. He would work for his mother tomorrow, help her out.

Vinnie was staring down at his plate, not eating. Gino said cheerily, "Boy, I'll bet you had it tough working for that bastid *Panettiere.* I saw you carrying a big basket. Where'd you bring it?"

"Nah," Vinnie said. "They got a store on Ninth Avenue. It ain't so bad. Just carrying the flour up the cellar." Gino looked at him. There was something wrong.

But already Vinnie was feeling better and he took in great mouthfuls of food, not knowing that what he had felt all that day was fear. That he had suffered a common cruelty—a child sent from the warmth of his family to be commanded by strangers to perform their drudgery. It was his first experience of selling part of his being for money, so unlike doing some-thing for his mother, or shining his big brother's shoes for a nickel.

But school would come in the fall and set him free, and he would forget how his mother and sister had sent him out of the family and its rule by love and blood. He no longer thought of how he could not play stickball in the summer morning sun, or wander aimlessly around the block talking with friends, hiding in the shade of 31st Street as he sleepily licked a pleated paper cup of lemon ice. He felt the terrible sadness that only children can feel, because they have no knowledge of the sadness of others, of the general human despair.

Gino cleaned the table and started to wash the dishes. Vin-nie helped him dry. Gino told of his adventures with the rail-road Bull, the empty house and rope, and playing cards with Joey; but he didn't say anything about his boat-sailing all the way around the block, because ten years old was too old for that kind of stuff.

There was one dirty pot caked with grease and soot, which Gino hid in the oven. Then the two boys went into the living room to look out over the Avenue. Gino sat on one window sill and Vinnie on the other. They were both at peace.

Gino asked, "Why the hell are Mom and Octavia mad at me? I just forgot. I'll do everything tomorra."

"They're just mad because Pop left. They don't know where he is. He musta run away."

They both smiled at Vinnie's joke. Only children ran away.

Far down Tenth Avenue they could see the red lantern of a dummy boy and behind it, like a small round ghost, the white dot of the trailing engine searchlight. The people below were shadows lit by lamp posts, by the blue and red streamer lights of the *Panettiere*'s lemon-ice stand, by the window bulbs of the grocery and candy stores.

Gino and Vincent, sit-sleeping on their childhood window sill, felt on their tired faces the fresh breeze from the Hudson River. It smelled of running water and, as if it had been carried great distances, of grass and trees and the other green things it had sprung from before it came to the city.

4

BY LATE AUGUST, everyone hated summer except the children. The days were filled with the smell of burning stone, melting street tar, gasoline, and manure from horse-drawn wagons hawking vegetables and fruit. Over the western wall of the city where the Angeluzzi-Corbos lived hung clouds of steam trailed by locomotives, air immobilized by heat. Black flakes flew out of burning fires as engines packed freight cars into neat long rows. On this Sunday afternoon, when everything was still, the abandoned yellow, brown, and black railroad cars made solid geometric blocks in the liquid golden sunshine, abstractions in a jungle of steel and iron, stone and brick. The gleaming silvery tracks snaked in and out.

Tenth Avenue, open all the way to the river at Twelfth, with no intervening wall to give shade, was lighter than the other avenues of the city and hotter during the day. Now it was de-serted. The enormous midday Sunday feast would last to four o'clock, what with the nuts and wine and telling of family leg-ends. Some people were visiting more fortunate relatives who had achieved success and moved to their own homes on Long Island or in Jersey. Others used the day for attending funerals, weddings, christenings, or—most important of all—bringing cheer and food to sick relatives in Bellevue.

The more Americanized might even take their families down to Coney Island, but they would not do this more than once a year. The trip was long, and the size of families demanded great expenditures for frankfurters and sodas, even though they took their own food and drink along in paper bags. The men hated going. These Italians had never stretched idle on a beach. They suffered the sun all week working on the tracks of the railroad. On Sunday they wanted the cool of a house or garden, they wanted their minds occupied and alert over a deck of cards, they wanted to sip wine, or listen to the gossip of women who would not let them move a finger. They might as well go to work as go to Coney Island.

Best of all was a Sunday afternoon without duties. Children at the movies, mother and father took a little nap together after the heavy meal and made love in complete privacy and relaxation. It was the one free day a week and was jealously treasured. Strength was restored. Family bonds healed. Not to be denied, it was a day set aside by God himself.

On this Sunday the streets, empty, beautiful, marched in straight lines away from Tenth Avenue. Since the neighborhood was too poor to own automobiles, none marred the symmetry of concrete pavement interspersed with blue-gray slate. The sun glinted on the smooth black tar, on the iron railings of the stoops, and on the coarse brownstone steps. All this seemed fixed forever in the blinding sun of summer; it was dazzling, as if unveiled on this one day by idle factory chimneys.

But Lucia Santa had picked this day to be a day of strife, to catch the enemy, the Le Cinglatas, unaware.

Everybody was out of the house. Octavia, dutiful Italian daughter that she was, had taken Sal and Baby Lena for a walk. Vincenzo and Gino had gone to the movies. Lucia Santa was free.

The eldest son, the shield and buckler of a fatherless family, had not shown the respect due to his blood or his mother. Lorenzo had not been present for the Sunday dinner. He had not been home to sleep for the last two nights, and came in each morning only to tell his mother that he had to work late and would sleep in the stable of the railroad. But Lucia Santa had found his good suit missing from the closet, and one of his two white shirts and a small suitcase were also gone. That was enough. *Bastanza.* Her word of decision.

A son of hers not yet eighteen, not married, not master of his own household, he dared to leave his own roof, his mother's domain? What a disgrace to the family name. What a blow to her prestige in the neighborhood. What defiance of her just powers. Rebellion. Rebellion not to be borne.

Dressed in black, respectable in Sunday hat and veil, pocketbooked as befitted a matron, and short legs in brown cotton stockings fastened by garters that cut into the thighs, Lucia Santa went out on the blazing streets and walked up Tenth Avenue to 36th Street, where the Le Cinglatas lived. As she walked she whipped up her anger for the scene she would have to make. That little slut, that mealymouth, who twenty years ago had cried in church, making such a fuss that she would have to sleep with a man she had never seen. *Del-i-cato.* Oh, how awful—oh, how terrible—oh, ah, ah. Lucia Santa smiled grimly. These people who gave themselves airs. That was the true instinct of the born whore. Marriage vows and legal papers so that you could hold your head up, look everyone in the eye, rich or poor, that was important. As long as there was no *disgrazia.* Then if someone insulted your honor you could do murder with a clear conscience. But this was not Italy. She put away these thoughts, bloodthirsty as any greenhorn's.

But truly, that was what America could do to a respectable Italian girl who no longer had parents to govern her. She was a woman now, the Le Cinglata. But what airs. What graces she had given herself. Oh, those were always the sly ones.

And her son. America or no America, seventeen years old

or not, working or not working, he would obey his mother or feel her hand on his mouth. Ah, if his natural father was alive there would be real blows—but then, Lorenzo would never have dared leave a paternal roof.

The shade of the Le Cinglata tenement brought relief. Lucia Santa rested in the cool dark hallway, with its familiar musty smell of rodents, and gathered up her strength for the climb up the stairs and the battle awaiting her. For a moment she felt a weakening despair, a great sudden awareness of her vulnerability to fate and life—her children alienated by foreign ways and a foreign tongue, a husband so erratic that he was a liability in the fight for survival.

But such thoughts led to disaster. She ascended. No son of hers would be a gangster, a criminal sucked-out jellyfish to an older woman without shame. For one moment in the dark hallway, in those murky stairwells, Lucia Santa had a terrible vision of electric chairs, of her son bleeding, stabbed by the Sicilian or the jealous husband. By the time the Le Cinglata door opened, her swiftly coursing fearful blood had made her ready for battle.

But from the very first she was given pause. In the door stood husband Le Cinglata, heavily gray-mustached, in a clean white shirt and black suspendered trousers swelled by his paunch. He was not even pale from his short stay in jail.

Now Lucia Santa was in doubt. With the husband home, what was her son doing here? Could it all be gossip? But that she did not believe, especially when she saw the woman Le Cinglata standing by the table. The look of an enemy was on that face, a defiant guilt mixed with a strange jealousy.

This woman dressed in black, except that her face was thinner and younger than Lucia Santa's, could be Lorenzo's mother. That a woman her age should dare corrupt a child. Could they both have been so young once and she so innocent?

"Ah, Signora," the man Le Cinglata was saying. "Come sit and have a glass of wine." He ushered her to a white metal-topped table. He poured a glass from a half-gallon jug. "The grapes were good last year. This wine smells of Italy." Then, with a wink, "This is not the wine I sell, believe me." It was understood that only a respected guest like Lucia Santa was served from such a harvest.

The woman Le Cinglata brought out a plate of *tarelle,* hard and crusty, flecked with dark dots of pepper. She put them on the table, then folded her arms. She did not drink.

Signor Le Cinglata poured himself a glass and said, "Drink, Lucia Santa," with such hearty friendliness that the mother was disarmed, as she always was by an unexpected courtesy. She drank. Then she said, in a gentler voice than she had intended, "I was passing by and thought Lorenzo might be here, helping Signora Le Cinglata with the customers."

The husband smiled and said, "No, no. Sunday afternoons we rest. No business until night time. After all, we're not Jews."

Lucia Santa said, a little more forcefully, "Forgive me for saying this. You must understand a mother. Lorenzo is still too young for such a business. He has no judgment. One night he beat a man old enough to be his father. And a Sicilian who may decide to kill him. Of course, Signor Le Cinglata, you know about this, all these things."

The husband was expansive, tolerant. "Ah, yes, I know. A good boy. *Bravo, bravo,* your Lorenzo. You have brought him up a good Italian, respectful to his elders, helpful, industrious. I know the good money we pay him he gives to his mother. There are not many people I would trust, give the freedom of my house, but with Lorenzo there could be no doubt. What an honest face he has." And so on.

Lucia Santa became impatient and she broke in. "But he is not an angel from heaven. He must obey. Am I right? Does a son show respect to his mother or not? And now some of his clothes are missing. So I thought you might know, perhaps he rested here one night."

For the first time the woman Le Cinglata spoke, and Lucia

Santa marveled at her brassiness, her lack of shame, her hard voice. "Ah," the woman said. "Your son is a man grown. He earns his own bread and some for your other children. We are not in Italy. You rule with too iron a hand, Signora."

Here, now, the Le Cinglata woman made her mistake. Met with rudeness, Lucia Santa could become angry and voice her true feelings. She said coldly, politely, "Ah, Signora, you don't know what trouble children make. How could you, you who are so fortunate not to have any? Ah, the worries of a mother, a cross pray to Christ you will never have to bear. But let me tell you this, my dear Le Cinglata. America or no America, Africa, or even England, it does not signify. My children sleep under my roof until they are married. My children do not become drunkards or fight with drunkards, or go to jail or go to the electric chairs."

Now the woman Le Cinglata was angry and shouted back. "What? What? You're saying that *we* are not respectable people? Your son is too good to visit here? But who are you? What part of Italy do you come from? In my province and yours there was not one of the nobility with the name of Angeluzzi or Corbo. And now my husband, the closest friend and fellow worker of your son's true father, almost a godfather, *he* is not to be a friend to Lorenzo? Is that what you are saying?"

Now Lucia Santa was trapped, and she cursed the other woman's slyness. She had an answer ready to hand but could not use it—that she objected not to the husband's friendship, but to the wife's. She did not dare. A jealous and deceived husband wreaked vengeance on wife and lover alike. She said defensively, "No, no, of course he can visit. But not work. Not stay so late amongst quarreling men. Not sleep here," she concluded dryly.

The Le Cinglata woman smiled. "My husband knows your son slept here. He does not listen to idle gossip. He does not believe his wife would disgrace herself with a mere boy. He is thankful for your son's protection. He gave your son twenty dollars for his good deeds. Now tell me. Does the boy's own mother believe the worst of him?"

With the husband looking down her throat, Lucia Santa perforce said hurriedly, "No, no. But people talk. Your husband is a sensible man, thank God." A fool and an idiot, she thought furiously. And as for a mother thinking the worst of her son, who had a better right?

But then, without knocking, entering as if it were his household, Lorenzo came in, stopped short, and the tableau that this made explained everything to the mother.

Larry smiled with genuine fondness at them all, his mother, then the paramour, then the husband he had made a cuckold. They smiled back. But the mother saw that the husband's smile had a falsity and contempt for youth; it was the smile of a man who was not deceived. And the female Le Cinglata—that a woman her age should have such a look on her face, the lips full and wet and red, the black eyes penetrating, looking directly into the youth's face.

Lucia Santa watched Lorenzo with grim irony. Her handsome son with the false heart. But he—his hair like blue-black silk, with his straight bronze heavy features, his big nose, heavily fleshed and masculine, his skin unbroken by adolescent blemish—he, the Judas, turned his head to view his mother with affectionate astonishment. He put down the suitcase he was carrying and asked, "Ma, what are you doing here? And I was just thinking what bad luck I missed you home."

She knew what had happened. He had waited to see her leave, watching from some hiding place. Never dreaming she was coming here. Then quick into the house to get his clean clothes. *Figlio de puttana,* she thought, how two-faced he is.

But she did not let her anger show. "Ah, my son," she said. "You're moving into your new home? Signor and Signora Le Cinglata are adopting you? My cooking doesn't please you? One of your blood has affronted you in some way? You're making a change, are you?"

Larry laughed and said, "Ah, come on, Ma, quit kidding." He was appreciative. He found her witty. He gave her his big flashing smile. "I told you I'm just gonna stay here and help out awhile. I want to give you some extra money. Zi' Le Cinglata has to go to court and then to the country and buy grapes. Don't worry, Ma, any money I get, it's yours."

"*Grazia,*" the mother said. They all smiled, even Signor Le Cinglata, that the youth thought himself so clever he could call his cuckold "Uncle."

Signor Le Cinglata fell into the spirit of the thing. "Lucia Santa," he said familiarly. "I look on Lorenzo as my very own son. Ah, what a *disgrazia* we have no children. But now who will protect my wife when I am away? This business is hard and dangerous for a woman alone. There must be a strong man in the house. Your son has his regular hours on the railroad. Then he comes here until early morning. He must sleep during the daytime. Your children run in and out, in and out. Why shouldn't he get his rest here, where everything is quiet? I have absolute trust in your son and I don't care about idle gossip. A man who makes the money I make need not worry about his neighbors' opinions."

It was all clear to the mother. She felt an overwhelming contempt for these people. Here was a husband, and an Italian, who for the sake of money let his wife cuckold him. Here was a wife who knew her husband cared more about the business and money than about her honor and good name, and made his wife his whore. Lucia Santa was truly shocked, for one of the few times in her life.

Where would it lead her son, living with such people? She said to Lorenzo, not even in anger, "Get all your things, *figlio mio,* and come back to your own roof. I don't leave here until you come."

Larry gave them all an embarrassed smile. "Come on, Ma," he said. "I been working five years now and bringing home money. I'm no kid."

Lucia Santa stood up, commandingly stout in black. She said dramatically, "I am your mother and you dare defy me before strangers?"

The female Le Cinglata said with savage contempt, "*Va, va, giovanetto.* Go with your mother. When a mother calls, children must obey."

Larry's face became red through the bronze and Lucia Santa saw the man's anger in his eyes. He looked like his dead father. "Like hell I will," Larry said.

The mother rushed across to him and hit him in the face, a good solid blow. He gave her a push that sent her staggering against the kitchen table.

The Le Cinglatas were aghast. There would be too much trouble now. They stepped between mother and son.

"Ahhh." Lucia Santa gave a long hiss of satisfaction. "A son strikes his mother. *Animale! Bestia! Sfachim! Figlio de puttana!* Thank God your father is dead. Thank God he does not see his son beating his own mother for the sake of strangers."

Larry's face had five red stripes, but he was no longer angry. He said sullenly, "Ah, Ma, I just pushed you away. Cut it out." He felt guilty, conscience-stricken, to see tears of humiliation in his mother's eyes.

Lucia Santa turned to the Le Cinglatas. "This is your pleasure, eh? Good. My son can stay here. But let me tell you this. My son will be in my house tonight. Or I will be in the police station. He is underage. I will send him to reform school and you people to prison. Selling wine and whisky is one thing, but here in America they protect children. As you said, Signora, we are not in Italy." She spoke to her son. "And you, stay with your friends. I wouldn't want your company in the street. Stay, enjoy yourself. But, dear son of mine, I warn you, sleep in my house tonight. Or big as you are I'll put you away." She made a dignified exit.

Walking home, she thought, Ah, that's how people make their fortunes. Money comes before everything. But what scum they are. What animals. And yet when they have money they dare look everyone in the eye.

That night, after the children had been put to bed, Octavia and the mother sat drinking coffee at the great round kitchen table. There was no sign of Larry. Octavia was a little frightened at her mother's determination to put Larry in reform school. She would not be able to go to work the next day. They would both have to go to the police station to swear out a summons. Octavia had never thought her mother could be so cruel and hard or so contemptuous of extra money earned by Larry at the Le Cinglatas'.

A knock on the door startled them, and Octavia went to open it. A tall, dark, good-looking man, dressed in a suit as beautiful as a movie star's, smiled at her. He asked in perfect Italian, "Is this the home of Signora Corbo?" Then he added, "I am from the Le Cinglatas, their lawyer; they asked me to see you."

Octavia brought him a cup of coffee. Friend or enemy, a guest was offered something to drink.

"Now," the young man said. "Signora Corbo, you are foolish to get so upset about your son. Everyone is bootlegging. It is not something wrong. The President himself has his little drink. And are you so rich you can't use a few dollars?"

"Mr. Lawyer," the mother said, "I don't care how or what you say." The young man was observing her intently, not taking offense. She went on. "My son sleeps in the house of his mother, his brothers, his sisters. Until he has a wife. That, or off he goes to reform school to enjoy his pleasure. At eighteen let him leave and I will not be his mother. But until he is of age I have no choice. None of my children will be pimps or jailbirds or murderers."

The young man was staring hard into her face. Then he said briskly, "Good. We understand each other. But perfectly, Signora. Now listen to me. On no account go to the police. I promise you that tomorrow without fail your son will be here.

This trouble will not trouble you again. Now, that's well said, is it not?"

"Tonight," Lucia Santa said.

"Eh," the young man replied. "I'm disappointed in you. Jesus Christ could not make your son come home tonight. You, a mother, with your experience of life—you must understand his pride. He thinks himself a man. Let him have this little victory."

The mother was pleased and flattered and recognized the truth. She nodded assent.

The young man rose quickly and said, "*Buona sera,* Signora." He bowed his head to Octavia and left.

"See?" the mother demanded grimly. "That is what I save your brother from."

Octavia was bewildered.

The mother went on, "A lawyer—ha, ha. They do business with the Black Hand. There was 'murder' written all over his face."

Octavia laughed with pure delight. She said, "Ma, you're crazy, you really are." And then she looked at her mother with love and respect. Her mother, a simple peasant, thinking this man a dangerous criminal, had not quailed or shown any fear. In fact, at the beginning she had looked as if she were going after the *Tackeril.*

"So now can I go to work tomorrow?" Octavia asked.

"Yes, yes," Lucia Santa said. "Go to work. Don't lose a day's pay. We can't afford it. People like us will never be rich."

5

HOLDING BABY LENA in her arms, Lucia Santa looked out the living room window into the blinding light of the late August morning. The streets were busy with traffic, and directly below her a peddler shouted his arrogant singsong. "Potatoes. Bananas. Spinach. Cheap. Cheap. Cheap." His wagon was filled with red, brown, green, and yellow square boxes of fruits and vegetables. Lucia Santa might have been staring down at a child's vivid, blotchy painting on her linoleum floor.

Across in the railroad yards she saw a crowd of people, men and young boys. Thank God Lorenzo was safe in his bed after the night shift, or she would have that terrible stabbing pain, the weakening fear in her legs and bowels. She watched the street intently.

She saw a small boy standing on top of a railroad car, staring down at the people below him. He was walking back and forth, a few steps at a time, quickly and frantically. The sun glinted on a blue rayon shirt laddered white across the chest. It could only be Gino. But what was he doing? What had happened? There were no engines near the car. He could not possibly be in danger.

Lucia Santa felt that power, that almost godlike sense of knowledge women feel looking down from windows at their children playing, observing and themselves unobserved. Like the legend of God peering out of a cloud at human children too engrossed to glance upward and catch him.

There was a glint of shiny black leather as the uniformed railroad policeman went up the ladder of the freight car, and the mother understood. She rushed into the bedroom and shouted, "Lorenzo, wake up. Hurry." She shook him. She gave her voice an urgent shrillness that would make him jump. Larry came bounding out of bed, all hairy chest and legs and BVDs, indecent to any woman but a mother, his hair tousled, his face greasy with the sweat of summer sleep. He followed his mother to the living room window. They were just in time to see Gino jump from the top of the railroad car to escape the Bull, who had climbed up to get him. They saw him grabbed by another black-uniformed Bull, who waited on the ground. When Gino dropped through the air, the mother let out a scream. Larry bawled, "Jesus Christ, how many times I told you make that kid stop stealing ice?" Then he rushed into the bedroom and put on his pants and sneakers and ran down the stairs.

When he came out of the building, his mother was shouting from the window, "Hurry, hurry, they're killing him." She had just seen one of the policemen give Gino a cuff on the ear. The whole group was walking toward the shanty on Tenth Avenue. Lucia Santa saw Larry run across the Avenue, rush toward them, and grab Gino's hand away from the policeman. In that moment she forgave his insults to her at the Le Cinglatas', forgave his sullen behavior of the last few weeks. He still knew what a brother meant; that there was no obligation more sacred than blood, that it came before country, church, wife, woman, and money. Like God, she watched the sinner redeem himself, and she rejoiced.

Larry Angeluzzi ran across the street like a man rushing to commit murder. He had been pushed around enough. During the past weeks he had lived with a feeling of rage, humiliation, and guilt. His image of himself had been shattered. He had actually struck his mother and shamed her before strangers. And all for the sake of people who had used him and then sent him away. A child sent to do errands, then brought to heel; an object of ridicule. In his mind he had become a villain, an angel fallen from his own heaven. Sometimes he could not believe he had acted in such a fashion and thought of it as an accident— that his mother had tripped and stumbled, that he had put his hand out to steady her and been clumsy. But behind this thought came a quick flush of shame. Now, not knowing he was seeking redemption, he grabbed Gino away from the Bull and felt, as if it were a physical touch, his watching mother's eye upon him.

Gino was crying, though not tears of pain or fear. Up to the last moment he had been sure he would escape. He had even dared to leap from the top of the railroad car to the hard gravel, and he had escaped injury. His tears were the tears of a little boy's baffled rage and lost pride on being made small and helpless and trapped.

Larry knew one of the Bulls, Charlie, but the other was a stranger. Larry had spent many a winter night in the shanty swapping stories with Charlie about the local girls, laughing at the bowlegged man's conceit. But now he said coldly to both of them. "What the hell you guys doing to my kid brother?" He had meant to be conciliating; he knew it was a time for friendliness and charm. But the words came out in a rough challenge.

The tall Bull, the stranger, said to Charlie Chaplin, "Who the hell is this guy?" and reached over to grab Gino. Larry pushed Gino behind him and said, "Go on home." Gino didn't move.

Charlie Chaplin said to his partner, "He's the dummy boy on the night shift." Then, "Listen, Larry, this kid brother of yours stole ice all summer. One time he throws rocks at me and tells me go fuck myself. A kid like that. Your brother or not, I'm gonna make his ass black and blue. Now step aside, kid, or get hurt. And out of a job in the bargain. You work for the railroad, too, don't forget. And *you are wrong, Jack.*"

One of the watching laborers said in Italian, "They gave your brother a few pretty slaps already."

Larry stepped backward until he felt pavement instead of gravel. They were out of the yard. He said, "We're off railroad property now. You guys got no jurisdiction." Larry decided to reason; he didn't want to lose his job. "But I'm surprised at you, Charlie. Since when you been a company man? Every kid on Tenth Avenue steals ice from the yards. Even your girl's kid brother. What the hell, you're not talking to a greenhorn. O.K., you hit my brother because he hit you with a rock. You're even." He saw out the corner of his eye, first the crowd, then Gino, dry-eyed and somber, his small boy's face wearing a look of thirsty vengeance that was comical. Larry said affectionately to his half brother, "You go in this yard again and I'll give you a beating. Now, come on."

It was well done. Everyone had saved face, he hadn't been too tough and made enemies, and he hadn't backed down. Larry was proud of his good judgment. But the tall, strange Bull spoiled everything. He said to Charlie Chaplin, "So you made me come all the way over here for nothing?" Charlie shrugged. The tall Bull reached out and gave Gino a backhanded slap in the face and said toughly, "Just let *me* see you in here." Larry hit him so hard that the black visored cap went flying through the crowd. The circle widened, and everyone waited for the bloody-mouthed Bull to get up. Without his cap he looked much older, and less menacing in his almost complete baldness. The Bull got up and faced Larry.

They stared at each other. The Bull took off his gun belt and gave it to Charlie along with his black jacket. He was long-chested in his tan shirt. He said quietly, "O.K., you're one of these tough guineas. Now you're gonna fight."

"Not here," Charlie said. "Let's get behind those cattle cars." They all walked back into the yard to a natural square of gravel. There was no idea of a trap. It was an affair of honor. Both Bulls lived on the West Side. To use their official authority now would disgrace them forever in the neighborhood.

Larry slipped out of the BVD top and stuffed it into his pants. Young as he was, he had a chest as hairy as and even broader than the older man's. Larry felt only one fear—that his mother would come down and make a scene. If she did that, he would leave the house for good. But glancing upward, he saw her figure still at the window.

For the first time in his life, Larry really wanted to fight, to hurt someone, to show himself the master of his world.

People were running across the Avenue to watch the fight. Heads were popping out of tenement windows. The *Panettiere*'s son, Guido, came to him and said, "I'll be your second." Behind him was Vinnie with a scared look on his face.

Larry and the Bull raised their hands against each other. In that moment Larry felt the full force of his mother watching at the window, and his two small brothers tense and wide-eyed in the crowd. He felt a great surge of power. He would never be humbled; they would never see him beaten. He sprang at the older man. They rained blows on each other, their fists sliding off each other's shoulders and arms. One of the Bull's defensive blows struck the onrushing Larry full in the face and left a long bloody gash on his cheek.

The *Panettiere*'s son rushed between them, yelling, "Take off the ring, you yellow bastard. Fight fair." The Bull flushed and took the rough gold wedding ring he had slipped up to his knuckle and threw it to Charlie Chaplin. The crowd jeered. The Bull rushed at Larry.

Larry, a little frightened at all the blood running down his face, yet filled with a murderous hatred, hit the Bull with a roundhouse right to the stomach. The Bull went down. The crowd yelled. Guido kept shouting, "Knock him out, Larry. Knock him out." The Bull got up and everyone was still. Larry heard his mother, far away, screaming, "Lorenzo, stoppa stoppa." Some of the people turned and looked across the Avenue and up toward the tenement window. Larry made a furious, imperious gesture for his mother to shut up.

The two men kept swinging at each other until the Bull went down again, not from the force of a blow, but to get rest. He was winded. When he got up, Larry knocked him down with a painful blow in the face.

The older man, furious with humiliation, grabbed Larry by the neck and tried to kick him. Larry flung him away. They were both exhausted, and neither was skillful enough to score a clear-cut victory. Charlie Chaplin grabbed the Bull and Guido grabbed Larry. Each held his friend back. The fight was over.

"O.K.," Charlie Chaplin said with authority. "It was a good fight. You both showed you ain't yellow. Shake hands and no hard feelings."

"Right," said Guido. Then, with a wink at Larry and with a voice filled with condescension for the Bulls, he said, "It's a draw." Some of the crowd shook Larry's hand and patted him on the shoulder. Everybody knew he had won the fight.

And then both Larry and the Bull had sheepish smiles on their faces. They shook hands laughing and grasped each other's shoulders to show their friendship. The Bull said huskily, "You're all right, kid." There were murmurs of approval. Larry put his arm around Gino and said, "Let's go, brudder." They crossed the Avenue and went up the stairs to the house. Guido and Vincent came with them.

When they came into the house the mother aimed one blow at Gino, which he dodged easily. Then she saw Larry's cheek. She wrung her hands and moaned, *"Marrone, marrone,"* and rushed to put a wet rag on the cut, meanwhile screaming at Gino, *"Sfachim,* because of you, your brother gets a beating."

"Ah, Ma," Larry said proudly and happily. "I won the fight—ask Guido."

"Sure," Guido said. "Your son could be a professional fighter, Mrs. Corbo. He knocked the hell out of that Bull. He wouldn't have a mark except for that ring."

Gino said excitedly, "Ma, Larry knocked that bastard down four times. That makes you win the fight, right, Larry?"

"Sure," Larry said. "But you cut out that cursing." He felt full of affection for his mother and brother and the whole family. "Nobody is gonna lay their hands on anybody in my family," he said. "I woulda killed the guy except for my job in the railroad."

Lucia Santa gave them all coffee. Then she said, "Lorenzo, go back to sleep. Remember you work tonight." Guido and Vinnie left for the bakery. Larry undressed and went to bed. Lying there, he could hear Gino telling his mother all about the fight in an excited happy voice.

Larry felt tired and at peace. He was no longer a villain. Tonight when he rode up Tenth Avenue on his horse, the great black engine and endless train behind him, people on the Avenue would look at him, shout to him, talk to him. He would be treated with respect. He had protected his brother and the family honor. No one would dare mistreat anyone in his family. He fell asleep.

In the kitchen the mother, her face awful with fury, said to Gino, "If you go into the railroad again, I'll kill you." Gino shrugged.

Lucia Santa was happy, but a little irritated by all the fuss about the fight, the masculine pride and hoopla, as if such things were really of great importance. Now she wanted to hear no more of it. She had that secret contempt for male heroism that many women feel but never dare express; they find masculine pride in heroics infantile, for after all, what man would risk his life day after day and year after year as all women do in the act of love? Let them bear children, let their bodies open up into a great bloody cavern year after year. They would not be so proud then of their trickling scarlet noses, their little knife cuts. Gino was still babbling about the fight. She picked him up by the scruff of the neck and threw him out the door like a kitten. She shouted after him, "Don't dare be late for supper."

THE REST OF the summer Lucia Santa had to do battle with Octavia in a cruel heat that was burnt out of concrete. The pavement and gutters were covered with the dust of dried manure flakes, soot—the debris of millions of people and animals. Even the great structures of inanimate stone seemed to shed gritty particles into the air as a dog sheds hair.

Octavia won. First she switched jobs and became a sewing teacher for the Melody Corporation, an organization promoting the sale of sewing machines. Octavia gave the free lessons that went with each purchase. The pay was three dollars a week less than she had been getting, but there would be promotions. Then, too, she could sew dresses for her mother and Baby Lena right at work. This last persuaded Lucia Santa. That was one victory.

Vinnie had become very thin during the summer. The mother worried, and so did her daughter. One day Octavia took her three little brothers to the free dental clinic at the Hudson Guild Settlement House. Earlier she had seen a sign saying that applications were open for the Herald Tribune Fresh Air Fund, which sent children to summer camp for two weeks or to special country homes. She had entered Vinnie's name. That was before the job with the *Panettiere*.

Now she broached the subject with her mother. Vinnie would only lose two weeks' pay. He would have to leave the job when school opened in the fall anyway. Here was an opportunity for him to spend two weeks in the country with a private farm family, all expenses paid. The mother protested, not because of the money, but because she could not grasp the basic principle that a city child ought to spend a few weeks in the fresh country air. Herself a peasant, she could not believe this. Also she found it hard to believe that a strange couple would agree to take an unknown child into their home for two weeks without making him work or earn his keep. When Octavia explained that people received a small payment, she understood. It must be a good sum.

Finally Lucia Santa consented. Gino would take Vincent's place in the bakery for two weeks. Vinnie was given a letter he could mail so that if he did not like it, Octavia would come and get him. Then Vincent didn't want to go. He was terrified of having to live with strange people. But Octavia became so angry and close to tears that he went.

Gino ruined the family reputation for industry and reliability working for the *Panettiere*. After a bread delivery he would not return for hours. He came late and left early. He threw flour sacks down the cellar stairs and dragged them up, ripping the bags, spilling the flour. He ate tons of pizza and lemon ice. Yet no one could be angry with him. The *Panettiere* merely informed the mother that Gino would not be an acceptable substitute for Vincenzo next summer and they both laughed, which made Octavia furious. God forbid, if Vinnie did what they were laughing at, the mother would beat him black and blue.

Octavia had her reward. Suddenly it was the end of summer, school was only a week away, and Vinnie came home. The change was astonishing. He had a new suitcase of shining brown leather. He wore new white flannel trousers, a white shirt, a blue tie, and a blue jacket. His face was tanned and full. He was at least an inch taller. He was quite the man of the world when the social workers dropped him off in a cab they had taken from Grand Central Station.

That night the Angeluzzi-Corbo family went indoors early.

When Vinnie told them all about the country, Gino and Sal were wide-eyed, and even Baby Lena seemed to be listening.

The country was a place without brick or pavement. The streets were made of dirt; apples, small and green, hung on trees all around. Raspberries grew on bushes wherever you went. You just ate everything when you felt like it. The country was a small white house made of wood, and the nights were so cold you had to use blankets. Everybody had a car because there were no subways or trolley cars. The mother was unimpressed. She had lived in the country. But Gino was stunned at the thought of what he had missed.

Then Vincent showed them his pajamas. He was the first one in the family to own a pair. They were yellow and black, and he had picked them out himself. The mother said, "But you sleep in these?" In winter everyone slept with heavy underwear and a knitted sweater of coarse wool. In hot weather there were BVDs. Pajamas were for the Chinese.

"But why did these people buy you all these clothes?" she asked. "Do they get that much money from the *Funda*?"

"No," Vinnie said proudly, "they like me. They want me back next year and they said I could bring Gino too. I told them all about the family. They're gonna write me letters and send me a Christmas present. So I'll have to send one to them too."

"So, they have no children?" the mother asked.

"No," said Vincent.

Seeing him happy, Octavia said impulsively, "You won't have to go back to the bakery, Vin. It's only a week before school. He can go to hell." Vinnie was delighted. They both looked toward Lucia Santa, but she smiled at them in agreement. Her face was thoughtful.

She was wondering. There were good people in the world, then, that made strange children happy. What kind of people were these? How safe they must be that they could squander love and money on a boy they had never seen and might never see again. Vaguely she sensed that outside her world was another as different as another planet. It was not a world that people like themselves could ever stay in. They entered by charity, and charity exhausted itself like a falling star, burned out. Ah, in Italy they eat the children of the poor alive, the rich, the fat landowners. But it was enough that for tonight her children were happy and had hope. She was content.

The summer ended badly for Octavia. Her boss, a portly, genial man, always very nice, called her into the office one evening.

"Miss Angeluzzi," he said, "I've had my eye on you. You are a fine teacher. The women who buy their machines and get their lessons from you are very happy with you. And they are very happy with their machines. And that is the rub, my dear girl."

Octavia was bewildered. "I don't know what you mean," she said.

"Well, you're young, you're obviously intelligent. That's good, very good. And you have determination. You get a job done. I noticed one woman having trouble, a very stupid woman, that was easy to see, and you stuck with her until she got the technique. I won't make any bones about it, you're the best girl we ever had." He patted her kindly on the arm, and she drew away. He smiled; her benighted Italian upbringing had betrayed her. A man only touched you for one reason.

Octavia's mind was spinning with pleasure at his praise. She was a real teacher after all. She had been right all the time.

"But, Octavia," the boss went on gently, "the Melody Sewing Machine Company is not in business to give sewing lessons. Or even to sell those inferior machines we advertise to make people come into the store. We want to sell the good machines. The best. Now that is what your job really is. I'm promoting you to saleslady, with a two-dollar raise. But you still do the same thing. Only be sociable." Her eyes suddenly flashed and he smiled. "No, not with me. Be sociable and go out with these ladies you teach. Have coffee with them, get to be real friendly. You speak Italian, and that helps. Now, we don't make money on the machines we advertise. Your job is to make these people switch to the better models. Understand? Just go on as you do now. Only be their friend, maybe even go out at night with them. Come to work a little late the next morning. If you sell good you make your own hours." He started to pat her arm again, stopped and gave her an amused, fatherly smile.

Octavia left the office impressed, happy, tremendously flattered. Now she had a good job, a job with a future. That afternoon she went out with some of the young married women when they had their coffee break, and they talked with her so respectfully and with such deference that she felt very important, just like a real teacher. When she asked one of them how the machine worked, the woman said it was fine, adding, "Your boss tried to make me change to that fancy expensive one. But why should I? I'm just making dresses for my kids and myself and saving a little money." Then Octavia saw clearly what her boss had asked her to do.

Once started on her job of selling, she had for the first time in her life to make a moral and intellectual decision that had nothing to do with her own personal relationships, her body, her sex, her family. She learned that to get ahead in the world meant despoiling her fellow human beings. She thought of her mother, a greenhorn, being cheated in such a fashion. If it had been a case of padding bills, overcharging to keep her job, she might have done so. But she still was so naïve that she felt that to use her personality, her smiles, her words of friendship, was like using her body for material gain. Sometimes she tried, but she was not capable of the final bullying that was needed to clinch a sale.

In two weeks she was fired. The boss stood near the door as she went out. He shook his head at her, smiling with gentle pity, and said, "You're a nice girl, Octavia." But she did not smile in return. Her black eyes flashed angrily and she gave him a look of contempt. He could afford to understand her. He had lost nothing, his way of life had conquered. His was the easy amiability of the victor over the vanquished. She could not afford such tolerance.

Octavia began to lose her dreams. Now it seemed that the teachers she had loved had really tricked her with their compliments, with their urgings to find a better life, a life she could not afford to seek. They had sold her an ideal too expensive for her world.

Octavia went back to the garment shops. When she had a new job she told her mother the whole story; the mother listened silently. She was combing little Sal's hair, holding the boy between her knees. She merely said, "People like you will never be rich."

Octavia said angrily, "I wouldn't do it to poor people. You wouldn't do it, either. Put money in those lousy bastards' pockets."

Lucia Santa said wearily, "I'm too old for such tricks. And I have no talent. I don't like people well enough to be nice to them, not even for money. But you, you're young, you can learn. It's not so hard. But no. My family, they read books, they go to movies, they think they can act like rich people. Have pride. Be poor. It's nothing to me. I was poor, my children can be poor." She pushed Sal toward the door.

Sal turned around and said, "Give me two cents for a soda, Ma." The mother, who always gave him two cents, said angrily, "Didn't you hear what I just told your sister? We are poor. Now *go.*"

Sal looked at her gravely. She thought with irritation that all her children were too serious. Then Sal said, with the perfect reasonableness of a child, "If you never give me two cents will you be rich?" Octavia let out a shriek of laughter. The mother took her pocketbook and with a straight face gave Sal a silver nickel. Sal ran out of the house without another word.

Lucia Santa shrugged and smiled at Octavia. And yet, the

mother thought, if I never gave my children two cents for soda, we might be rich. If I never gave them money for the moving pictures and baseballs, if I made meat only once a week and put on the electric light only when it was pitch dark. If I sent my children to work all year round instead of waiting till they finish high school, if I made them sew buttons on cards at night instead of reading and listening to the radio—who knows?

Thousands of houses had been bought on Long Island by miserly thrift. But it would never work with her family. They would all be miserable, including herself. And it was her fault. She had not rubbed their noses in poverty as a good mother should.

She had no illusions about human beings. They were not evil, not deliberately malicious. But money was God. Money could make you free. Money could give you hope. Money could make you safe. Renounce money? As well ask a man to give up his gun in the wild jungle.

Money guarded the lives of your children. Money lifted them out of darkness. Who has not wept for lack of money? Who has not wept for money? Who comes when money calls? Doctors, priests, dutiful sons.

Money was a new homeland. Lying awake at night thinking of the growing sums in the bank, Lucia Santa felt the sudden physical chilling sharpness mixed with fear that a prisoner feels when counting the days to stay behind walls.

And money was friends, respectful relatives. A new Jesus could never rise to reproach those with money.

Not to be rich, but to have money; to have money like a wall to put your back to, and then face the world.

Octavia knew her mother was thinking about money. Money for doctors, money for clothes, money for the oil stove, money for school books, money for Communion suits. Money for a house on Long Island, and maybe little Sal would be the one to go to college.

And yet, Octavia thought, with all this her mother was

careless with money. She bought the best olive oil, expensive cheese, imported prosciutto. She served meat at least three times a week. And many times she called a doctor for the ailing children, where other families would give home remedies and wait for the fever or cold to pass. At Easter time each child had a new suit or dress.

But every few weeks there was five or ten dollars that the mother would give Octavia to put away. There was now over fifteen hundred dollars in the postal savings book that no one knew about except her and her mother. Octavia wondered what the magic signal would be that would make her mother decide to take one of the great steps in a family's life and buy a house on Long Island.

IT WAS AUTUMN, the children going to school, the nights too chilly to sit on the Avenue, and too much work to do to spend a whole evening in gossip. There were clothes to wash and press, shoes to shine, buttons to be sewn on cards to earn extra money. Oil stoves were brought out of hiding from backyard and cellar. The city changed its lights; the sun became a chilly yellow, the pavements and gutters steely gray. The buildings became taller and thinner and more distinct from each other. You could no longer smell the stone and tar. The air lost its summer solidity of dust and heat. White smoke from bull engines in the railroad yard smelled of nature. It was on the morning of such a day that Frank Corbo came home to his family.

6

T HE BIG CHILDREN were off to school and work. Zia
Louche was having a coffee with Lucia Santa. They both
heard steps on the stairs and when the door opened, Frank
Corbo, proud, but like a child waiting for a sign of welcome,
stood for a few moments before entering the apartment. He
looked well, his face brown and full, the eyes gentler. Lucia
Santa said coolly, "Ah, you're home finally." But there was a
note of welcome in her voice despite the resigned, unspoken
protest. Zia Louche, being older, knew how to treat a returning husband. She said, "Ah, Frank, how well you look. How
good it is to see you looking so well." And she bustled around
to get him a cup of coffee. Frank Corbo sat at the table opposite his wife.

They looked into each other's eyes for a moment. There
was nothing either could say. What he had done had been impossible not to do. He could make no apology, no plea for understanding. She must accept it as she must accept sickness
and death. And just as impossible was it that she could forgive

him. She rose and went to the door where he had left his suit-case, as if he might not stay, and put it in the farthest corner of the room. Then she made him a quick omelet to go with his coffee.

When she bent her head over to serve him, he kissed her cheek and she accepted the kiss. It was an act of two people who have betrayed each other and with this kiss pledged them-selves never to seek vengeance.

The two women and the man sat around drinking coffee. Zia Louche asked, "So how was it to go back on the land? Ah, work, real work is the best thing for a man. In Italy people work sixteen hours a day and never get sick. But you, you look very fine. The land agreed with you, then?"

The father nodded his head. He was polite. "It was good," he said.

The two small children, Sal and Baby Lena, came down the corridor from the front room, where they had been playing. When they saw their father, they stopped and held each other's hand. They stared at him.

Zia Louche said sharply, "Go kiss your father, go." But the father was looking at the children with the same helpless vul-nerable ghost of remembered love, a kind of wonder, remem-brance mixed with wariness, of danger. When they came to him he bent and kissed their foreheads with an infinite gentle-ness. After he had done this his wife saw that stricken look in his eyes that had always troubled her so.

From his pocket the father took two small brown paper bags of candy and gave one to each of the children. They sat on the floor beside his chair, to open the bags and explore their gifts, brushing against the father's legs like cats. He drank his coffee, seemingly unaware, making no gesture to touch them again.

Zia Louche left. When the door closed, the father took a roll of bills from his pocket, kept two for himself, and gave the rest to Lucia Santa. There was a hundred dollars.

She was overwhelmed. "Maybe you did the right thing. You look better. How do you feel, Frank?" Her voice was touched with concern, a little apprehensive.

"Better," the husband said. "I was sick. I didn't want to fight before I left, so I couldn't tell you. The noise in the city, in the house. My head hurt all the time. Out there it was quiet. I worked hard all day and at night I slept without dreams. What man could want more?"

They were both silent. At last he said, as if in apology, "That's not much money, but it's everything I earned. I didn't spend a penny on myself. My boss gave me the suitcase, the clothes, and my living. Better than staying here and washing your stairs."

The mother said quietly, reassuringly, "It is a lot of money." But she could not help adding, "Gino did your stairs for you." She expected him to be angry. But Frank nodded his head and said in a reasonable, gentle voice, without irony, "Children must suffer for the sins of their fathers."

He spoke like a churchgoer, a Christian, and, in confirmation of her suspicion, he took a red-edged holy book from the pocket of his jacket.

"You see this?" he asked. "This book has the truth and I can't even read it. It's in Italian and still I cannot read it. When Gino comes home from school he can read to me. The places are marked."

The mother watched him intently. "You must be tired," she said. "Go on to bed and sleep. I'll send the children down to play in the street."

When he had undressed and gone to bed she brought him a wet towel so that he could wipe his face and hands. He made no attempt to possess her or show any desire, and when he closed his eyes and sank back into the bed, it seemed as if he were closing his eyes against the world he had re-entered. Lucia Santa sensed something terribly wrong beneath the external health, the seeming good fortune. Looking down at him, she felt a strange pity for this man she had loved, who had been her husband so many years. As if in the course of every day, with each second, each minute, each day she had spun out his fate, as if he were her prisoner dying in his cell. She was an innocent jailer, she had not pursued him, she had not condemned him, she had not sentenced him. But she could never let him escape. Lucia Santa sat on the bed and put her hand on his. He was already asleep. She sat so for a time, in some way glad that he would be sleeping safe in his bed when the rest of the family returned home, that Octavia, Larry, Gino, and Vinnie would see him for the first time defenseless, and so they could pity him.

That evening the family was at supper when the father rose and joined them. Octavia said "Hello" very coldly. Larry was warm in his greeting, saying with utmost sincerity, "You're looking good, Pop. We missed you around here."

Gino and Vincent gazed at him curiously. The father asked Gino, "Have you been good to your mother while I was away?" Gino nodded. The father sat down and then, as an afterthought, he took the two one-dollar bills from his pocket and without a word gave them to Gino and Vincent.

Octavia was angry that he had not asked Vincent if he had been good. She understood Vincent and knew that he had been hurt, that the dollar would not make up for this. It made her even angrier because she understood that her stepfather had not done this intentionally.

Suddenly the father made a statement that startled all of them.

"Some of my friends are visiting me tonight," he said. He had never brought friends to the house. As if he knew or felt in some way that this was not really his home, that he could never be the chief of this family. He had not even brought card-playing cronies home for a glass of wine. Tonight Larry had to go to work, but Octavia decided to stay and meet these people, and give her mother support if they were in league with her stepfather against the family.

THE HOUSE WAS neat, the dishes washed, fresh coffee on the stove, and store-bought cake on the table when the visitors came. They were Mr. and Mrs. John Colucci and their nine-year-old son, Job.

The Coluccis were young, in their early thirties. Mr. Colucci was thin and saturnine, with only a slight accent to show that he was not born in America. He wore a shirt, tie, and jacket. His wife was heavy and voluptuous, but not fat. She had no accent, but she seemed more Italian than her husband.

The whole Angelucci-Corbo family was surprised at the affection the Coluccis showed for Frank Corbo. They shook his hand warmly, inquired after him tenderly, said, "And this is your wife" in admiring tones, and "These are your children?" as if awe-struck and incredulous. They treated him as if he were a rich uncle, Lucia Santa thought. And she could see her husband reacting to their love. He was never demonstrative, but she could tell by his tone, by his respectful voice, in which for the first time since their marriage she heard that note which means that the speaker will bow to the wishes and opinions of his listeners. He was nervous, anxious to please. For the first time, he seemed to want people to think well of him. He poured the coffee himself.

They all sat around the great kitchen table. Octavia was charming in the best American style, with frequent smiles and a low sweet voice. The Coluccis had perfect manners. It was obvious that Mr. Colucci worked in an office and not with his hands. Mrs. Colucci spoke a refined Italian she could never have learned in Italy. They were not the children of mountain peasants but from the class of officials, of long generations of civil servants in Italy. Mr. Colucci was one of the few Italians whose family had emigrated to America for religious reasons instead of poverty. They were Protestants, and here in America they had formed a new sect, the Literal Baptist Church.

It had of course been the will of God that they met Frank Corbo. The farm owner was a first cousin of the Coluccis' and they spent their summer vacation on the farm for the sake of their son's health. Lucia Santa, a reconstructed peasant, raised her eyebrows at this repetition of a theme she had heard so much during the past summer. But, Mr. Colucci went on, what showed the hand of God was that they lived only a few blocks away from each other in the city, and every morning he passed the house of Frank Corbo. Mr. Colucci worked in the Runkel chocolate factory around the corner on 31st Street. Best of all, he was sure he could get Frank Corbo a job in the factory, but it was not for that they had come to visit.

No. Mr. Colucci had promised he would teach Frank Corbo to read and write. They would use the Bible as text. They had come tonight to keep their promise to visit him, to teach him, not only reading and writing, but about Jesus Christ. He would have to come to their class in the chapel of the Literal Baptist Church. Mr. Colucci wanted to make sure that Mrs. Lucia Santa Corbo would not object, would not be offended, if her husband came three nights a week to the chapel. He knew the respect, the consideration due an Italian wife and mother of children. He made no mention of religious objections, as if he knew there would be none.

Lucia Santa looked at him with a more kindly eye. She gathered that her husband would become a Protestant, but to her this was unimportant in every sense. He was a grown man. But the job at Runkel's. He would bring home free chocolate and cocoa. The pay would not be insignificant. This was good fortune. Her husband could become a Jew if he wished. She gave not her assent, for that was not hers to give; the father could not be vetoed. She gave her blessing.

The tension relaxed, they talked about themselves, told each other what part of Italy they had come from, when and why they had left. The Coluccis did not smoke or drink. Religion was their life, for they believed in a living God. They told wondrous tales of the miracles their faith had wrought. At their meetings in chapel, believers fell to the ground in a trance and spoke in strange tongues; drunkards became total abstainers, evil men who regularly tattooed their wives and children black and blue became sweet as saints. Lucia Santa raised her eyebrows in polite astonishment. Mr. Colucci went on. "Sinners become God-like. I myself was a great sinner, in what manner I would rather not say." His wife bowed her head for a moment, and when she looked up there was a small, grim smile on her lips. But Mr. Colucci had not said this boastingly. His was the manner of a man who had been the victim of a terrible misfortune and who after great suffering had been rescued through no virtue of his own.

Mr. Colucci went on to make himself clear. Even now, if Frank did not feel the faith, it did not matter. They were his friends, they would do everything to help him. Out of love for him and God. Faith would come in its own time.

The family was impressed, despite the words "love" and "God." They had never met or even heard of a man like Mr. Colucci. Lucia Santa waited for some request, some trick that would exact payment for this good fortune. But there was none. She rose to make fresh coffee and bring out the *tarelle*. The father watched them all, impassive but seemingly content.

There could be no doubt. Everything was in harmony. Mr. Colucci sensed this and was carried away. He explained more about their religion. Everyone should love each other, no one should desire worldly goods. Shortly, Armageddon would come, God would wipe out the world, and only the chosen, the true believers, would be saved. Mrs. Colucci nodded her head. Her beautiful mouth, with its natural, dark, bloody red color, was tight with conviction, her magnificent dark eyes flashed around the room.

The children, sensing they had been lost track of, sneaked away. Gino, Vincent, and Job went down the corridor to the front room. Mr. Colucci went on. Lucia Santa listened with polite calm. These people were going to get her husband work. *Bravo.* They could have his prayers. All her children except Sal and Lena had already made their Communion and Confirmation in the Catholic Church, but she had done this as she dressed them in new clothes on Easter Sunday, as part of a primitive social rite. She herself had long ceased to think of God except to automatically curse his name for some misfortune. There was no question; when she died she would prudently take the last rites of her church. But now she did not go to Mass even for Christmas or Easter.

Octavia was more impressed. She was young and a belief in goodness and a desire to do good works inspired respect in her. She wished she were as beautiful as Mrs. Colucci and she thought for a moment that it was a good thing that Larry wasn't home to exercise his charms on her, as he surely would.

The father watched and listened, as if he expected Mr. Colucci to say something he desperately wished to hear, as if Mr. Colucci were very close to saying some magic words that would be a key for him. He kept waiting.

In the front room Gino took his deck of cards from the round hole of the wall that housed the stovepipe in winter. "You wanta play Seven-and-a-half?" he asked Job. Vinnie was already sitting on the floor and taking pennies out of his pocket. Gino sat down opposite him.

"Card playing is a sin," Job said. He was a small earnest boy, almost pretty, resembling his mother, but in no way effeminate. He sat down on the floor and watched.

"You want a hand for Chrissake?" Gino asked mildly.

"Swearing is a sin," Job said.

"Bullshit," Vinnie said. He never swore himself, but who did this snotnose think he was, telling Gino not to swear?

Gino tilted his head and looked at Job wisely. "You talk like that on this block, kiddo, they take off your pants and hang them on the lamp post. You have to run home and every-

body sees your bare ass." The frightened look on Job's face satisfied them. They played cards and became absorbed in the
game.

Job said suddenly, "Well, all right, but you two will go to
hell, and pretty soon, too."

Gino and Vinnie couldn't be bothered.

Job said calmly, "My father said the End of the World is
coming."

Gino and Vinnie stopped playing for a minute. Mr. Colucci
had impressed them.

Job smiled with confidence. "It's people like you that will
cause it. You make God mad because you do bad things like
gamble and curse. If people like you did everything that me
and my father told you, maybe God wouldn't make the world
end."

Gino frowned. He had made his Communion and Confirmation the year before and the nuns who taught him the cate-
chism had said nothing about this. "When does it happen?" he
asked.

"Soon," Job said.

"Tell us when," Gino insisted, still respectful.

"It's gonna be by fires and floods and guns coming out of
the sky. Everything is gonna explode. The earth is gonna open
up and swallow people into hell and the ocean's gonna cover
everything. And everybody is gonna burn in hell. Except just a
few who believe and act good. And then God is gonna love
everybody again."

"Yeah, but when?" Gino was stubborn. He always wanted
an answer when he asked a question, no matter what it was.

"Twenty years from now," Job said.

Gino counted his pennies. "I'll bet a nickel," he said to Vincent. Vinnie dealt. Anything could happen in twenty years.

Vinnie lost. Old enough to be witty, he said, "If I had a
name like Job the world couldn't end too soon for me."

The two brothers watched Job slyly and for the first time he became angry. He said, "I'm named after one of the greatest people in the Bible. You know what Job did? He believed. So God tested him. God killed his children, and then made his wife run away. Then God made him blind and gave him millions of pimples. Then God took all his money and his house. Then you know what? God sent a devil to Job's house to ask Job if he still loved God. You know what Job said?" He paused dramatically. "The Lord giveth, and the Lord taketh away. I love my God."

Vinnie was impressed and watched Job intently. Gino was outraged and asked, "Did he really mean it? Or was he afraid he was gonna get killed?"

"Sure he meant it," Job said. "And then God gave him a lot of good luck to make up for it because he believed. My father says that Job was the first Literal Baptist. That's why the Literal Baptists get saved when the world ends and everybody who doesn't listen to us is gonna get buried for a million years. Or even more. You two had just better stop playing cards and swearing."

But since he was just a nutty little kid, Gino riffled the cards, humping them and letting them cascade into place. Job watched, fascinated by such expertness. Gino looked at him and said, "You wanta try it?" He thrust the deck into Job's hands. Job tried to riffle the cards and they scattered across the floor. He picked them up and tried again, his face intent and serious. Suddenly an enormous shadow spread across the room. Mrs. Colucci was watching them; they had not heard her come down the corridor of bedrooms.

Vinnie and Gino were fascinated by her beauty. They stared. She was looking her son up and down very coolly, with one eyebrow raised.

Job stuttered, "Mother, I wasn't playing, Gino was just showing me how to shuffle. I just watched them play."

Gino said warmly, "He ain't lying, Mrs. Colucci, he just watched. You know," he said with enormous wonder, "he wouldn't play no matter what I said."

Mrs. Colucci smiled and said, "I know my son never lies to me, Gino. But touching cards is a beginning. His father will be very angry with him."

Gino smiled at her confidentially. "You don't have to tell his father."

Mrs. Colucci said coldly, "Of course I won't tell him. But Job certainly will." Gino was surprised and looked at Job questioningly. Mrs. Colucci said in a more gentle voice, "Mr. Colucci is the head of our house, as God rules over the world. You wouldn't keep secrets from God, would you, Gino?" Gino looked at her thoughtfully.

Vinnie was angrily shuffling cards. He was mad at Gino for not seeing through these people, for acting as if they liked him, being fooled by their good manners. On Mrs. Colucci's beautiful face he had seen a look of disgust at their playing cards, as though she had caught them in something shameful that you never talked about. "Stop butting in, Gino," he said. He dealt out a hand.

Gino, intrigued by something he could not understand, said to Job, "You gonna tell your father? No kidding? If you don't tell him, your mother won't tell. Right, Mrs. Colucci?" The look of physical disgust came over the woman's face, but she said nothing.

Job didn't answer, but tears came out of his eyes. Gino was stunned. He said, "I'll tell your father I pushed the cards into your hands. That's what I did. Right, Vin? Come on, I'll tell him."

Mrs. Colucci said sharply, "His father will believe everything Job tells him. Good night, children. Say good night to your friends, Job." Job said nothing, and they both went down the corridor to the kitchen.

The two brothers had no heart for more cards. Gino went to one window, opened it, and sat on the sill. Vincent went to the other window and did the same.

The railroad yard was dark except for a headlight of one working, black, invisible engine, grinding steel on steel. Even the Hudson River was almost blue-black beneath the faint autumn moon, and the cliffs of the Palisades were shadowy mountains beyond. Tenth Avenue below the window was dark and still, swept clean of smells and people by a cold October night wind. Only on the corner of 31st Street was there life, a bonfire with some half-grown boys around it.

Gino and Vincent saw their father come out of the building with the Coluccis. He was walking them to the trolley car on Ninth Avenue. They watched till he came back. They saw him stand by the bonfire, staring into its flames for a long time. They kept their eyes on him. Finally he walked down the Avenue and into the house.

Gino and Vincent left their windows. They unfolded their bed and made it. Vinnie put on his pajamas from the country. Watching him, Gino said, "That Job, he's a nice kid, but he's sure lucky he don't live on our block."

Mr. Colucci was not just a talker, he was a doer. Frank Corbo was working in Runkel's chocolate factory the next week, and his homecoming at night was a delight for the children. He returned with his person and clothes scented with cocoa. Always he would have a great jagged boulder of chocolate in his pocket. It was pure chocolate, much more delicious than candy-store chocolate. He would give this to Gino to share among the children. Gino would hack it with a knife, give half to Vinnie and half to himself. Then they would each give a piece to Sal and Baby Lena. Gino always thought of his father as working on a great mountain rock of chocolate with a pickax, breaking it up into little pieces.

The father was to be baptized in the new faith at Easter time. Every night he went to the Coluccis' for reading lessons, and then to the chapel for services and more lessons. Sometimes he would make Gino read to him from the Bible, but Gino always protested; he read badly and with obvious distaste, especially his father's favorite passages, in which man was brought to book by a wrathful and revengeful God. Gino read this in such a voice, so unimpressed and bored, that he only irritated his father. One day Frank Corbo said to him gently and with a smile, "*Animale!* Don't you believe in God then? Aren't you afraid of dying and going to hell?"

Gino was surprised and confused. "I made my Communion and Confirmation," he said. The father looked at him, shrugged, and never asked him to read again.

For the next two months everything went smoothly. There were no quarrels.

But then Lucia Santa, seeing her husband so well, working, quiet, well-behaved, thought there was no excuse for him not to be better. She complained that he was always out of the house, that his children never saw him, that he did not take her to visit relatives. And it was as if the father had been waiting for such a complaint, as if his new character had not really pleased him. There was a scene; he struck a blow, there were screams and shouts, Octavia threatened her father with a kitchen knife. It was like old times again. The father left the house and did not come back until the next morning.

He changed gradually. He did not go to chapel so often. Many nights he came straight home and went directly to bed without eating. He would lie in the bed staring up at the ceiling, not sleeping, not speaking. Lucia Santa would bring him a hot dish; sometimes he would eat, sometimes he would strike it out of her hand, soiling the bed covers. Then he would not let her change the bed sheets that night.

He would fall asleep for a bit; then wake near midnight, moaning and tossing about. He had terrifying headaches and Lucia Santa would bathe his temples with alcohol. Nevertheless, the next morning he would be well enough to go to work. Nothing kept him from his job.

That winter the nights were like a nightmare. The father's cries would wake the baby. Gino, Vincent, and Sal would huddle together, Gino and Vincent curious and subdued, but Sal so frightened that he trembled. Octavia would wake and lie in her bed raging over her mother's patience with the father. Larry missed it all, for he worked at night and stayed out until the early morning hours.

The father became worse. He would wake in the middle of the night and curse his wife, first in a slow, then a quickening, rhythm—the rhythms of the Bible. Everyone would be asleep, the house would be dark, when suddenly, rising out of the pitch blackness, the father's voice would fill the apartment, vibrant, alive. "Whore" . . . "Bitch" . . . "Lousy, dir-ty, rot-ten, lying bastard" . . . Then, on a higher note and faster, "Fiend of hell—child of a whore—mother of a whore." Last came a long stream of filth that ended in a great moan of pain and a terrifying cry for help, "*Gesù, Gesù,* help me, help me."

Everyone awake, frightened, sitting up in bed, would wait, never knowing what he would do next. The mother would soothe him, talking in a low voice, pleading with him to be quiet so that the family could sleep. She would bathe his temples with alcohol until the apartment was filled with its burning smell.

Octavia and Lucia Santa quarreled about sending him to the hospital. Lucia Santa refused to consider it. Octavia, fatigued from lack of sleep and worry, became hysterical, and her mother had to slap her face. One night when the father began to moan *"Gesù, Gesù,"* from behind Octavia's bedroom door came a mocking moan in answer. When the father cursed in Italian, Octavia shrieked back, aping his dialect, the filthy words in the foreign tongue, shrill in the darkness, more shocking than the cursing of the father. Sal and Baby Lena began to cry. Vinnie and Gino sat on the edge of their bed, stunned with sleep and fright. Lucia Santa pounded on her daughter's bedroom door, pleading with her to stop. But Octavia was beyond control, and it was the father who stopped first.

Next morning the father did not go to work. Lucia Santa let him rest while she sent the children off to school. Then she brought her husband breakfast.

He was rigid as wood. His eyes stared emptily at the ceiling. When she shook him, he spoke in hollow tones. "I'm dead, don't let them bury me without clothes. Put my good shoes on my feet. God has called me. I'm dead." The mother was so frightened she felt his limbs. They were icy cold and stiff. Then the father began to call out, "*Gesù, Gesù.* Mercy. *Aiuto, aiuto.*"

She tried to hold his hand. "Frank, let me call the doctor," she said. "You're sick, Frank."

The father became as angry as a dead man could. In hollow menacing tones, he answered. "If the doctor comes, I'll throw him out the window." But the threat was reassuring to Lucia Santa, for now the cold blue eyes were alive with rage. Heat flowed into the limbs she touched. Then she heard someone coming up the stairs and into the house. It was Larry home from the night shift.

She called out, "Lorenzo, come here and see your father." The tone of her voice brought Larry quickly down the corridor to the bedroom.

"Look how sick he is, and he won't see the doctor," the mother said. "Talk to him."

Larry was shocked by his stepfather's appearance. He had not noticed the change, the thinning of the face into gauntness, the tension in the mouth, the cording of the face into lines of madness. He said gently, "Come on, Pop. We gotta get a doc even if you're dead. Maybe people will say Ma poisoned you or something. See? We gotta get a certificate." He smiled at his stepfather.

But Frank Corbo gave him a look of contempt, as if the son were feeble-minded or insane. "No doctors," he said. "Let me rest." He closed his eyes.

Lucia Santa and Larry went into the kitchen at the other end of the apartment. The mother said, "Lorenzo, go to Runkel's and get Mr. Colucci. He can talk to Frank. Last night he was so bad again. If this keeps up—no, get Mr. Colucci."

Larry was dead tired and wanted to get to bed. But he saw

that his mother, always so strong and confident, was near to tears she was too proud to shed. He felt an overwhelming love and pity for her, and yet a curious distaste for being involved in the affair, as if it was a tragedy that did not concern him. He patted his mother's arm and said, "O.K., Ma," and left the house in search of Mr. Colucci.

MR. COLUCCI, DESPITE the fact that he was an office worker, could not get off from work. He came at five o'clock, bringing with him three other men. Their clothes smelled of cocoa. They went in to see Frank Corbo lying lifeless in his bed.

They ringed themselves around him like disciples. "Frank, Frank," Mr. Colucci said gently. "What is this? What are you doing? You cannot leave your wife and children. Who will give them bread? God would not call you now; there is too much good for you to do. Frank, come now, rise up, listen to a friend who loves you. The time is not yet." The other men murmured "Amen" as though to a prayer. "We must get you a doctor for your headaches," Mr. Colucci said.

The father raised himself up on one elbow. He spoke in a low, angry voice, full of life now. He said, "You told me there was never any need for doctors, that God decides, man believes. Now you are false. You are Judas." And he pointed, arm extended, forefinger almost in the Colucci eye. He was a picture on the wall.

Mr. Colucci was stunned. He sat down on the bed and took Frank Corbo's hand in his. He said, "My brother, listen to me. I believe. But when I see your wife and children to be left so, my faith wavers. Even mine. I cannot make my faith your destruction. You are ill. You have these headaches. You suffer. Dear brother, you do not believe. You say God has called you and you say you are dead. You blaspheme. Live now. Suffer a little longer. God will have mercy on you at Armageddon. Rise now and come to my home for supper. Then we will go to chapel and pray together for your deliverance." Mr. Colucci was weeping. The other men bowed their heads. The father looked at them wide-eyed, seemingly rational.

"I will rise," he said formally and motioned them to leave so that he could dress. Colucci and the other men went into the kitchen and sat at the table to drink the coffee Lucia Santa set before them.

Mr. Colucci stared silently at the wooden table. He was in terrible distress. What he had seen in that bed was a caricature of Christ and the true believer, the belief carried to its logical conclusion; the lying down to die. He said to Lucia Santa, "Signora Corbo, your husband will be home at nine this evening. Have the doctor come. Have no fear, I will stay with him." He put his hand on her shoulder. "Signora, believe in me. Your husband has true friends. He will have prayers. He will be cured. And his soul will be saved."

Lucia Santa became coldly, implacably angry at his touch. Who was this man with his single child, a stranger to her grief and suffering, to presume to comfort her? Callow, criminal in his meddlesome religiosity—he was the cause of her husband's illness. He and his friends had disordered her husband's mind with their foolishness, their obscene and obsequious familiarity with God. And beyond that she had a feeling of disgust for Mr. Colucci. In some profound way she felt that he cared nothing for life or for his fellow man; that with a beautiful wife he showed a deep distrust and lack of faith by resting with one child. Remembering his weeping at her husband's bed, she felt an overpowering contempt for him and all men who sought something beyond life, some grandeur. As if life, life itself, were not enough. What airs they gave themselves. She looked away from Mr. Colucci, his pity, his suffering, so that he could not see her face. She hated him. It was she who would feel the anguish, the rage of the sufferer who must bow to fate; as for Mr. Colucci, his would be the easy tears of compassion.

7

THE DOCTOR WAS a son of the landlord who owned many tenements on Tenth Avenue. That Italian peasant father had not strained and sweated, had not left his homeland, had not squeezed every penny out of his compatriot tenants, had not supped on *pasta* and *fagioli* four times a week so that his son could become a Samaritan. Dr. Silvio Barbato was young, but he had no illusions about the Hippocratic oath. He had too much respect for his father, was too intelligent in his own right to be sentimental about these southern Italians who lived like rats along the western wall of the city. But still he was young enough to think of suffering as unnatural. Pity had not been squeezed out of him.

He knew Lucia Santa. As a boy, before his father had become wealthy, he had lived on Tenth Avenue and shown her the respect due an older woman. He had lived as she did not, with his spaghetti on Thursdays and Sundays; *pasta* and *fagioli* on Tuesdays, Wednesdays, Fridays, and Saturdays; and *scarola* on Mondays to clean out the bowels. He could not overawe her and act completely professional. But whenever he entered a home like this, he blessed his father.

His escape was complete. His father had been shrewd to make him a doctor. People always became sick, there were always hospitals, work came. The air was filled with germs, bad times or good. Some escaped for a while but there was always the long process of dying. Everyone alive had money that would find its way into a doctor's pocket.

He sat down for his cup of coffee. He must, or they would never call him again. The icebox in the hall was probably full of cockroaches. The daughter—what was her name?—was old enough to work and she was so developed that marriage was imperative or she would get in trouble. There were too many people explaining things about the patient. The family friends and advisers had gathered round—that most irritating thing to doctors. The old women cronies were the worst.

At last he saw the patient, who was in bed. He seemed calm. Dr. Barbato felt the pulse, took the blood pressure. It was enough. Behind that calm, harsh face there must be an unbearable tension. From other doctors he had heard about cases like this one. It was always the men who crumbled under the glories of the new land, never the women. There were many cases of Italian men who became insane and had to be committed, as if in leaving their homeland they had torn a vital root from their minds.

Dr. Barbato knew what to do here. Frank Corbo should be hospitalized, given a long period of rest, removed from pressure. But this man had to work, he had children to feed. They would all have to gamble. Dr. Barbato continued his examination. Drawing back the sheet, he was startled to see a pair of hideously deformed feet and felt an almost superstitious fear. "How did this happen?" he asked in Italian. His voice was polite but firm, demanding an answer.

The father rose on his elbows and drew the sheet back over his legs. "They are not your concern," he said. "They do not trouble me in any way." This was an enemy.

"You have headaches then," the doctor said.

"Yes," the father said.

"For how long?"

"Forever," the father said.

There was nothing to be done here. Dr. Barbato wrote out a prescription for a heavy sedative. He waited patiently for his fee while the mother scurried into another room to take money out of its hiding place. He felt a little uncomfortable. He always wished that the people who gave him money were a little better dressed, that they had better furniture. Then he noticed the radio and his compunctions vanished. If they could afford such a luxury, they could afford an illness.

Frank Corbo went back to work the next week. He was a great deal better. Sometimes at night he moaned and cursed aloud, but only for a few minutes, and after midnight he would always remain asleep. But before another week was ended, he came home one day just before lunch. He stood in the doorway and said to his wife, "The *padrone* sent me home," he said, "I'm too sick to work." To Lucia Santa's horror, he began to weep.

She sat him at the kitchen table and brought him coffee. His body was very thin. He talked as he had never talked since their marriage year. He asked her in a frightened voice, "Am I that ill? The *padrone* says I stop work too much and I forget the machine. That I should take a long rest and then come see him. But I'm not that sick, I'm just getting better, I'm controlling myself. I take care of myself now. Isn't it true?"

Lucia Santa said, "Don't worry about work, rest a little. You have to get well. This afternoon go for a walk, bring Lena for some air in the park." She looked down at his bowed head. Was he better or worse? There was nothing she could do but wait.

When he left with Baby Lena, the mother gave him a dollar for candy and cigars. She knew he loved having some money in his pocket and that it would cheer him up. He was gone the whole afternoon and came back just in time for supper.

The whole family was gathered around the table, Octavia,

Larry, Vincent, Gino, and Sal. They all knew their father had lost his work and they were subdued. But he was quiet, and so well behaved and helpful to his wife that soon everyone was at ease. It seemed as if the shock of losing his job had knocked all the other nonsense out of his head. Everyone chattered. Larry tricked the boys by saying that the cockroaches were playing baseball on the wall and when Sal and Gino turned around he stole potatoes from their dishes. Octavia fed Baby Lena and held her on her lap. Vinnie watched everything. Larry couldn't fool him. He touched his mother's dress as she went by, serving food, and she stopped and served him first.

When everyone left the table, Lucia Santa asked her husband if he was going to chapel. He answered that he did not need Mr. Colucci any more. The mother was astonished. Could it be that her husband, who, to his family's detriment, had never been cunning, had used the Coluccis just to get work? But then why the illness? The contradiction troubled her.

Later, when bedtime came, Lucia Santa settled in her kitchen chair to sew until midnight. Now she always wanted to be fully dressed and ready when her husband had his attacks. If by midnight nothing had happened, it would be safe to go to bed; the danger would be over.

Frank Corbo watched her and, with what for him was tenderness, said, "Go. Go get some rest. I'll stay up a bit and then come to bed." She knew he meant until after midnight. It was nearly eleven now. Everyone else was asleep and Larry had gone to work. Lucia Santa felt a great surge of relief and pride that her judgment had proven sound. He was better. Men had these spells, but they passed. "I'll finish this little bit," she said. As she sewed, he smoked his cigar. He served her a glass of wine and even took one for himself, though it was against the Colucci religion. It was after midnight when they went to bed, with Baby Lena lying between them. It was very dark, the very black heart of night, when Lucia Santa woke to hear her husband repeating in a clear, even tone, "What is this doll doing en us? Quick, before I throw it out the window." Lucia put one arm over the sleeping baby and said in a low, urgent voice, "Frank, what is it? What's the matter?" Still stunned with sleep, she could not comprehend.

The father asked in a low, menacing tone, "Why did you put this doll between us?"

Lucia Santa tried to keep her voice low. She whispered, "Frank, Frank, it's your baby daughter. Wake up, Frank."

There was a long silence, but Lucia Santa did not dare go back to sleep. Suddenly the whole bed shook violently.

He rose like an avenging angel. Light flooded the bedroom and the front room where the children slept, and there stood the father fully dressed. His face was almost black with the blood of rage. His voice was like thunder as he shouted, "OUT OF THIS HOUSE. BASTARDS, SONS OF WHORES AND BITCHES. OUT OF THIS HOUSE BEFORE I KILL YOU ALL."

The mother sprang out of bed in her nightgown, the baby clutched in her arms. She went into the front room and told the frightened Gino and Vincent, "Quick, get dressed and get Salvatore and go to Zia Louche. Quickly now."

The father was raving, cursing, but when he saw Vincent about to leave he said, "No, Vincenzo can stay. Vincenzo is an angel." But the mother pushed Vincent down the corridor.

Father and mother were face to face. There was no mercy in the father's eyes. He said quietly, but with real hatred, "Take your doll and get out of this house." Lucia Santa looked at the only bedroom door, Octavia's.

The father saw her look. He said, "Don't make me knock on your daughter's door. Get her down on the street where she belongs."

The door opened. Octavia stood there, already dressed, and holding her dressmaker's scissors in her right hand.

The mother said quickly, "Octavia, come with me." Octavia was not afraid; she had come out of her room ready to do battle to protect her mother and the children. But now she saw on her stepfather's face such a look of cruel delight that for the first time she was frightened. She took Baby Lena from her mother's arms and, still holding the scissors, ran to the kitchen. Vinnie, Sal, and Gino were huddled together wearing only their coats over winter underwear. She herded them down the stairs and out of the house. Lucia Santa was left alone with her husband.

She put on clothes over her nightgown, asking him, her voice shaking, "Frank, what is it? You were so good all day, what is it now?"

The blue eyes were opaque, the harsh face calm. He repeated again, "Everyone out of this house." He moved close to her and pushed her down the corridor of rooms toward the door.

Larry and the *Panettiere* burst into the apartment and came between them. The father grabbed Larry by the throat and pushed him against the wall, shouting, "Just because you gave me a dollar today you think you can interfere?" He threw a handful of change at his stepson.

Larry was watchful, alert. He said carefully, "Pop, I come to help. The cops are coming. You gotta quiet down." A siren suddenly wailed. The father ran to the front room to look out the window.

In the street below he could see his three small children huddled in overcoats, surrounding Octavia, and Octavia pointing up toward him as the police came out of the car. He saw the two policemen running into the tenement. He became very quiet and went back down the corridor of rooms to the kitchen and said to them all in a very reasonable tone, "The police have clubs. No one can stand against the police. Not even God can stand against clubs." He sat on a kitchen chair.

The two burly policemen, both Irish and tall, came into the open apartment cautiously and calmly. Larry took them aside and spoke to them in a low voice. The father watched them all. Then Larry came over and sat by his father. There were tears of anxiety in his eyes. He said, "Listen to me, Pop. There's an ambulance coming. You're sick, see? Now don't make any trouble. For Mom and the kids."

Frank Corbo gave him a violent push. Immediately the two policemen came forward, but the mother was ahead of them. "No, wait, wait," she said.

She went to her husband and spoke quietly, as if the *Panettiere* and the policemen could not hear. Octavia and the children had come out of the cold of the street and stood on the other side of the room watching them. The mother said, "Frank, go to the hospital. They will make you well. What will the children feel when they see the police beat you and drag you down the stairs? Frank, Frank, be reasonable. I'll come to see you every day. In a week, two weeks, you'll be well. Come now."

The father rose. As he did so, two white-jacketed interns came over the top of the stairway and into the open door of the apartment. The father stood by the table, head down, brooding. Then he raised his head and said briskly, "Everyone must have coffee. I'll make it myself." The two white jackets started toward him, but the mother moved across their path. Larry went beside her. The mother said to the interns and policemen, "Humor him, please. He will go if you humor him. But if you use force he will be an animal."

While the coffee was perking, the father began to shave at the kitchen faucet. The interns were tense and alert. The policemen stood ready with nightsticks. The father finished quickly and set cups of coffee on the table. The children and Octavia were on the far side of the table. While they drank to please him, he made his wife fetch him a clean shirt. Then he surveyed them all with a sardonic gleam in his eyes.

"Figlio de puttana," he began. "Evil men. I know you two policemen. At night, late, you go into the bakery and drink whisky. That's how you work? And you, *Panettiere*. You make whisky in your back room against the law. Oh, I see you all at night when everyone sleeps. I see everything. At night I'm

everywhere. I see the sins of the world. Monsters—fiends—murderers—sons and daughters of whores—I know you all. You think you can overcome *me*?" He was shouting rapidly, incoherently, and he gave the kitchen table a push, knocking over all the coffee cups.

He seemed to rise on his toes; he grew tall and menacing. Larry and the mother shrank away from him. The two white-jacketed interns formed a line with the two policemen and came toward him. Suddenly the father saw across the huge wooden table his son Gino's face, the skin white with terror, the eyes almost blank, extinguished of sensibility. With his back to his enemies, the father winked one eye at his son. He saw the color flood back into Gino's face, the fear relieved by surprise.

But now the comedy was over. The four men surrounded the father, not yet touching him. The father raised both his palms toward them as if beseeching them to halt, to listen to something important he was going to say. But he did not speak. He reached into his pocket and gave his wife the key to the apartment and then his billfold. Lucia Santa grasped him by the arm and pulled him out of the apartment and down the stairs. Larry took the father's other arm. The police and white-jacketed men followed close behind.

Tenth Avenue was empty. The wind whipped around the ambulance and the police car parked before the tenement. Frank Corbo faced his wife in the dark street. He said in a low voice, "Lucia Santa, let me come home. Don't let them take me away. They will kill me." Across the street an engine hooted. The wife bowed her head. She dropped his arm and stepped away from him. Without warning, the two white-jacketed interns pounced on the father, slipped something over his arms, and half thrust, half lifted him into the ambulance. One of the police jumped in to help. There was not a sound. The father did not cry out. There was just a flying about of many blue-and-white-clad arms. The mother bit her fist, and Larry stood paralyzed. The ambulance drove away, and then the remaining policeman came over to them.

The cloudiness of early dawn veiled the stars, but it was not yet really light. Lucia Santa wept in the street as Larry gave the policeman their names, his father's name, the names of the children and everyone in the house that night, and told how it had all begun.

IT WAS NOT until the next Sunday that anyone was permitted to visit the father. After dinner Lucia Santa said to her daughter, "Do you think I should let him come home, do you think it safe?" Octavia shrugged, afraid to give an honest answer. She was amazed at her mother's optimism.

Larry assumed command as the eldest male of the family. He spoke as a man with contempt for the cowardice of women. "You mean you'll let Pop rot in Bellevue just because he went off a little one night? Let's get him the hell out of there. He'll be all right, don't worry."

Octavia said, "It's easy for you to talk like a big-hearted big shot. You're never home. You're out chasing floozies, your stupid little tramps. Then while you're having your nice little fun, Mom and the kids and me are getting our throats cut. And you'll be so-o-o sorry when you come home. But you'll be alive and we'll be dead. You're not so dumb, Larry."

"Ah, you're always making a big thing outa nothing," Larry said. "After the old man gets a taste of Bellevue, he'll never get sick again." Then, seriously and without malice, "Your trouble, Sis, is you never liked him."

"Why should I?" Octavia said angrily. "He never did anything for Vinnie or even for his own kids. How many times did he hit Mamma? He even hit her once when she was pregnant, and I'll never forget that."

Lucia Santa listened to them both, her face somber, her black brows knit. Their arguments were the irrelevant arguments of children, their talk meant nothing to her. They were not competent, emotionally or mentally.

Like many others this illiterate, untrained peasant woman had the power of life and death over the human beings nearest to her. On every day in every year people must condemn and betray their loved ones. Lucia Santa did not think in terms of sentiment. But love and pity had value, a certain weight in life.

The man who had fathered her children, rescued her from a desperate and helpless widowhood, and wakened her to delight, was no longer of any real value to her. He would bring war into the family. Octavia might leave; she would marry early to escape him. He would be a liability in the battle against life. She had her duty to her children, big and small. She dismissed love that was personal, an emotion of luxury, of uncomplicated lives.

But beyond love there was honor, there was duty, there was a union against the world. Frank Corbo had never betrayed that honor; he had only not been able to fulfill it. And he was the father of three of these children. There was blood there. In the future years she must look these children in the eye. She would have to account to them, for he had given them life, they were in his debt. Lurking behind this was the primitive dread that parents have of their own fate when they are old and helpless and become their children's children, and in their turn seek mercy.

Gino, who all this time had been twisting and turning and quarreling with Sal and Vinnie, and seemingly inattentive to the conversation, suddenly said to his mother, "Poppa winked at me that night."

The mother, bewildered, did not understand the word "wink." Octavia explained.

Lucia Santa became excited. "See?" she said. "He was putting it on. He knew what he was doing but he was weak-headed, he couldn't help himself."

"You know," Larry said. "He saw Gino looking so scared, that's why. I told you it wasn't anything serious. He's a little sick, that's all. Let's get him home."

The mother said to Octavia, "Eh, well?" She had already

made up her mind but wanted her daughter's consent. Octavia looked at Gino, who turned his head away.

"Let's try it," she said. "I'll do my best."

They all helped the mother get ready. The packing of the food, spaghetti in a small bowl, fruit, half a loaf of real bread. Just in case he could not come home this very day. They even made jokes. Lucia Santa said, "Ah, that night when he called Vincenzo an angel, then I knew he was crazy." It was a bitter joke that would last through the years.

At last she was ready to leave. Gino asked her, "Is Pop really coming home today?"

The mother looked down at him. There was some sort of fear on his face she could not understand. She said, "If not today, then tomorrow, don't worry." She saw the anxiety vanish from his eyes, and his absolute trust gave her that familiar warm sense of power and love.

Vinnie, hearing his mother's words to Gino, shouted with loyal happiness, "Hurrah! Hurrah!" Octavia said to her mother, "I'll clean up the kids and have them dressed up in front of the house."

Larry was going with her. Before they left, he told the children, "Now if we bring Pop home today, nobody bother him, let him rest. Just do everything he asks you to do." Listening, the mother felt a great buoyancy of spirit; she believed that everything would end well, that the terrible night was not so significant as it had appeared. The strain had grown too great, everyone had been carried away by emotion. Really, there had been no need to call the police or the ambulance or have him taken to the hospital. But maybe it was for the best. Now the air was clear and they would all be the better for it.

Stout in black, and carrying the bundle of food herself, Lucia Santa walked to 23rd Street for the crosstown trolley car to Bellevue, her eldest son on her arm like a good, dutiful child.

Lucia Santa and her son went to a crowded reception desk

and waited. After a long time they were told they must see the doctor, and they followed directions to his office.

It has been said of this great hospital that its professional staff is the finest in the world, that its nurses are more efficient and hard-working than any other nurses and that its medical care for the indigent is as good as can be had. But for Lucia Santa these things mattered little on this Sunday afternoon. To her, it seemed, Bellevue was the terror of the poor, the last painful and shameful indignity they suffered from life before they went to their death. It was filled with the dregs, the helpless of humanity, the poverty-stricken. Tuberculars sat on cheerless balconies sucking in soot-filled air, watching the stone city distill the poison which devoured their lungs. The senile aged lay unattended except by visiting relatives, who brought them food to eat and tried to fan alive a breath of hope. In some wards were those enraged by life, God, humanity, who had swallowed lye or done some other terrible injury to their bodies in their lust for death. Now, with physical agony to relieve their other sufferings, they clung to life. And then there were those insane who had rushed out of the world into some kinder darkness.

Lucia Santa reflected that whatever else you might say of the place, you must say the truth: that it was a hospital of charity. It owed her and people like her nothing and would receive nothing from them. Its dark tiled corridors were noisy with children waiting for drugs, treatment, stitches. In one ward children crippled by automobiles and drunken parents fought over a solitary wheelchair.

In some beds were the righteously ill—men whose labor had earned bread for their wives and children, whose fear of death was compounded by the vision of their helpless, unprotected families.

It was a hospital where people brought food every day to their loved ones—casseroles of spaghetti, bags of oranges, and towels and decent soap and fresh linen. It was a factory for the human vessel to be glued together without pity, tenderness, or love. It was a place to make an animal fit to take up his burden. It was heedless of the hurt spirit; it gave a grudging charity that on principle would never dispense flowers. It hung on the eastern wall of the city, medieval in its tower-like formation and iron gates, a symbol of hell. The pious poor crossed themselves when they entered those gates; the gravely ill resigned themselves to death.

Lucia Santa and her son found the doctor's office and entered. The mother could not believe that such a young man in his ill-fitting white jacket held power over her husband. As soon as they were seated, he told her that she could not see her husband that day; it would be best if she signed certain necessary papers.

The mother said to Larry in a low voice, in Italian, "Tell him about the wink." The doctor said in Italian, "No, Signora, you tell me." The mother was surprised, he looked so American.

He spoke the Italian of the rich and he treated her with gentlemanly courtesy. Lucia Santa explained to him how at the height of madness that terrible night her husband had winked his eye at his oldest natural son. To reassure him, to show he was not really crazy. It was clear, he had let himself go out of weakness or exasperation with his family, or despair at his fate. They were poor. He was really too ill to earn a living. This was the reason, sometimes, that men behaved so strangely. And he had gone all winter without a hat. His brains had been chilled with the cold. And she must not forget that, digging the new subway for Eighth Avenue, he had been buried alive a few minutes and hurt his head.

She went on and on to show that the illness was physical, external, subject to simple care, but she always came back to the winking of the eye. He had fooled them all that night. They had everyone been taken in, even the doctors.

The doctor listened with grave courtesy and tact, nodding

his head in agreement that the winking of the eye was very strange, that the cold, the blow on the head might be at fault, murmuring encouragement. The mother did not realize that this courtesy was an expression of pity and compassion. When she finished, he spoke in his beautiful Italian, revealing himself as an enemy.

"Signora," he said, "your husband is very ill. Too ill for this hospital. Too ill for your home. He must be sent away. Perhaps in a year or two he will be well. No one knows. These things are still a mystery."

The mother said in a low voice, "I will not sign any papers. I want to see my husband."

The doctor glanced at Larry and shook his head. Larry said, "Come on, Ma, I'll bring you back tomorrow, maybe we can see Pop then."

Lucia Santa sat still, dumb as an animal. The doctor said in a gentle, hopeless voice, "Signora, if your husband had a fever, an ague, you would not send him out to earn his living, you would not drive him out to cold and labor. If his legs were broken you would not make him walk. For him to go out in the world is too much. It is too painful for him. The illness is a signal so that he will not go to his death. You can show your love for your husband by signing these papers." He touched a yellow manila folder on his desk.

The mother raised her head and stared at him. She said in rude Italian, "I will never sign."

The doctor flushed. Then he said gravely, "I see you have a package for your husband. Do you wish to take it to him yourself? You will not be able to stay, but you can speak for a moment." The mother flushed in her turn at his kindness, and nodded. The doctor picked up the phone on his desk and spoke to someone. Then he rose and said to Lucia Santa, "Come with me." When Larry rose from his chair the doctor said, "I think you had better wait for your mother here."

Lucia Santa followed the white jacket through dark,

prison-like corridors, up steps and down, until after going a long distance they came to a door which opened into a huge tiled room scattered over with bathtubs, some of which were curtained from view. She followed the doctor across the room toward another door in the far corner. But suddenly the doctor stopped by one of the curtained bathtubs. With his right hand he grasped her firmly by the arm, as if to save her from tripping or falling. With his left hand he pulled back the curtain on its rod of metal.

A naked man, his arms bound to his side, sat in a tub of clear water. The mother cried out, "Frank!" And the narrow skull turned toward her, the face elongated in the bare-toothed grimace of a wild animal trapped in terror. The blue eyes were like glass, glittering in soulless rage. They looked not at her, but at the invisible sky above. It was a face of hopeless satanic madness, and the doctor let the curtain fall as the woman's long helpless wail of anguish brought attendants running to them. The brown paper fell to the tiled floor, breaking, soiling Lucia Santa's stockings and shoes.

She was sitting in the office again. Larry was trying to stop her weeping. But she wept for herself who must be a widow again, who must sleep forever in a lonely bed; for her other children, who must be fatherless, too; she wept that she had been conquered, overcome by fate. And she wept because for the first time in many years she had been terrified; she had loved a man, borne his children, and then seen him, not dead, but with his soul torn from his body.

She signed all the papers. She thanked the doctor for his kindness. When they left the hospital, Larry took her home in a taxi. He was worried about her. But when they got out on Tenth Avenue, she was completely recovered; he did not even have to help her up the stairs. They never noticed the children, Gino, Vinnie and Sal, waiting on the corner of the Avenue.

PART
TWO

8

THE FIRST FINE Saturday of spring Octavia decided to give the house a good cleaning. Vinnie and Gino were sent off to janitor the building—to wash the halls and stairs, and clean the backyard of the tenement. Little Sal and Baby Lena were given rags to dust the chairs and the great wooden table; the chairs with their many ringed rungs, the table with its great mysterious arches of wood beneath it, forming caves in which the two little children could sit and hide. With the great greasy bottle of lemon oil, they made everything shiny and green-black and slick so that Octavia had to go over it with a dry rag.

Everything was taken out of all the closets, and the shelves were lined with fresh clean newspaper. All the china was spread over the kitchen table to be washed of its film of dirt.

In an hour Vincent and Gino were back in the apartment with their broom and mop and pail and the kettle for hot soapy water. Gino said, "We're all finished. I gotta go out and play stickball."

Octavia's head jerked out of the closet. She was angry.

There had been a change in Gino the last few months. He had always been irresponsible; but pinned down, with no chance to disappear, he had worked cheerfully and well. Now he was sullen, defiant. He spoiled everything. She frowned at them both. Vinnie was getting just as bad.

Octavia called out, "Ma, look. They washed the whole building with one kettle of hot water. Four flights of stairs and four halls and the ground-floor marble with one lousy kettle of hot water." She laughed contemptuously.

Lucia Santa said from the kitchen, "Eh, well, as long as it looks a little clean."

Octavia almost screamed. "How the hell could it look clean with one kettle of hot water?" She heard her mother laugh and she laughed herself. It was such a beautiful morning. The apartment was flooded with yellow light.

The two boys standing there with the mops and pail looked so comical, they hated it so. Their faces were all twisted up with disgust. "All right," Octavia said, "Vinnie, you help me with the closets; Gino, you wash the windows on the inside. Then you and Vinnie can bring all the junk down in the yard and I'll finish the windows."

"Like hell I will," Gino said.

Octavia didn't even look at him. "Don't be smart."

"I'm going out," Gino said.

Vinnie and Sal were aghast at Gino's audacity. None of the brothers ever dared defy Octavia; even Larry took orders from her sometimes. She always pulled their hair and slapped them when they were fresh and did not obey. Once she even hit Larry on the head with a milk bottle.

Octavia was kneeling half in the closet. She said over her shoulder, "Don't make me get up."

"I don't care," Gino said. "I ain't washing any goddamn windows, I'm playing stickball."

Octavia leaped up from the floor and was upon him. With one hand she grabbed his hair, with the other gave him two good slaps in the face. He tried to get away, but she was too strong for him. She held him fast. She pummeled him, though she did not really hurt him. She screamed, "Now you little bastard, say you won't wash the windows and I'll kill you."

Gino didn't answer. He tore himself free of her with an unexpected burst of strength. He looked at her, not with hate or fear, but with his painfully disarming surprise, his nakedly defenseless bewilderment. Octavia could never get used to that look. She beat Vinnie worse sometimes, so it was not guilt that she felt. And despite her feelings about the stepfather, she never thought of Lena, Sal, and Gino as half sister and brothers. They were her mother's children.

Lucia Santa came out of the kitchen. She said to Octavia, "Enough, no more. Gino, just wash the two front windows and then go out and play."

But Gino's thin dark face was filled now with stubbornness and rage. He said, "I'm not washing no son-of-a-bitch windows." He waited to see what they would do.

Conciliatingly, tentatively, Lucia Santa said, "Don't curse, a small boy like you."

Gino yelled, "Octavia curses all the time. And she's a girl. You never say anything about her. And with other people she's such a phony lady." The mother smiled and Octavia turned her face away to keep from laughing outright. It was true. The boy friends, especially the *Panettiere*'s son, never dreamed how she swore. They would not dare use words in her presence that she used at home when irritated with her mother or her little brothers. Sometimes, when she was hysterical with rage, she shocked even herself. One of her girl friends had called her the "filthy-mouthed virgin."

"Good, good," the mother said. "Just help until lunchtime; then you can go out. The food will be ready soon." She was aware that Octavia was angry at being overruled, but things had been going so well that she wanted peace in the family.

To her surprise, Gino said defiantly, "I ain't hungry. I'm

going out right now. The hell with lunch." He took his stick-ball bat out of the corner and turned to leave. He was just in time to receive his mother's hand, flush in his mouth.

She was angry. She shouted, "*Animale.* Hard head. You're just like your father. Now stay in the house all day."

He did not come up to her chin. She looked into his eyes, two great black pools of rage, crazy with a small boy's frustration. He lifted up the stickball bat and threw it blindly, but carefully aimed not to hit anyone. The long thin stick arched gracefully and swept the table clean of its pile of china. There was a tremendous crash. Painted bits of dishes and cups flew around the room.

A moment of great stunned silence followed. Gino gave one startled look at his mother and Octavia, turned, and fled. Out the door, down the stairs, and into Tenth Avenue and the fresh spring sunlight. His mother recovered enough to shout down the dark hallway, through the smell of peppers, frying garlic, and olive oil, "*Figlio de puttana!* Beast! Animal! Don't come home to eat."

Gino felt a lot better walking up 31st Street. The hell with everybody. The hell with his mother and sister. They could all go to hell. He jumped when he felt a tug on his arm, but it was only Vinnie.

"Come on home," Vinnie said. "Octavia says I gotta bring you home."

Gino turned around. He gave Vinnie a push and said, "You wanna fight, you son-of-a-bitch?"

Vinnie looked at him gravely and said, "Come on, I'll help with the windows. Then we'll play ball."

Gino ran up toward Ninth Avenue, and though Vinnie was a faster runner, there was no sound of anyone chasing him.

HE WAS FREE, but he felt a strange discontent. He wasn't even mad. He just wasn't going to do what anybody told him, not even Larry. The thought of Larry made him pause. He would have to get out of the neighborhood. Sure as hell they would send Larry after him.

On Ninth Avenue Gino hitched on the back of a horse and wagon going uptown. After a couple of blocks, the driver, a burly mustached Italian, saw him and flicked his whip. Gino jumped off, picked up a rock, and sailed it in the direction of the wagon. He had not taken aim really, but it came close. There was a roar of curses, the wagon stopped, and Gino fled toward Eighth Avenue. There he hitched on the back of a taxi. The driver saw him and went fast so that he couldn't hop off until Central Park. The driver thumbed his nose and grinned at Gino.

For the first time in his life, he went into Central Park. He saw a fountain near a horse trough and took a drink of warm water. He did not even have a penny for a soda. He walked deeper into the park, as far as he could from west to east, until he saw the great white square stones that housed the rich. They meant nothing to him. His childish dreams did not include thoughts of money. He dreamed of bravery on a battlefield, of greatness on a baseball diamond. He dreamed of his own uniqueness.

Gino tried to find a spot in the park where he could sit against a tree and not see stone against the sky or, darting through the screen of leaves, the black shadows of moving cars and wagons. He searched for the illusion of a forest. But no matter where he stood or sat, whenever he made a complete turn, he found at least one facade of stone above the trees, a billboard suspended near the sky, the sound of honking horns, or the clatter of horses' hoofs. The smell of gasoline mingled with the scent of grass and trees. Finaly, exhausted, Gino lay down by a lake that had concrete banks, and, lidding his eyes, made the tall buildings lose their solidity and become airy, suspended above the trees like a picture in a fairy tale. Later he would come out of the forest and enter the city. Without warning, he fell asleep.

He slept an enchanted sleep. He knew people walked by and looked at him, a ball bounced near him, and two feather merchants came after it and stood looking down at him. But he could never wake up enough to really see them. The seasons changed as if years were going by. First it was very hot and Gino rolled along the grass to the shade of a tree. Then there were light sunny rains and he got wet, and then he was cold and it was dark, and then it was sunny again like summer. But he was too tired to ever get up. Cradling his head in his arms, burying his nose and eyes in fresh grass, he slept his life away, but when he awoke it was only one afternoon that had vanished.

The suspended spires of the city were all blue with approaching twilight; there were no yellow sun rays in the air. The park was black and green. Gino would have to hurry to get home before dark.

He got out of Central Park at 72nd Street. He was worried now. He wanted to get home to his own house, his own neighborhood; he wanted to see his brothers and sisters and his mother again. It was the longest he had ever been away from them. He hitched on a taxi. He was lucky; it went downtown and then over to Ninth Avenue. But at 31st Street the taxi was going too fast. Gino jumped anyway, pumping his feet before they touched the ground. He kept his balance, running swiftly. Suddenly he heard a shriek of metal behind him. He felt a shock and found himself lifted off his feet and flying through the air. He hit the pavement and jumped up. He wasn't hurt, but he was frightened because he knew he had been run over.

A big blue car was half on the sidewalk, half in the gutter. A tall man got out of it and ran toward Gino. He had blue eyes and thin hair, and his face showed such a look of fright and concern that Gino felt sorry for him. He said immediately, "I'm O.K., mister." But the man began feeling him all over his body for broken bones. There was only a big rip in the leg of his dungarees and blood coming out of it.

The man said with almost panicky nervousness, "Are you all right, sonny? How do you feel?"

Gino said, "My knee hurts." The man looked at it. There was a deep scrape where blood was welling slowly. The man picked up Gino as if he were a baby and put him in the front seat of the car. To the people who had gathered around he said, "I'm bringing this kid to the hospital."

In front of the French Hospital on 30th Street, the man parked his car and lit a cigarette. He looked at Gino intently, studying his face. "Now tell me the truth, kid, how do you feel?"

"I'm O.K.," Gino said. His stomach felt weak. He was a little scared at being hit by a car.

"Let me see your knee," the man said.

Gino rolled up his trousers leg. The bleeding had stopped and there was a raw scab beginning to form over the whole knee. "I never bleed when I get hurt," Gino said proudly. "I always get a scab quick."

The man sighed and said, "I guess we better go in."

Gino said quickly, "Those hospitals, they always make you wait and I gotta get home or my mother will be real mad. I'm O.K., mister." He got out of the car. "Besides, it wasn't your fault." His tone was that of one equal reassuring another. He limped away from the car.

The man called out, "Wait a minute, kid." He leaned out of the window, extending a bill. It was five dollars.

Gino was embarrassed. "Nah," he said. "It was my fault. I don't want no money."

"You take it," the man said sternly. "Don't make your old lady spend her dough on new pants because you wanta be a big shot." He looked like Lindbergh when he was serious. When Gino took the money the man shook his hand, smiled, and said, in a relieved, flattering voice, "You're O.K., kid."

All Gino had to do to get home now was cross Ninth Avenue under the El and walk down 30th Street to Tenth Avenue.

He turned the corner feeling a great sense of happiness. Sal was playing in the street, his mother was sitting on her backless chair in front of the tenement, Zia Louche and another woman with her. Octavia was standing by the lemon ice stand talking with the *Panettiere*'s son. Gino walked past her and they made believe they didn't see each other. In front of the tenement he stopped and faced his mother when she spoke to him.

She wasn't mad, he could tell that. *"Buona sera,"* she said calmly. "You've decided to come home? Your supper is in the oven." She glanced away quickly and talked to Zia Louche. Gino thought bitterly, She didn't even notice my leg.

He limped up the stairs. He was relieved. Everything seemed to be forgotten. And now for the first time he was conscious of a dull throbbing ache in his knee. His mouth was dry and salty, his eyes hurt a little, and his legs were shaky.

Vinnie was reading in the kitchen. When he saw Gino, he took a plate of peppers and eggs and potatoes out of the oven and put it on the table. Then he went out into the hall to the icebox and brought back a bottle of milk. Gino took a slug right from the bottle. Then he sat down to eat.

Vinnie said quietly, but a little accusingly, "Where were you all day? Mom and Octavia were worried and Larry looked all over for you. They were worried about you."

"Yeah, sure," Gino said sarcastically. But he felt better. After a few mouthfuls he couldn't eat any more. He put his leg up on the chair. It was stiff. He pulled up his pants leg. The scab was huge and bloody, and blown up like a black cake.

"Wow." Vinnie was impressed. "You better put some iodine on that. And on your face and hands, too. You get in a fight?"

"Nah," Gino said, "I just got hit by a car." He almost cried when he said it. He went to the sink and washed. Then he went into the front room and unfolded the bed and undressed. He was cold, so he put a blanket over his body. He took the five-dollar bill from his pants and held it. His stomach quivered, his face felt hot. He saw the car now as he had not seen it then, rushing up and hitting him, and his body flying through the air. Vinnie was sitting on the bed near him. "I got hit by a car," Gino said in a trembling voice. "See? The guy gave me five dollars. He was a nice guy. He even wanted me to go to a hospital, but I wasn't hurt. I was just hitching and jumped off right in front of him. It was all my fault." He opened his hand. "See? Five bucks."

Both boys stared at the money. It was a fortune. Vinnie had a five-dollar gold piece for his Confirmation from Zia Louche, but he would never be allowed to spend it. "Gee," Vinnie said, "what are you gonna do with it, give it to Ma?"

"Like hell," Gino said. "If she knows I got hit by a car I'll get a beating." Then, seriously, "Let's make those bottles of root beer like you always wanted to, Vinnie, and sell it and make money. Remember? Maybe we could build up a good business."

Vinnie was delighted. It had always been his dream. "No kidding?" he asked. And when Gino nodded, Vinnie said, "You better let me hold the money. Ma might take it off you and make you save it."

"No, sir," Gino said suspiciously. "I'm gonna hold this money myself."

Vinnie was surprised and hurt. Gino always let him hold his money, the ice money, the winnings from Seven-and-a-half.

"C'mon," Vinnie said. "Let me hold the five dollars. You'll lose it."

Gino said spitefully, "I got hit by the car, you didn't. You didn't even come with me. You were on Octavia's side. You're lucky I made you a partner."

He lay back on his pillow. Vinnie watched him carefully. Gino had never acted this way before. "O.K.," he said. "You hold the money."

Gino lay back on the pillow and said almost absently, "And

I have to be the boss making the root beer. It's my money."

This hurt Vinnie's feelings. He was the older and it was his idea. He nearly said, "You and your five dollars can go to hell." But instead he said, "O.K., you'll be the boss. You want a bandage on your knee?"

"Nah, it don't hurt," Gino said. "Let's talk about how to make that root beer. And remember, don't tell anybody I got hit by a car. I'll just get a beating."

Vinnie said, "I'll go get a paper and pencil to figure expenses." He went into the kitchen and cleaned the table and washed the dishes. The mother had given strict orders that Gino was to clean up after eating supper. Then he got the pencil and pad from his schoolbag.

When Vinnie got back to the front room it was almost dark, the last shreds of twilight. In the dimness he saw Gino's relaxed hand on the blanket. The crumpled five-dollar bill was on the floor. Gino was sound asleep, his body completely inert, his eyes closed.

But there were strange sounds coming from the bed. Vinnie went closer and saw that his brother was crying in his sleep, tears streaming down his face. Vinnie shook him to wake him out of the nightmare, but his brother kept sleeping, breathing easily and deeply. The sounds of crying stopped finally, leaving only his face and eyelashes wet. Vinnie waited for a while beside the bed in case his brother should wake up and want the five dollars back. Then he put the money in their secret hiding place in the wall.

Vinnie sat on the window sill in the darkness. It was a very still night, too early in the spring for the people on the Avenue to stay down late. Even the railroad yards were quiet; there were no engines moving, no ringing of steel. Vinnie kept looking at the bed to make sure his brother was all right, and figuring where they could get the bottles for the root beer they would make. He knew that Gino would let him be the boss.

9

THE SMOKY GRAY light of autumn made the city all lines and shadows. The bridge over Tenth Avenue was half obscured, as if it were over some bottomless gorge, not just two stories above a cobblestone street ruled with twin lines of steel. Underneath the bridge, from the direction of 29th Street, came a wagon, flat-bedded, drawn by a heavy brown horse. The wagon was loaded with thin crates made of splintery wood, the crates filled with purple wine-grapes.

The wagon parked midway between 30th and 31st Streets. Driver and helper stacked twenty crates in front of one tenement. The driver leaned back and called up to the city sky, as if singing a note, "Ca-te-rin-a, your grapes are waiting for you." Four stories up a window opened, children leaned out, men and women. Seconds later, as if they had flown down the stairs, people erupted from the tenement. A man walked around the cases, sniffing like a dog at the clusters between the slats. "They are good this year?" he asked the driver. The driver did not bother to answer. He held out his hand for money. The man paid.

Meanwhile the wife posted two children as guards, while she and the other children each took a crate and carried them into the cellar. The father ripped a slat off a box, partially exposing its contents, and took out a great blue-black cluster of grapes to eat. When the children and wife came back from their load, they and the guards were each given a cluster. In front of each tenement this scene was repeated, the children eating pear-cluster blue-black grapes, the father leaning happily against his stack of crates while other men not so fortunate flocked around to wish him luck with his wine. They licked their lips, thinking of the great jugs, red-black, stacked against the walls of their cellars.

Gino was envious of the other children, those fortunate ones whose fathers made wine. He stood beside Joey Bianco's father, but Joey was too cheap to give him grapes and so was his father. Joey's father was too cheap to open a box for sampling even for relatives and close friends.

But now the *Panettiere,* fat and round, wearing his baker's white hat, came to receive three towering stacks of crates in front of his shop. He opened two of the crates and handed out great clusters to all the children. Gino jumped in and got his share. The *Panettiere* said in his great booming voice, "*Ragazzi,* help carry and there will be pizza for all." Like ants, the children swarmed over the three stacks of crates and they magically disappeared underground into the cellar. Gino was left without anything to carry.

The *Panettiere* looked at him reprovingly, "Ah, Gino, *figlio mio,* what will become of you? Work eludes you, try how you may. You must learn now; those who do not work do not eat. Away."

The *Panettiere* started to turn but the angry look in the young boy's eyes stopped him. "Ah," he said. "It's not your fault. You just do not move quickly toward work. If there had been one left you would have carried it, eh?" When Gino nodded, the *Panettiere* motioned him into the shop. By the time the other children had come up from the cellar to get their reward, Gino was already out on the Avenue eating his pizza, the hot tomato sauce cutting the sweet juice of the grape from his mouth and palate.

In the falling dusk the children, their mouths purple with grape and red with tomato sauce, ran screaming up and down the Avenue, raced up and down the steps of the bridge like howling demons, danced in the steam of the locomotive passing underneath, and reappeared in a shower of sparks. The stone city towered above them black with winter. It was their last frenzy before being called from windows to flee the falling night. They piled empty crates in the gutter, and one of the older boys set a match to the paper around the pile to make a bonfire. Tenth Avenue burst into beacons of orange light, and around them the children made a great circle. The calls from mothers leaning out of windows echoed throughout the cold twilight canyon streets, long and drawn out, shepherds down a mountainside.

Lucia Santa, like God behind a cloud, watched from her window on the top floor of 358 Tenth Avenue, her elbows resting on an unsheeted pillow. She regarded her children and the others eating grapes running over the bridge, halved in the light of orange bonfires, shredded into fluttering shadows by the chilly, windy autumn night. The cold was coming early this year. The summer, blessed season of rest for city people, had come to an end.

Now school would begin. There must be white shirts for the children, trousers mended and pressed. Shoes must be worn instead of sneakers patched with tape. Hair must be cut and combed. Winter's gloves, always lost, must be bought; hats and coats. The stove must be put up in the living room next to the kitchen; it must be checked and kept filled. Money must be put aside for winter tribute to the doctor. In the back of her mind Lucia Santa thought of saving money by having Sal steal coal from the railroad yards. But Salvatore was too timid; he didn't enjoy it. With Gino it was no longer possible. He was getting too big; he could be treated like a criminal. This Lucia Santa thought out with the cunning of the poor.

Now in the orange light she could see a small boy go out a little way from the sidewalk into the gutter and then run and jump over the bonfire. Gino. Determined to ruin his clothing. Then an even smaller boy tried it, and this one landed on the edge of the fire, setting up a shower of sparks. When Lucia Santa saw Gino back off for a second try she said aloud, *"Mannaggia Gesù Crist."* She ran down the corridor of rooms to the kitchen, grabbed the black *Tackeril* and rushed down the stairs. Octavia looked up from the book she was reading.

As Lucia Santa burst out of the tenement door, Gino was sailing over the bonfire for the third time. In mid-air he saw his mother, then hit the ground, and tried to twist away. The thin black club caught him on the ribs, sharp and stinging. He let out a howl to satisfy his mother and ran up to the house. Then the mother saw Sal sailing over the fire, and when he ran past her, his trousers smelled burnt. She gave him time to duck before she swung the *Tackeril* but caught him flush just the same. Sal wailed and ran into the house after Gino. By the time Lucia Santa had climbed the stairs they had taken off their jackets and caps and hidden under the beds. They would be quiet, at least for a half hour. A time of day had come to an end, a season, a piece of the fabric of her life.

"Put your book away," the mother said. "Help with the children." Octavia sighed and put away her book. She always helped on Sunday night, in atonement for her Sabbath day of rest. She always felt a special kind of peace on Sunday night.

Octavia took down the drying clothes over the bathtub, cleaned the tub, and ran hot water into it. Then she went into her room and called under the bed. "Come on out, you two." Gino and Sal crawled out. Sal said, "Is Mamma still mad?" Octavia said sternly, "No, but if you don't behave she will be. Now no fighting in the tub, or you'll both get killed."

In the kitchen Lucia Santa prepared supper. Vinnie had come home from the movies and was helping her set the table. He would take his bath later.

When Gino and Sal came out their winter underwear was waiting for them, with its long legs and arms. From some forgotten hiding place their schoolbags appeared, battered but usable. Also waiting for them were meatball sandwiches and glasses of cream soda, for their mother refused to serve milk with food cooked in tomato sauce.

After supper Octavia gave them all a lecture—Sal, Gino, and Vinnie. It was familiar. "Now," she said, "none of you kids are stupid. I want to see good report cards this term, and in conduct, too. Vinnie, you did all right last year, but you have to do better now you're in second term high. You want to go to C.C.N.Y., don't you? If your marks are good enough you can go free." There could never be any question of paying for college. Vinnie would be lucky if he didn't have to go to work right after high school. But Octavia had her own plans and her own money on this score. Vinnie would go to college, to C.C.N.Y. She would take care of the family. It was this that had made her at last give up any ideas of teaching.

She went on. "Gino, if you get conduct marks like last term, I'll put you in the hospital, I'll beat you black and blue. And your school work could be a lot better. Now behave, or you'll wind up in reform school and disgrace the whole family." She was laying it on too thick; Gino had never behaved badly enough to go to reform school, he never failed in conduct, and never got any D's.

She had her audience. Even Baby Aileen sat up in her crib and climbed out to sit on a chair by the table. Octavia reached over and put the baby on her lap. "Sal," she said, "you did all right last term. But now school will get harder for you. I'll help with your homework, so don't worry. I'm nearly as good a teacher as the ones in school," she said with almost a little girl's bragging pride. "One thing. I want everybody upstairs from the street when I come from work. By that time it will be dark and there's no reason for you to be out anyway. Anybody not in this house by six o'clock will get the hell knocked out of them. And no card playing or fooling around until the homework is done and I check it. And you, Vinnie, Gino, Sal, take a night each helping your mother with the dishes. Give her a break."

She gave one last warning, blood-chilling in its simplicity and sincerity, delivered without any flourish or preamble. "If you don't get promoted, if you get left back, I'll kill you." Aileen moved uneasily in her lap. "Nobody is going to disgrace this family name, and you're not growing up ignorant guineas to live on Tenth Avenue the rest of your life."

Lucia Santa broke in, irritated by her daughter's phrase. "*Bastanza.* Enough. They're not going to a war, after all." Then, to the kids, "But remember this, *mascalzoni* that you are. I would give anything to have gone to school, to be able to read and write. Only the sons of the rich went to school in Italy. At your age I was chasing goats and digging vegetables and shoveling manure. I killed chickens and washed dishes and cleaned houses. School to me would have been like movie pictures. If your father could have gone to school he would have had better work, and—who knows—might not have become ill. So: know your good fortune, or you will be taught how lucky you are with the *Tackeril.*"

Sal was wide-eyed. Gino and Vinnie were composed, though a little impressed. Sal said in a scared voice, "But, Ma, what if I can't learn, what if I'm not smart enough? That ain't my fault." He was so serious that the two women smiled.

Octavia said gently, "Don't worry, everybody in this family is smart enough to pass. You just do your best. I'll help you, and I was the smartest girl in my graduating class from high school."

Vinnie and Gino said, "Ha, ha," together, lured by her gentle, sad tone into teasing her. Octavia's great dark eyes flashed, but she smiled and said to Lucia Santa, "Well, I was, wasn't I, Ma?" This wistfulness for some glory unknown to them did more to persuade the children than any of her threats, except the one to kill them if they got left back. That threat they did not doubt for a moment.

Lucia Santa watched her daughter. She remembered how Octavia had loved to go to school, and it was this that made Lucia Santa tolerate such American airs, making education so important. She distrusted high ambition, high aims. For, the greater the reward, it followed, the greater the risks. You could become helpless in a shattering defeat. Better a modest safety. But Lucia Santa paid this deference to her daughter.

The mother said gravely to her children, "Yes, your sister could have been a schoolteacher if it had not been for your father." She saw Gino looking directly into her eyes, intent. "Yes," she said, speaking to him. "If your father had done his duty, supported his family, Octavia could have stopped work. But he never thought of anyone else, and you, *figlio de puttana* that you are, take after him. Tonight you jump over the fire. You spoil your good clothes and make your little brother a bad example. Now I have to buy new pants for school. *Animale* that you are. You never think of anyone. But I warn you—"

Octavia broke in quickly, "All right, Ma, that's something else. The big thing is that they know how important school is to their life. If you learn something at school you can be somebody. Otherwise you'll be just a slob down on the docks or in the railroad like Larry."

When the children were in bed the mother became very busy ironing the wash for the next week, sewing up holes in clothing. She had a basket piled so high that she had only to reach out without stooping. Octavia propped her book against the big sugar bowl. There was absolute quiet, except for the creak of bedsprings from the bedroom whenever one of the children turned over restlessly in sleep. The women were in perfect ease and contentment, chiefs of an obedient tribe.

Everything was running smoothly; they were both in rapport—the daughter a faithful but powerful underling; the mother undisputed chief, but showing her respect and admiration for a clever and faithful daughter's help. It was never said, but the father's banishment had relieved them of a great deal of tension and worry. They were almost happy he was gone, and their rule now absolute.

The mother rose to put coffee on the fire, for Octavia in her book would forget about everything. The mother wondered, What could be in these books that stunned her daughter into some magic oblivion? It was something she would never know, and if she had been younger she would have felt some envy or regret. But she was a busy woman with important work to be done for many years and could not make herself unhappy over pleasures of which she did not know the taste. She had enough regrets about pleasures whose taste she had known. But there was nothing to be done about that, either. She grimaced from the steam and her thoughts.

She had to go down to the other end of the hall to get the milk from the icebox again, and some good Italian peppered ham to tempt Octavia, who was getting too thin. Lucia Santa heard someone coming slowly up the steps, but whoever it was could only be on the second floor. She left the door of the apartment open, to get a little air from the ironing. Anyway, no one could go past their door to the icebox and bureau and then up the roof and escape. She sat at the table with her daughter, both of them drinking coffee, eating the prosciutto and coarse bread. They could both hear the steps coming up close, and then the shawled head of Zia Louche rose slowly and cautiously over the last step of the stairs and the old lady hobbled into the apartment, cursing terribly in Italian.

They were too intimate with her to give the usual greetings of formal courtesy. Lucia Santa rose to set another cup and slice more bread, though she knew the old dame never ate before other people. Octavia said pleasantly in Italian and with respect, "How are you feeling, Zia Louche?"

The old woman made a gesture of angry impatience, the gesture of a person who waits for a death that is in the present and therefore finds such a question not polite, in poor taste. They sat in silence.

"Work, work," Lucia Santa said. "This school, what miracles they make over it. The children must dress like the President himself, and I must wash and iron like a slave."

Zia Louche said, "Eh, eh," and made another impatient gesture as if to brush away all people who expected life to run smooth. She took off her shabby black coat and then the long knitted sweater with its buttons down to her knees.

Under those gimlet eyes Octavia felt she could no longer read; it would not be respectful. She rose and began to iron slowly. The mother reached out and closed the book, which was lying open on the table, so the daughter could not look down at it and read while ironing. Then Octavia was aware that she was being accorded the rare honor of a direct address from Zia Louche.

"Young lady of mine," Zia Louche said, with the rough familiarity of the old, "your handsome brother, has he appeared at all today?"

"No, Zia Louche," Octavia replied demurely. If anyone else had used this tone with her she would have spat in her face, especially the smug fat matrons, those guineas who always spoke to young girls with voices filled with sly pity because they had never tasted the pleasures of a marriage bed.

"And you, Lucia Santa?" Zia Louche asked. When the mother shook her head the old woman continued sharply, "Then you have no concern for this beautiful son of yours, a boy of seventeen years, in a country like this? You have no fears for him?" Octavia saw her mother's face contort in a frown of anxiety.

Lucia Santa shrugged helplessly. "What is now with that *disgrazia*? Saturday nights he never sleeps at home. Nothing has happened?"

Zia Louche gave a short harsh laugh. "Oh, yes, something

has happened. A whole comedy has been played. And, as usual in America, the mother is the last to know. Calm, Lucia Santa, your beautiful son is safe, alive. The Lady Killer—" she said this last in American, with incredible relish—"has finally met a girl who is very much alive. Congratulations, Lucia Santa, on your son's marriage and your new daughter-in-law—American style."

The stunning effect of this was such that Octavia and her mother could only stare. The old lady, in her taunting way, hoped to draw some of their rage on herself, but now she had to give way to gales and gales of laughter that shook her old skeleton in its flesh of black cloth, gasping out, "No, no, Lucia Santa, you must forgive me, you have all my love in this, but oh, what a villain your Lorenzo is, *cue mascalzone*. It's too much, it's really too much." But then she saw the stony face of her friend, the tight lips, the almost mortal insult that she had given. She composed herself. She held the wrinkled bones of her face in a gravity suitable to her years. But she could not hide a certain contempt for their anxiety.

"Again forgive me," Zia Louche said. "But with a son who is such a whoremaster, what did you expect, after all? Would you rather see him beaten or dead? Your son is not stupid, Lucia Santa. Signora Le Cinglata, twenty years barren, and Signor Le Cinglata, married twice, forty years a husband and never a father, finally they are blessed." She bowed her head mockingly. "Thanks be to the good God. But the man Le Cinglata thinks he owes his thanks to someone nearer and sharpens his knife to repay this debt. And the shameless woman Le Cinglata had a dream of marrying your son. Is this possible of a woman born and raised in Italy? Oh America—shameless land." At this Lucia Santa raised a threatening hand to heaven in a wordless curse on the brazen Le Cinglata, but she leaned forward to hear more.

Zia Louche went on. "Your son finally is trapped by the tigers he has so thoughtlessly tamed. A word from the Le

Cinglata to her husband and he is a dead man. But if he gives hope to the old whore, what may happen? What disgrace? She may even poison the old man and bring them both to the electric chair. But you know your son, he is clever and will do anything to avoid saying 'No' to anyone. So away he scampers to City Hall and marries a young innocent Italian girl who has watched him ride his horse on Tenth Avenue since she was in pigtails, without ever speaking to him. No one even knew he was acquainted with this bride, they had never even spoke together in public. Her people live on 31st Street, the family of Marconozzi, respectable, but the poorest of the poor. Oh, he is sly, your son, he will be a priest."

The mother asked quietly, "Has the girl a good reputation?"

Zia Louche grinned lewdly. "Men like your son marry only those girls who are irreproachable. That is their philosophy. Who values the virgin more than the whoremaster? But she is a stick." The old dame held up a bony skeleton forefinger, the gnarled bones lewder than any rounded flesh. "Dear God of mine, he'll split her in two like a piece of kindling." She crossed herself.

Octavia was furious, shamed by this marriage so typical of the poor, at the scandal, the sordidness of her brother's life. The disgusting sex madness they were all infected with. She saw with surprise that her mother was now in no way disturbed and was even smiling faintly. Octavia did not understand that this news, while surprising, disconcerting, something that it was better should not have happened, was not really bad news. How could it be for a woman who waited for more terrible dreams to become a reality? The fear of mysterious illness, murderous deeds of passion, prison, the electric chair—all were perfectly possible, all discernible. Lorenzo could have married a whore, or a slattern, or even one of the Irish. So he had married in haste, a common occurrence with the sons of the poor and no disgrace; the disgrace lay with the parents of the girl. "Everyone will think the worst," Octavia said aloud. "The rotten bastard."

But Lucia Santa was laughing outright now, at the thwarting of the Le Cinglatas, at her son's slyness. "Where is he now, this beautiful son of mine?" she asked Zia Louche.

Zia Louche said, "Let me finish. The man Le Cinglata now believes himself the father. A woman has only to hold a man on his knees by both ears and then she can lead him anywhere. But there is another question. The girl's mother, ah, the mother of the bride, she must be told. There is the problem. They are as proud as they are poor. They will consider their daughter shamed."

Lucia Santa made an impatient gesture. "I will go and tell them. We are as proud, and certainly as poor. We will understand each other. But now, where are they?"

The old woman rose, groaning as her bones creaked. She hobbled out the door and shouted down the stairwell, "Lorenzo, Louisa, come up."

As the three women waited for the bridal pair to ascend the stairs, they pondered on this new change in fortune. The mother suddenly realized that the loss of her son's income would be a serious blow to the family. But until he had children, he would be made to contribute something to his fatherless brothers and sisters. She was determined on that. Next, the second-floor apartment would be vacant soon; they could move into it, so she could watch her new daughter-in-law, help the couple in their early troubles, and with the babies to come—for she had no doubt she would soon be a grandmother. And then she had a great curiosity to see the looks of the girl her handsome son had finally chosen, the one who had finally put the bit in his mouth.

Octavia, too, was thinking now about money. That bastard Larry, deserting the family just when they needed the money most. And suddenly she was convinced that this was the real reason for his marriage, that the mother had ruled with too iron a hand, taking most of his pay check, restricting his freedom, so he had chosen this means of shedding his bonds. And now that the family was in trouble, Larry could see no future in it. Octavia prepared to welcome him as a brazen traitor and let his floozy have no doubts about her position with this family.

Zia Louche waited. Without a shred of malice, she was delighted to witness such a fine comedy.

Larry's handsome dark head rose first above the stairs. The girl was almost invisible behind him. Larry had an embarrassed grin that was charming; its usual confidence was touched by an alien bit of shyness. His mother waited for him with a smile of welcome touched with forgiving contempt.

Larry said quickly, "Mom, Sis, I want you to meet my wife." He brought the thin girl out from behind him. "Lou, this is my mother and sister Octavia."

The mother embraced the young girl and made her sit down. At the sight of the beautiful, pale, thin face with the great haunting brown eyes, the immature figure, Octavia felt an overwhelming pity for the girl. This was just a kid, she would never be able to handle Larry, she didn't know the life she would lead. Octavia, looking at her brother, his strong body, sleek black hair, knowing his romantic belief in himself, felt pity for him too; that this would be the end of his dreams; that his life had come to an end. She remembered him riding up Tenth Avenue on his black horse, sparks flying from cobblestones and steel tracks; the way he talked about himself as if he alone saw some great destiny. She understood that his goodness—his going early to work to help his mother, his leaving school and not preparing his mind for the life struggle—had left him without weapons to fight his fate. Now he would have children, the years would fly by as swiftly as the horse passed under the bridge, and he would be middle-aged. And since he was Larry, still dreaming. She had loved him once when they were children together, and now her pity made her kind to his child wife. She kissed Larry on the cheek and hugged her new sister-in-law, feeling the other's body stiff with fright.

They all sat down to a wedding feast of coffee and dry buns and arranged that the newly married couple would sleep there until the apartment on the second floor was vacant. Larry became animated, talking cheerfully; everything was going well. He was perfectly at ease. But suddenly Louisa buried her face in her hands and began to weep, saying between low, choking sobs, "I've got to go home and tell my mother."

Lucia Santa rose and said with determination, "We will all go. We should know each other, all of us, since we are related."

Larry said tentatively, "Gee, Ma, I gotta go on the night shift. You go over with Lou, and then I'll go over tomorrow."

The young bride looked at him with fearful surprise. Octavia burst out angrily, "Like hell you will, Larry. Your wedding night is a good excuse for a day off from work. You go with Mom and Louisa to her house and stick up for your wife."

Louisa looked at her wide-eyed, as if she had committed some blasphemy. Larry laughed and said, "Sis, come on, stop making a big deal out of the whole thing. You want me to go, Lou?" The girl nodded her head. He put a hand on her back protectively and said, "Then I'll come."

When the girl said, "Thanks, Larry," Octavia laughed loudly. She was surprised that her mother gave her such a threatening look, surprised that her mother had not forced Larry to do what was right. But when Lucia Santa said courteously to her son, "I think it better if you come with us, Lorenzo," she realized that her mother had accepted a new role; that she no longer considered herself the master of this particular child, and in some chilling way she was casting him out of her heart—not with anger or malice or lack of love, but as a burden to be dropped, to leave more strength for other burdens. When they all left, Octavia was so depressed that she ironed all the wash and did not reopen her book.

• • •

LIFE IS SO full of surprises for small boys that Gino was not surprised the next morning to see the long black hair of a girl in his brother Larry's bed. Standing in his modest winter underwear, Gino studied them. Larry looked different, and the girl didn't look right, either. The two pale faces, dead white with sleep in the chilly apartment, defenseless in a terribly deep unconsciousness, a tragic exhaustion, held the drawn purity of death. Both had jet-black hair, all scattered and untidy and flowing into each other as if it were a single silky mass of black grown together over both their faces. Then Larry stirred; strength and power and life came flowing back, blood rose from his body and tinged his cheeks. The heavy straight black eyebrows moved, his eyes opened, and the dark eyes flashed. Larry jerked his head away from the girl's so that now their hair did not intermingle and he was separate. He saw Gino watching them and grinned.

Vinnie had already taken the top of the milk bottle, the first inch of frozen icy cream that was a prize for the early bird. Gino tried to open another milk bottle, but his mother made his hand sting with the flat of a knife.

When Gino went back through the bedroom to finish dressing, his brother Larry was sitting up, head resting on the bedspread, smoking a cigarette, and the girl was sleeping with her face to the wall, her back small and hunched against the world. The straps of a white slip showed, framing the shoulder bones that protruded like chicken wings from the skin. As Gino went by, Larry reached out and pulled up the blanket to cover his wife from the cold, showing his own hairy chest over the long, heavy underwear as he did so.

GINO NEVER FORGOT that year. So many things happened, starting with Larry's marriage.

One day coming home from school he saw Joey Bianco sitting on Runkel's platform, all his schoolbooks scattered on the sidewalk. To his astonishment, Joey was crying; but under his tears his face was set in a brooding rage. Gino approached cautiously and asked, "What's the matter, Joey? Something happen to your father or mother?"

Joey shook his head, still crying. Gino sat down beside him hoisting himself up onto the platform. "You wanta play Seven-and-a-half?" Gino asked. "I got sixteen cents."

"I got no money to play," Joey said roughly. Then he wailed aloud. "I lost all my money. My father told me to put it in the bank and now the bank lost all my money. The lousy bastards. And my father doesn't even care, he laughs at me. They all said I could have the money for myself when I get big, and then they stole it off me. And now they all laugh at me." He was crying and cursing, heartbroken.

Gino was shaken. He, more than anyone else, knew what a terrible blow this was. How many times had Gino bought lemon ice and given Joey a lick because Joey wanted to save the two cents? How many times had Joey stayed home on Sunday afternoons to save the movie money and put it in the bank? How many times had Joey turned away from the hot dog vendor and his three-wheeled cart with the orange-striped umbrella, clutching a nickel firmly in his pocket, while Gino bit into the soft long bun, the juicy red hot dog, the white greasy sauerkraut and gobs of yellow mustard, all in one soul-filling mouthful? Gino felt the loss, too, for in some way it was his money. Though the other kids laughed at Joey, Gino had always respected him and given him at least one bite of hot dog, one taste of pizza, one lick of lemon ice to help him past temptation. And even at Easter, when everybody bought pink and white sugar eggs for a dime, even then Joey held fast, though Easter came but once a year. Gino was proud that his friend was the richest kid in Chelsea maybe, and certainly the richest kid on Tenth Avenue. So he asked slowly and fearfully, "Joey, how much did you lose?"

Joey said with desperate, dignified calmness, almost awe-stricken, "Two hundred and thirteen dollars."

The two of them looked at each other absolutely aghast. Gino had never dreamed it would be so much. For the first time Joey realized the extent and finality of his tragedy. "Oh, Jesus," he said. Gino said, "Come on, Joey, pick up your books. Joey, let's go home."

Joey jumped off the platform and kicked all the books savagely, kicked them until they were scattered yards apart in the gutter. He screamed, "Fuck the books. Fuck school. I'll get even with everybody. I'm never going home." He ran up toward Ninth Avenue and disappeared among the gray iron winter shadows of the El.

Gino picked up the schoolbooks. They were torn and dirty and smeared with grains of horse manure. He cleaned them against his pants and then went down to Tenth Avenue and up to Joey's house at 356.

The Biancos lived on the third floor. After Gino knocked he heard a woman weeping and wanted to run down the stairs, but the door opened too quickly. Joey's squat little mother, all in black, motioned him in.

Gino was surprised to see Joey's father home already and sitting at the kitchen table. He was a little hunched-up man with enormous mustaches, who always wore a crumpled gray fedora in the street and for some reason was wearing it now at table. Before him stood a jug of dark red wine, and a glass half full beside it.

"I brought Joey's books home," Gino said. "He's coming home after he helps the teacher."

He put the books on the table. The little man looked up and said with drunken kindness, "*Buono giovanetto,* good boy. You're the son of Lucia Santa and Joey's friend, a good boy. You never listen to anyone, eh? You go your own way. Very good. Very good. Have a glass of wine with me. And thank God you have no father."

"I don't drink, Zi' Pasquale," Gino said. "Thanks anyway." He was sorry for Mr. Bianco's feeling so bad over his son's loss. The mother sat at the table watching her husband.

"Drink, drink," said Zi' Pasquale Bianco. The woman produced a small wineglass and the man filled it. "To America," the little man said. "To those American presidents of the banks, may they one day eat the guts of their mothers."

"Quiet, quiet," Mrs. Bianco said soothingly.

In earlier days Gino had seen Zi' Pasquale in his daily resurrection, his glory and his triumph.

First the little bent man, gnarled, a body of lumps and knots, trudged wearily from the railroad yard over the sunken steel rails embedded in Tenth Avenue. How tired he was, how dusty and dirty, the sweat drying and sealing the pores. The round fedora, dirty gray and rimmed with black, repelled the dangerous rays of the sun; the empty lunch pail swung on the right side of his body as he came up the dark stairs of the tenement and into the apartment.

Off came his upper garments, out came warm water and soap, and Zia Bianco wiped his broad knotted back with a wet cloth. Then on with a clean blue shirt, a quick glass of wine as he took the jug from beneath the sink, and then to table.

First Zi' Pasquale would look them all in the eye, almost accusingly, even Gino, and then he would give a little shake of his head to show he did not blame them for some mysterious woe. Then a sip of wine from his glass. Slowly, carefully, his spine straightened as if the strength were pouring back into his body. Then his wife bent over him with a great deep plate of beans and pasta cloudy with a steam of garlic and brown bean sauce. Zi' Pasquale picked up a spoon as he would a shovel, scooped in, and with an expert laborer's flip the mound of beans and pasta disappeared behind that enormous mustached mouth, and after three such thrusts he put down his spoon and tore off a great chunk from the loaf of bread.

Spoon in one hand, bread in the other, he poured life and energy into his very soul. With each mouthful he grew visibly stronger, more powerful. He grew taller in his chair, over them all. The skin of his face became pink, there was a flash of white teeth and even a trace of the black-red lips as the mustache soaked flat with sauce. The brown crusty bread crackled like gunfire between his teeth, the great metal spoon flashed like a sword around their heads. He drained his glass of wine. And as if he had crushed everything on the table to its primal state, there was the smell of grape and flour and raw bean roots in earth.

Finally Zi' Pasquale took a knife from his wife and cut off a hunk of crumbly grainy cheese from the black-skinned wheel. He held it up to the light so all could fall under the spell of its aroma. His other hand plucked the remainder of the bread loaf from the table and then, powerful, serene, almost with holy authority, he actually smiled at them all and asked in his rough southern Italian, "Who's better than me?"

His wife would give out a short "Eh" of agreement as if he were confirming a belief of her own that he himself had denied. But the two boys would always stare at him very thoughtfully, trying to understand.

They saw. Whose food tasted sweeter this night, whose wine coursed more strongly through the blood? Whose flesh and bones and nerves became at peace with such merciful repose? Zi' Pasquale groaned with comfort as the pain of fatigue eased out of him. He raised himself a little to fart and a sigh of serious relief softly followed. At this very moment, who in all the world tasted more bliss?

Tonight Gino tried to say something comforting. "It's all right, Zi' Pasquale, Joey can save up again. I'll help sell coal from the railroad and next summer we can sell ice. It won't take long."

The great mustaches began to quiver and the face wrinkled into laughter. "My son and his money. Ah, *figlio mio,* if that were all. Do you know what I lost, does my son know what I lost? Five thousand dollars. Twenty years of rising in the dark, working in the bitter cold and this terrible American heat. Insulted by the boss, my very name changed, a name existing a thousand years in Italy, the name of Baccalona"—his voice thundered the name—"from the town of Salerno, Italy. I gave it all up. And my son is crying in the street." He drank another full glass of wine. "Five thousand dollars, twenty years of my life. My bones hurt with that money sweated out of their marrow. Damn heaven and Jesus Christ! They stole it from me without a gun, without a knife, in broad daylight. How is it possible?"

The woman said, "Pasquale, stop drinking. You have to go to work tomorrow, you did not work today. Many are losing their jobs in this Depression. Eat a little and go to sleep. Come now."

Zi' Pasquale said gently, "Don't worry, woman, I'll go to work tomorrow. Never fear. Didn't I go to work when our little daughter died? Eh? Didn't I go to work when you had the babies? When you were sick and the children sick? I'll go to work, never fear. But you, poor woman, who never put on the electricity until it was too dark to see, just to save a penny! The times you ate spinach without meat and wore sweaters in the house to save coal. This means nothing to you? Ah, woman, you are made of iron. Hear me, little Gino, fear them." Zi' Pasquale drained one full glass of wine and fell unconscious to the floor without another word.

The woman, sure her husband could not hear now, let out lamentations. Gino helped her drag Mr. Bianco to the bedroom as she wept and cried out her woes. He watched her undress her husband until he was just a pathetic, huddled figure in long yellow-white underwear snoring drunkenly through his mustaches, funny enough for the comics.

The woman made Gino sit in the kitchen with her. Where was Joey? she asked. Then went on. Her poor husband, he was their hope, their salvation, he must not bend to the Furies. The money was lost—terrible, but not death.

America, America, what dreams are dreamed in your name? What sacrilegious thoughts of happiness do you give birth to? There is a price to be paid, yet one dreams that happiness can come without the terrible payments. Here there was hope, in Italy none. They would start again, he was only a man of forty-eight. He still had twenty years of work in his body. For each human body is a gold mine. The ore of labor yields mountains of food, shelter from the cold, wedding feasts and funeral wreaths to hang on the tenement door. That comical little gnarled body in long winter underwear and gray mustaches still held a treasure to yield up, and with a woman's practical sense Mrs. Bianco was worried more about her husband than about the money they had lost.

After a long time, Gino made his escape.

He was late arriving home; everyone was already at the table. How good it was to come into that warm kitchen that smelled of garlic and olive oil and tomato sauce bubbling like dark hot wine in the pot.

They all filled their dishes from the central bowl heaped high with spaghetti. There were no meatballs for the Thursday pasta, just a piece of cheap chuck beef, so tender from simmering in the sauce that you could lift out shredded pieces with a fork. As they were eating, Larry and his wife came from the apartment below to join them at table.

They were all glad to see Larry, especially the young boys. He always made things lively with jokes and stories about the railroad, he knew all the gossip about the families on the Avenue. Octavia and Lucia Santa were always cheerful and animated when he was there and would not scold the children.

Gino noticed that Louisa was getting fat, but her head was getting smaller.

"Yeah," Larry was saying, "the *Panettiere* lost ten thousand dollars in the stock market and some more money in the bank, but he doesn't have to worry with his store. A lot of people on the Avenue lost money. Thank God you're poor, Mom."

Octavia and her mother smiled at each other. The money was a secret from everyone, and it was in postal savings besides. Lucia Santa said to Louisa, "Eat more, you have to keep up your strength." She took a great chunk of beef from

Larry's plate and put it on Louisa's. She said to Larry, "You *animale,* you are strong enough. Eat spaghetti, your wife needs meat."

A strange look of pleasure came over the young girl's face. She was very quiet, she seldom spoke, but now she said timidly, "Thank you, Mom." Gino and Vincent looked at each other; something struck them both as not quite right. They knew their mother inside out. She had not been sincere, she did not really like the girl, and the girl had been too woebegone in her thanks.

Larry grinned at the boys and winked. He took up a spoonful of sauce and said in great astonishment, "Look at the cockroaches on the wall." It was the old, old game he played to steal their roast potatoes on Saturday nights. Vinnie and Gino refused to turn their heads, but Louisa looked around quickly, and in that moment Larry speared the piece of beef on her dish and took a bite out of it before putting it back. The children laughed, but Louisa, realizing she had been tricked, burst into tears. Everybody was astounded.

Larry said, "Ah, come on, that's an old joke in our family. I was only kidding." The mother and Octavia made sounds of sympathy, Octavia saying, "Leave her alone when she's like that, Larry." The mother said, "Louisa, your animal of a husband plays like the beast he is. Next time—the hot sauce in his face."

But Louisa rose from the table and ran down the stairs to her apartment on the second floor.

"Lorenzo, go after her, bring her down something to eat," Lucia Santa said.

Larry had folded his arms. "Like hell I will," he said. He started to eat his spaghetti again. No one said anything. Finally Gino said, "Joey Bianco lost two hundred and thirteen dollars in the bank and his father lost five thousand dollars."

He saw his mother's face take on a grim light of triumph. It was the same look she had when she heard about the *Panet-*

tiere's losing money. But when Gino told how Zi' Pasquale had got drunk, his mother's face changed and she said wearily, "Even clever people aren't safe in this world, that's how it is." She and Octavia exchanged another glance of satisfaction. It had been the merest chance, pure luck, that they had put their money in postal savings. When they had opened the account they had been too shy to go through the white-pillared entrance and the great marble lobby of the bank with their little money.

The mother said, with impersonal sadness, as if her malicious triumph made her feel guilty, "Poor man, he loved money so much, he married a miser out of true affection. They were happy. A perfect marriage. But then nothing goes right, no matter what you do."

No one paid attention to Lucia Santa. They knew her. In her speech and in her thinking she was pessimistic about life. Yet she lived like a true believer in good fortune. She rose in the morning with gladness, she bit into bread knowing it would be sweet. Her hope was a physical energy, replenished by her love for her children and the necessity to do battle for them. They all believed that she could never be afraid. So her words meant little, they were merely superstition. They ate in peace. When they finished, Larry lolled back with a cigarette and Octavia and the mother talked with him, telling stories about his escapades as a youth. Vinnie took Louisa's plate of spaghetti and put the piece of beef in the hot sauce for a moment. Then he covered it with another plate.

Lucia Santa said, "Good boy, bring something to eat to your sister-in-law." Vinnie went down the stairs with the two plates and a half-full bottle of cream soda. A few minutes later he came back empty-handed and sat at the table.

Larry looked at him for a moment and asked, "Is she O.K.?" When Vinnie nodded, Larry went on with the story he was telling.

10

O N A LATE March Sunday afternoon, Octavia Angeluzzi stood in the kitchen, gazing down into the backyards below. Inside the block of tenements there was a great
hollow square, which was cut up by wooden fences into many
separate yards.

Octavia looked down on stone gardens, concrete loam.
Some homesick *paesano* had left a box like a three-cornered
hat filled with hairy dirt, and out of it grew a bony stick. At its
foot little stems, like toes, wore deathly yellow leaves. In the silvery light of winter an empty red flowerpot rose out of a gray
cemented flower bed. Above them, filling the air and criss-
crossing so that not even a witch could have flown over the
backyards, were innumerable frayed dirty white clotheslines
stretching from windows to distant tall wooden poles.

Octavia felt terribly tired. It was the cold, she thought, the
long winter without sunshine and the long hours at work.
With the Depression, rates of pay had gone down. Now she
had to work longer hours for less money. At night she and the

mother sewed buttons on cards in their own home, sometimes with the kids helping. But the boys sneered at the low rate of pay, a penny a card, and would rarely work. She had to laugh at them. Children could afford to be independent.

There was an ache in her chest and in her eyes and head. She felt hot all over. And there was the constant refrain running through her mind, what were they going to come to with Larry's money gone and the four kids to bring up? Every week now she had to go to the postal savings and take out money. The dream was shattered; they had slipped back in savings, receded years from owning a house.

Looking down at the desolate landscape, which was given a touch of strange humanity by a cat walking the top of a fence, she thought of Gino and Sal, growing up to be stupid laborers, loutish, coarse, living in slums, breeding children into the sack of poverty. A wild surge of anxiety rose in her, followed by a physical nausea and fear. She would see them cringe and suck for charity as their parents had done before them. The poor beg to stay alive.

And what about Vinnie? With shock Octavia realized that she had already written his future off. He would have to go to work early to help his brothers and sisters. There was no other way.

Oh, that lousy bastard Larry—leaving the family when they needed his help the most. And having the nerve to come up from the second floor to eat. But men were lousy. She had a sudden vision of a man—hairy, gorilla-like, naked and with penis enormous and erect—man the very image. Her cheeks flushed and she was so weak she could not stand. She went to the kitchen table and sat down. She felt a suffocating pain in her chest and realized with quiet terror that she was ill.

It was Gino who first came up and found Octavia leaning over the table, crying with fear and pain, spitting little red flecks of blood on the white and blue oilcloth. Octavia whispered, "Go call Mamma at Zia Louche." Gino was so frightened that he turned and flew down the stairs without a word.

When the two of them got back, Octavia had recovered her strength and was sitting up straight. She had not cleaned the oilcloth. She had started to, so as not to alarm her mother, but some need for sympathy, a fear that she would be thought a malingerer in the family fight, had unconsciously persuaded her to leave everything untouched.

Lucia Santa rushed into the room. She saw at once her daughter's woebegone, sick, and guilty face, and then the flecks of blood. She wrung her hands and cried out, "Oh, God of mine," and burst into tears. These dramatics irritated Octavia and made Gino, behind her, mutter, "For Chrissakes."

But that was for the moment. The mother immediately gained control, took her daughter by the hand, and led her down the row of bedrooms. She shouted back to Gino, "Run. Quick, to Dr. Barbato." Gino, delighted with the excitement and his own importance, sped down the four flights of stairs again.

With Octavia safely in bed, Lucia Santa got a bottle of rubbing alcohol and went to watch over her daughter until the doctor came. She poured the alcohol liberally into her cupped hand, bathed Octavia's hot forehead and face. They were both composed now, but Octavia noticed that familiar look of stern anxiety on her mother's face, that look that seemed to close out the world. She tried to joke. "Don't worry, Ma," she said. "I'll be all right. At least I'm not having a baby without a husband. I'm still *a good Italian girl.*"

But in times like these Lucia Santa had no sense of humor. Life had taught her a certain respect for the frowns of fate.

She sat beside her daughter's bed like a small black-clad Buddha. As she waited for the doctor, her mind raced ahead to what this illness would mean, what new woe it would bring. She felt overcome by disaster—her husband being sent away, her son marrying at an early age, the Depression with its lack of work, and now her daughter's illness. She sat there gathering up her strength, for there was no question now of individual misfortune. The entire family was in danger, its whole fabric, its life. It was no longer a matter of single defeats; now there was danger of annihilation, of sinking to the lowest depth of existence.

Dr. Barbato followed Gino up the stairs into the apartment and through the rooms to where Octavia rested. As always he was beautifully dressed, and his mustache was trim. He had tickets for the opera at the Brooklyn Academy of Music and he was in a hurry. He had nearly not come, nearly told the boy to call Bellevue.

When he saw the girl and heard the story he knew his coming had been a waste of time. She would have to go to the hospital. But he sat down beside the bed, noticing she was embarrassed at being examined by so young a man, and that she was conscious of the mother who was keeping a watchful eye upon him. He thought with disgust, These Italians think men would screw a woman on her deathbed. He forced himself to say quietly, "Now, Signora, I will have to examine your daughter. Have the young boy leave us." He prepared to pull down the sheet.

The mother turned and saw Gino wide-eyed. She gave him a backhanded slap and said, "Disappear. For once with my permission." And Gino, who had expected praise for all his swift running in this emergency, went back to the kitchen muttering curses.

Dr. Barbato put his stethoscope on Octavia's chest and stared off into space professionally, but really taking a good look at the girl's body. He saw with surprise that she was very thin. The full bosom and wide, rounded hips were deceiving. She had lost a lot of weight. Her heavy, planed face did not show this loss, for, though finely drawn, it could never be haggard. The eyes, a great liquid brown, watched him with fearful intensity. The doctor's mind registered, too, without desire, how ripe the body was for love. She looked like the great nude paintings he had seen in Italy on his graduation trip. She was a classical type, made for children and heavy duty on the connubial couch. She had better get married soon, sick or not.

He rose, covering the girl again with the bed sheet. He said with quiet reassurance, "You'll be all right," and motioned the mother to the other bedroom.

He was surprised when Octavia said, "Doctor, please talk in front of me. My mother will have to tell me, anyway. She won't know what to do."

The doctor had learned that the little niceties of the profession were lost on these people, and with reason. He said quietly to both of them, "You have pleurisy, not much, but you must go to the hospital for rest and X-rays. That blood you coughed up is serious. There may be something with the lungs." For a moment this brought to his mind the opera he would see tonight. The heroine dying of TB, singing like mad beneath bright lights; her only loss a lover, a loss of pleasure; her death treated in such a way as to make it frivolous. He said truthfully, "Now don't be alarmed; even if it is the lungs, it can't be too serious. Don't have any foolish fears. The worst that can happen is that your daughter will get a few months' rest. So tomorrow, bring her to Bellevue Hospital Clinic. I'll give her something for tonight." He took out one of the samples sent him by the drug houses and gave it to the mother. "Now remember, tomorrow without fail, off to Bellevue. This flat is cold, the children too noisy, she needs rest. The X-rays are important. Now, Signora, don't fail me." In a gentler tone he added, "Don't worry."

The doctor left, feeling a mixture of self-disgust and satisfaction. He could have made fifteen dollars instead of a lousy two. He could have treated her for the next week, taken the X-rays in his office, the whole business. But he knew the poverty of the family. Later on he was angry with himself, feeling frustration that the skills he had learned must be given so cheaply, that the sacrifices made by his father should bear such sour fruit. He was a man with a powerful economic weapon he could not use at full strength. What lousy luck it hadn't been the daughter of the *Panettiere*. He would have milked the baker dry, he would have wrung him out to the last drop. And with every justification, without really cheating, with all fairness. Oh, someday he would move into a practice, a neighborhood, where he could work and make his fortune with a clear conscience. Dr. Barbato was simply a man who could not stand the sight and smell of poverty. His sudden acts of compassion made him unhappy for days afterward. He seriously regarded them as a vice and not a virtue.

In the kitchen, Sal and Vinnie, finally home after the Sunday movie, sat quietly eating great slabs of crusty bread doused with vinegar and olive oil. Gino was sulking at a corner of the table, doing his homework. Lucia Santa watched them all somberly. "Gino," she said, "go take a ten cents from my pocketbook for yourself. Then go call your brother Lorenzo to come upstairs—*subito*." She felt a sudden surge of love at his happy springing to do her wishes, his quick forgetting of a quarrel balm to her spirit.

The next morning Lucia Santa committed an act so monstrous that it lost her the sympathy of the whole of Tenth Avenue, of everyone who would have commisserated with her in this new misfortune. It made Dr. Barbato so angry that he cursed in Italian for the first time since entering medical school. Even Zia Louche scolded Lucia Santa. It was a foolish act, immoral, shocking; and yet it was merely an act of love. Lucia Santa did not take her daughter to Bellevue's charity hospital; instead she had Larry drive them to the French Hospital on 30th Street between Ninth and Eighth Avenues, a little more than a block away. It was a cheerful, clean, and expensive hospital. The nurses there would be polite, the doctors charming, the clerical workers subservient. There would be no waiting for hours in dim halls for admittance. Lucia Santa's daughter would be treated like a human being, that is, as a solvent member of society.

No one was more surprised than Lucia Santa herself. It

was a fantastically foolish step that would wipe out the savings of years just at the time when they were most desperately needed. There would be no breadwinner in the home. It was an act of pure arrogance.

But there were reasons. Lucia Santa had lain awake all that night and, without sleeping, had suffered nightmares. She saw her beautiful young daughter imprisoned in the towers of Bellevue, lost in the dismal corridors, spat upon like an animal. And then there was superstition. Her husband had entered Bellevue and never returned. It was a charnel house; her daughter would die and they would cut her into little pieces and put her flesh in bottles.

So in the early morning hours Lucia Santa made her decision, and felt such a tremendous relief that she cared nothing of what the world would think—her friends, her relatives or her neighbors. In the darkness of her bed she had wept, the solitary terrible weeping that must be done alone with no one to see; not a show of grief, but a release of anguish that takes the place of consolation from a friend or loved one. Lucia Santa wept for strength because there was no one in the world to draw strength from. Hers was the terrible act of those who cannot show their need for pity. In daylight she composed herself, and when she rose from her bed, her face was strong and confident.

After the kids had been sent to school, Larry came up and they wrapped Octavia, already warmly dressed, in blankets. They helped her down the stairs and into Larry's car. When Lucia Santa got into the car she said to her son, "Drive to the French Hospital." Octavia started to protest, but the mother shouted with rage, "Quiet. Don't say a word."

The formalities were over quickly. Octavia was put in a quiet, clean, lovely room with another young girl. There were pictures on the wall. On the way home Larry told his mother, feeling the jealousy he always felt for his sister, that he would give five dollars a week for the family until Octavia was working again. His mother reached out and touched him for a moment, and said in Italian, "Ah, you're a good boy, Lorenzo." But in her tone Larry recognized his dismissal; she did not count him, did not trust him, she had no respect for him in this crisis. But if he had been in Octavia's place he would never have broken down, if she had picked him instead of her.

11

LUCIA SANTA ANGELUZZI-Corbo, a beleaguered general, pondered the fate and travails of her family, planned tactics, mulled strategy, counted resources, measured the loyalties of her allies. Octavia would be away at a rest home for six months. She would not be able to work for possibly a year. A year's wages lost.

Lorenzo gave five dollars a week, sometimes two or three dollars more. Vincenzo would work in the bakery—another five dollars a week and money saved on bread. Gino was worthless, Sal and Aileen too young.

And Lorenzo's wife was pregnant, another chink in the armor. Perhaps better not count on the money from Lorenzo, either.

No, think another way. Vincenzo had three years to go to finish high school. Was it necessary for him to graduate? Gino was headstrong, he must be tamed, he must help, she was too lenient with him.

The mother realized more than ever how important Octavia was to the family in things besides money. It was Octavia who made the children get good marks in school, brought them to the free dental clinic in the Hudson Guild. It was Octavia who planned how to save money and hide it in the post office, no matter how much they needed it for food and clothing. It was Octavia who gave her strength, on whom she leaned, who supported her in moments of weakness.

And now, Lucia Santa thought, she was alone again. The terrible battles were to be fought again. But older, tougher, experienced, she did not feel the helpless despair and terror she had known as a young widow. She was a hardened veteran to disaster and her spirit was not weakened by young and foolish dreams. She fought now as one desperately fights merely to remain alive.

Lucia Santa came to the decision she had to come to. There was nothing for it but to apply for welfare, to go on the home relief. And the struggle to come to this decision involved many things.

In no way did it involve conscience, or a concern for giving the authorities fair play. She had been born in a land where the people and the state were implacable enemies. No, there was a better reason.

Charity is salt in the wound. It is painful. The state gives charity with the bitter hatred of a victim to his blackmailer. The receiver of free money is subjected to harassment, insult, and profound humiliation. Newspapers are enlisted to heap scorn on the arrogant bastards who choose to beg instead of starve or let their children starve. It is made clear that the poor seek charity as a great and sordid chicanery in which they delight. And there are some who do. As there are some people who delight in sticking hot needles deep into their abdomens, swallow pieces of broken bottles. A special taste. Speaking for humanity in general, the poor accept charity with a shame and loss of self-respect that is truly pitiful.

Larry arranged for the investigator to come to the house,

but he would not stay for the interview. His male pride was affronted. He would not be a party to it, he disassociated himself from the whole thing. Lucia Santa found a hiding place for the imported Italian olive oil she did not dream of doing without; it would be a telling blow against her.

THE INVESTIGATOR CAME late in the afternoon. He was a solemn, comical-looking young man with great round black eyes. Those eyes had thick round eyebrows above them and dark circles beneath them so that he looked like an olive owl. But he was polite. He knocked at the door politely. He inspected the apartment with apologies, opening cupboard doors and closets and wandering through the apartment more like a prospective tenant than a home relief investigator. He addressed Lucia Santa as "Signora," and his own name had a touch of elegance; he was called La Fortezza.

He listened to Lucia Santa's story and wrote down all the particulars in his notebook, nodding and murmuring expressions of regret in Italian when she told about a particular misfortune. He spoke college Italian, but he could be understood.

Forms were spread out, questions asked. No, no; she had no money in the bank, nor did her children; she owned nothing, no insurance; nothing. She had no jewelry to sell except her wedding ring but he assured her that that was exempt. When they were finished, Mr. La Fortezza sat on his chair and leaned his body forward, his hands clasping the edge of the table like talons, his black-circled round eyes reproachful.

"Signora Corbo," he said, "it displeases me greatly to inform you there will be difficulties. Each of your three eldest children has money in trust from the unfortunate accident to their father. Strictly speaking, that money must vanish before you can get welfare. That is the law. And if I do not report this money you have, I will be in trouble." He looked at her gravely.

Lucia Santa was taken completely by surprise. That this polite young man, an Italian boy, had acted the spy, had gone to neighbors for information, then set a trap—this enraged her. She said bitterly, "Good. I'll throw the money in the streets."

He smiled at her joke and waited. She sensed all was not lost. "Isn't there something you can do for me?" she asked.

Mr. La Fortezza had a slightly uncomfortable look, an owl swallowing a particularly vigorous mouse. "Ah, Signora," he said, "one hand does not wash itself alone." Then, still a little embarrassed (he was still too young to be comfortable in dishonesty), he explained that he would risk his job to get her sixteen dollars every two weeks, but that when he brought the check she would have to give him three dollars. After all, it was money she should not receive, he was breaking the law, and so on. The bargain was struck. Lucia Santa was so grateful that she served coffee with cake, though coffee alone was enough for the laws of hospitality. And over the coffee Mr. La Fortezza told his woes. How he had taken his degree in law after many sacrifices by his parents, people like herself; now there was no work, and he had to take this lowly job with the city. How could he ever repay his father on his salary? It pained him to work in such a fashion, but how could he ever hope to have his own practice unless he made a little extra money? And after all, they both profited, since the signora was not really entitled to an allowance from the welfare. And so on. They parted friends.

Mr. La Fortezza came every two weeks with the check. There would be a ceremony. Gino would be sent down to the grocery to pay the outstanding bill and get the check cashed. He would also buy a quarter-pound of American ham, picture pink in its rectangular border of white, creamy, sweet fat; some soft, sliced, American bread; and yellow American cheese. For Mr. La Fortezza had a weak stomach and turned up his nose at honest Italian salami and pepperoni, the tingling sharp provolone, the crusty gum-cutting Italian bread.

Gino would watch wide-eyed at the little scene to be played. The thin pink and yellow slices laid out on a long ceremonial platter, the large mug of coffee, and Mr. La Fortezza at his ease, resting his swollen feet on another chair as he talked to Lucia Santa of his trials and tribulations, the mother shaking her head in sympathy. For the poor man climbed countless flights of stairs, quarreled with those low-class Italians who tried to conceal their sons' working and cursed because he would not approve their applications for relief, saying that he was a Jew and not an Italian, for no Italian would serve this government against his own kinfolk. "Ah," Mr. La Fortezza said always, "was it for this my poor parents pinched each penny? Ate *scarola* and *pasta* and beans every day of the week? For their son to earn his bread at the cost of his health?" Lucia Santa would cluck with pity.

The owl eyes were sad. Mr. La Fortezza was out in all kinds of weather. He was not well. Four years at the university studying hard. "Signora," he said, "I am not one of the clever ones; after all, my people were illiterate peasants for a thousand years, and even now it is enough for them that I do not have to work with my hands."

The ham and cheese eaten, he would stand, ready to take his leave. Lucia Santa would give him the three dollars with an exquisite tactfulness, picking up his hand and thrusting the money into it as if he would absolutely refuse if she did not press him. Mr. La Fortezza would make a gesture of reluctance, pushing back the money; then he would sigh and raise an eyebrow and say "Eh" in a hopeless voice to show that his circumstances were so desperate that refusal was impossible.

It was true, they were fond of each other. He liked the older woman for her courtesy, her regard for his feelings, her little thoughtful snack with the coffee. She on her part felt a real sympathy for the sad-looking boy, thanking God that none of her sons showed so little joy in life. She felt no resentment that she must pay tribute.

In a few weeks Mr. La Fortezza got Lucia Santa a fifteen-dollar-a-month rental allowance. Without being asked, Lucia Santa put a five-dollar bill in his hand instead of three dollars. It was an understanding with a foundation like a rock.

It grew. He got her another four dollars a week. Lucia Santa made it a point to have a little parcel of groceries for him to take home, a pound of the pink sweet ham, a bottle of homemade fiery anisette to help his digestion. Now that Larry had a ramshackle tin lizzie that he tinkered with when he was not working, the mother had her son drive Mr. La Fortezza home all the way to the Bronx on Arthur Avenue.

The three of them, Larry, Mr. La Fortezza, and Gino, would ride in the bouncing rattling car, darting between horses and wagons and trolleys and automobiles. Gino noticed that Larry was always polite, but had a contempt for the young lawyer that came out in little kidding remarks. Mr. La Fortezza obviously did not dream that he was being kidded. He would earnestly tell his misfortunes like beads. How little the welfare paid its investigators, the payments that must be made on the house in the Bronx, how his parents were now getting so old they could not work, and he would have to support them and discharge the mortgage. There was real fear, almost terror, in his voice when he spoke of his desperate need for money, and this puzzled Gino. For Mr. La Fortezza was rich. He had been to college, he owned a two-family house, his family went away in the summer for vacation. What people on Tenth Avenue dreamed of achieving after forty years of heavy toil, this young man already had; he lived the dream and he was more terrified than the meanest laborer in Gino's tenements.

When Mr. La Fortezza got out of the car, his little brown bag of groceries under his arm, Larry lit a cigarette and winked at his kid brother. Gino winked back. They drove home to Tenth Avenue in some way cheered and confident, as if the world was theirs to conquer.

DR. BARBATO, CLIMBING the four flights to the Angeluzzi-Corbo apartment, was a man grimly determined that by Jesus Christ this time this family would pay his due. Try to help them and someone else made the money. Why should he lose money to the French Hospital?

So Bellevue Hospital was too good for these poor ignorant guinea bastards? They wanted the best of medical care, did they? Who the hell did they think they were, these *miserabili,* these beggars without a pot to piss in, on home relief and the daughter in the sanitarium at Raybrook.

The door was open as the doctor came over the top stair. Sentineled there was little Sal, looking very solemn. In the kitchen the supper dishes were scattered all over the table, the yellow oilcloth dotted with scraps of French-fried potatoes and eggs. Gino and Vincent were playing a game of cards on this table. A fine pair of bandits, the doctor thought angrily, but he was softened when Vincent left the table to lead him through the string of rooms, doing so with a natural, shy courtesy, and saying in a gentle voice, "My mother is sick."

In the dark, windowless bedroom lay the heavy figure Lucia Santa. Standing beside her was the small girl Aileen, letting her face and hands be washed by the cloth the mother took from a water basin beside her bed. The scene reminded the doctor of some of the religious pictures he had seen in Italy, not for any sentimentality, but because of the composition of the reposing mother tending the child and the lighting of the room, with the dim yellow of the electric bulb casting a beatific glow on the dark-colored walls.

He tried to isolate the resemblance. Then he realized from his reading that it was simply a peasant upbringing, the child's complete reliance on its mother. These were the people that famous painters had used.

Dr. Barbato stood at the foot of the bed and said gravely, "Ah, Signora Corbo, you're having bad luck this winter." It was an expression of sympathy and a reminder of how badly she had behaved with Octavia.

Even lying flat on her back, Lucia Santa could become so violently angry that her cheeks flushed and her great black eyes flashed. But the reverence of the poor for so exalted a personage as the doctor made her hold her tongue, though she could have reminded him that he too had eaten from her hand a slice of coarse bread soaked in wine vinegar and olive oil. She said meekly, "Ah, Doctor, my back, my legs, I can't walk or work."

The doctor said, "First send the child to the kitchen." The little girl stood closer to the bed and put one arm out to her mother's head. The mother said gently, "Go, Lena, go in the kitchen and help your brothers with the dishes." The doctor smiled and Lucia Santa, seeing the smile, called out in Italian, "Vincenzo, Gino, *mascalzoni* that you are, have you started the dishes? Have you left the kitchen a mess for the doctor to see? Wait—I'll cripple both of you. Lena, go, and tell me if they don't work."

The little girl, delighted with her role of spy, ran to the kitchen.

Dr. Barbato walked around the bed and sat on it. He pulled down the blanket and put his stethoscope to her chest, first on top of the nightgown. As he was about to tell her to raise her nightgown the little girl was beside him, dark brown eyes curious. She said to her mother, "Gino and Vincent are washing the dishes and Sal is cleaning the table."

The mother saw the doctor's annoyance. "Good, good, Lena, and now you go help them and watch them. No one is to come in here until I call. Tell them that." The little girl scampered away.

Lucia Santa had put out her hand to touch her daughter's head, and the doctor, seeing the swollen wrists, knew what he could expect. When they were alone he told her to turn over on her stomach, and then he rolled up the plain woolen nightgown. He saw the knobby bumps at the base of the spine and said with a reassuring laugh, "Ah, Signora, you have arthritis. A month in Florida would make you a new woman. You need sunlight, heat, rest." He examined her thoroughly and firmly, pressing parts of her body to see where she felt pain. He was conscious of the swelling buttocks of this peasant woman in her forties. Like her daughter's they were the buttocks of the sensual Italian nudes hung in Florence, great, rounded, as deep as they were wide, but they aroused no desire in him. None of these women could. In his mind they were unclean, unclean with poverty. He pulled down the nightgown.

The woman turned around. The doctor looked at her gravely and said sternly, "What is this, Signora, you can't walk, you can't work in the house? It is not that serious. True, you need rest, but you should be able to walk. Your joints are swollen on the wrists and legs and your back, but it is not that serious."

Lucia Santa looked at him for a long moment before she said, "Help me up." Gingerly she swung her legs over the side of the bed and he tried to help her stand. As she began to straighten her back, she gave a muted shout of pain and slumped to a dead weight on his arms. He let her down gently to the bed. There was no question of a fake.

"Well, then, you have to rest, Signora," Dr. Barbato said. "But this should pass. Not altogether, you will always have trouble, but I'll soon have you at the stove again."

Lucia Santa smiled at his little joke. "Many thanks," she said.

WHEN DR. BARBATO left the Corbo house he took the fresh air on Tenth Avenue and pondered the world and humanity. He felt something resembling awe. With mock humor he recounted the misfortunes of this family. The husband in the cuckoo house, the daughter with that big white worm eating away behind those gorgeous tits (and don't forget the first husband killed in that accident), the son with a dismal marriage to a poverty-stricken immature girl. Now the woman, burdened with half-grown children, become crippled herself. Lying there on that great beautiful ass and that heavy marble-like body, and having the nerve to get angry at his remarks.

He looked down the row of tenements, the windows burning little square fires against the wintry sky. Feeling sick, he muttered without knowing what he meant, "What the hell are they trying to do?" The cold wind came across the railroad yards from the Hudson and set his blood racing. He felt angry, challenged, that this had been permitted to happen in his sight, as if his face had been slapped, as if he were being dared to interfere in some cosmological bullying. His blood churned. This was too much. Too much. All right, he thought, let's see what you can do. His blood now turned hot, so that despite the snapping cold, he had to loosen the collar of his coat and the wool scarf that his mother had knitted for him.

For the next two months Dr. Barbato, out of pure rage, practiced the art of healing. He visited Lucia Santa every second day, gave her injections, gave her heat treatments and chatted over old times with her for at least twenty minutes as he gave her massages. She was getting better, but still she could not rise from her bed. Dr. Barbato talked about Octavia, how she would be coming home from the sanitarium, and how distressed the daughter would be to find her mother so ill. A few days before Octavia was to come home he gave Lucia Santa shots of vitamins and stimulants, and the night before her return he found the mother sitting in the kitchen ironing clothes on the kitchen table, her children sitting around her, fetching water at her commands, and folding up the clothes for her. "Well, well, good, very good," Dr. Barbato said cheerfully. "A sure sign of health if one can work, eh Signora?"

Lucia Santa smiled at him. It was a smile that acknowledged her debt and denied his wit. If there was work, people would get up from a deathbed to work, they both knew. As Dr. Barbato prepared to give her an injection she murmured in Italian, "Ah, Doctor, how am I going to pay you?" For once he was not angry. With a comforting smile he said, "Just invite me to your daughter's wedding." Implying that there were joys in living, that rewards must follow suffering, good fortune follow bad; that all would be well, the daughter would recover, the children grow, time pass.

12

OCTAVIA HAD BEEN away for six months. In that time Lucia Santa had never visited her daughter; it had been impossible. The trip was too long, her duties at home too great, and she did not trust Larry and his battered car. To leave the children alone was not even considered.

The day Octavia returned, Larry and Vinnie went to meet her at Grand Central Station. The rest of the family waited in the apartment, the children dressed in their Sunday clothes, Lucia Santa in her finest black dress. Zia Louche scurried around the kitchen replenishing boiling water, stirring tomato sauce.

Gino watched out the front window. At last he flew to the kitchen yelling, "Ma, here they come."

Lucia Santa wiped away the tears that sprang to her eyes. Zia Louche started throwing the ravioli into the pot of boiling water. The door of the apartment was open and the children went to the stairhead, leaned over the banister and listened to the tread of feet coming up the stairs.

When Octavia appeared, they almost did not recognize her. They had been prepared for someone pale, invalid-like, someone they could tenderly minister to; crushed, risen from the dead. They saw an American girl, full blown. Octavia no longer even had her usual sallow skin. Her cheeks were rosy red, her hair waved in a permanent, American style. She was wearing a skirt and sweater with a belted jacket over it. But most of all, what made them feel like strangers was her voice, her speech, and her manner of greeting them.

She smiled sweetly, her teeth showing between her controlled lips. She let out a cry that was delightful yet subdued, hugged Sal and Aileen, and said to each of them, "Oh, darling, darling, how I missed you." Then she went to Lucia Santa and kissed her on the cheek instead of on the mouth and said with a pretty, coquettish air, "Oh, I'm so glad to be home."

Larry and Vincenzo came up over the stairwell, each carrying a suitcase and looking a little embarrassed.

Octavia gave Gino a peck on the cheek and said, "*My,* you're getting handsome." Gino backed away. Everyone stared. What had happened to her?

The only ones delighted with this new personality were the two small children, Sal and Aileen. They would not leave her side, they devoured her sweetness with their eyes and ears and bodies, stood trembling with pleasure as she ran her fingers through their hair and hugged them over and over, repeating in a most charming way, "Oh, how big you've grown."

Lucia Santa made Octavia sit down at once. She paid no attention to these new airs. She wanted her daughter to rest from the climb up the four flights of stairs. Zia Louche, already serving dinner, said to Octavia, "Ah, thank God you're back, young woman, your mother needs you." She bustled back to the stove before Octavia could answer.

The meal was the most uncomfortable one ever eaten in the Angeluzzi-Corbo household. The conversation was a polite exchange of information among strangers. Gino and Vinnie did not fight at the table. Sal and Eileen were absolute angels, never quarreling over who got the biggest meatballs. Louisa came up with the baby and kissed Octavia gingerly behind the ear so as not to get any infection. She sat down next to Larry, holding the baby away from Octavia. Octavia cooed over the baby but did not touch him. Larry ate, made excuses, and then left to go to work on the four-to-midnight shift. He hurried away.

When Octavia made a motion to start clearing the table, everyone rose in horror. Even Gino leaped to his feet and grabbed dishes to take to the sink. Lucia Santa cried out, "What are you trying to do, get sick again?" So Octavia sat, with little Sal and Aileen resting against her legs and looking up adoringly at her.

Only the mother sensed the sadness behind Octavia's smiles and gay talk. For sitting in the apartment again, seeing the rooms crammed with beds and clothes closets and strewn with the belongings of children, had made Octavia feel a wave of despair. As the afternoon wore on into evening, she watched her mother perform all the remembered, endless chores—the dish washing; the ironing of fresh clothes; lighting the kerosene stove in the kitchen and the coal stove in the front room; with twilight, the putting on of the gaslight that caged the room with shadows; and finally, preparing the children for bed. Octavia thought of what she would be doing at the sanitarium now, this minute. They would be in the garden taking a walk, she and her girl friend. They would be in their rooms waiting for dinner and gossiping about the romances going on. They would all be eating together and afterward playing bridge in the game room. Octavia felt nostalgic for the life she had left, the only life she had known devoted to the care of one's self, health and pleasure, without worry and responsibility. She felt awkward in her own home, and her family seemed strangers to her. She was so absorbed in her thoughts that she never noticed how stiffly her mother moved about the house.

At bedtime, when Gino and Vinnie were undressing by the

folding bed in the front room, Gino whispered to Vinnie, "She didn't curse one time the whole day."

Vinnie said, "I guess you can't curse in the hospital and she forgot."

Gino said, "I hope so. It sounds lousy when a girl curses, especially your own sister."

SO NOW THEY were alone in the kitchen, Octavia and Lucia Santa. They sat at the great round table with its yellow oilcloth cover. The coffee cups glared white before them. The ironing waited for Lucia Santa in a corner of the room. A pot of water hissed on the kerosene stove. From down the hallway of bedrooms came the soft sighing breath of the sleeping children. In the pale yellow light of the kitchen they faced each other, and the mother told of the troubles of the past six months. How disobedient Gino had been, and even Vinnie and the small ones. How Larry and his wife, Louisa, had not helped as much as they should, and how she herself had been ill but had never had anything put in the letters to Octavia that would distress her.

It was a long recital and Octavia only interrupted to say at intervals, "Ma, why didn't you write me, why didn't you tell me?" The mother replied, "I wanted you to get well."

There was no gesture of affection between them. Octavia said gently, "Don't worry, Mom, I'll be back to work next week. And I'll see that the kids do all right in school and help in the house." She felt a surge of strength and confidence and pride in her mother's need of her. In that moment all her strangeness fell away. She was home. When Lucia Santa began to iron, Octavia went to her room and got a book to read to keep her mother company.

When Octavia had been home a week, she and the welfare investigator finally met. Octavia had been sweet; happy to be home, she did not show her old bossiness, and never cursed or screamed.

She bustled into the apartment about four in the afternoon

and was surprised to see Mr. La Fortezza, his feet on a chair, sipping his light coffee and eating his ham sandwich. Mr. La Fortezza took a good look at her boldly handsome face and put aside his delicacies. He rose to his feet like a gentleman. "This is my daughter," Lucia Santa said, "Octavia. My eldest."

Mr. La Fortezza, abandoning his Italian manner, said in a friendly American voice, briskly, casually, "I've heard a lot about you, Octavia. Your mother and I have had some good long talks. We're old friends."

Octavia nodded coldly and her great dark eyes made the gesture one of dislike, a dislike she had not meant to betray.

Lucia Santa, anxious at this discourtesy, said, "Come have some coffee and talk to the young man." To Mr. La Fortezza she added, "This is the smart one, she reads books all the time."

"Yes, do have some coffee," Mr. La Fortezza said. "I would enjoy talking to you, Octavia."

Octavia was so offended she nearly cursed. The condescending use of her first name, his familiarity, made her spit, but into her handkerchief, as befitted a newly recovered lung patient. They watched her with sympathetic understanding. So she sat and listened to her mother toady to the welfare investigator.

Now he had read novels, Mr. La Fortezza had, in which the poor working girl had only to be smiled at and condescended to by a young man of the higher classes and the lucky female would fall flat on her back, legs waving in the air like a dog. Understand, not because of the money, but the recognition of nobility. Alas, Mr. La Fortezza did not have that flashing air, that smiling blondness, that slim American debonair charm, or the million dollars (always the million dollars), which of course meant nothing to heroines. And so La Fortezza became more and more animated, loquacious, and as charming as his two dark circled owl eyes would permit. Octavia looked at him more and more coldly. Gino and Vincent came into the house and, seeing their sister's face, lounged around the room, happily expectant.

La Fortezza spoke now of literature. "Ah, Zola, he knew how to write about the poor. A great artist, you know. A Frenchman."

Octavia said quietly, "I know." But La Fortezza went on. "I would like to see him alive today to write about how the poor must live on the few pennies the welfare gives. What a farce. Now there is a man whose books your daughter should read, Signora Corbo. That would be an education in itself. And it would make you understand yourself Octavia, and your environment."

Octavia, itching to spit in his eye, nodded quietly.

La Fortezza was gratified, as was the mother. With solemn eyes he said, "Why, you are an intelligent girl. Would you like to see a play with me sometime? I ask you in front of your mother to show my respect. I'm old-fashioned myself as your mother can tell you. Signora, isn't it true?"

Lucia Santa smiled and nodded. She had visions of her daughter marrying a lawyer with a good city job. For mothers, even in books, do not set their sights so high as heroines. She said benignly, "He's a good Italian boy."

La Fortezza went on. "We've had many long talks together, your mother and I, and we understand each other. I'm sure she would not object to our having a friendly date. The city gets us the theater tickets cut-rate. It will be a new experience for you instead of the movies."

Octavia had been to the theater with her girl friends many times. The dressmaking shops got cut-rate tickets, too. Octavia had read the same novels and always had a supreme contempt for the heroines, those generous, witless maidens who exposed themselves to shame while serving pleasure to men who flaunted their wealth as bait. But that this stupid starving guinea college kid thought he could screw her. Her eyes began to flash and she spat out shrilly in answer to his invitation,

"You can go shit in your hat, you lousy bastard." Gino, in a corner with Vinnie, said, "Ooh-oh, there she goes." Lucia Santa, like an innocent sitting on a lit powder keg and only now seeing the sputtering fuse, looked around dazedly as if wondering where to run. A surge of blood coursed through Mr. La Fortezza's face, even his owl eyes turned red. He was petrified.

For there is nothing more blood-curdling than a young Italian shrew. Octavia's voice in a high, strong, soprano note berated him. "You take eight dollars a month from my poor mother, who has four little kids to feed and a sick daughter. You bleed a family with all our trouble and you have the nerve to ask me out? You are a lousy son-of-a-bitch, a lousy, creepy sneak. My kid brothers and sister do without candy and movies so my mother can pay you off, and I'm supposed to go out with you?" Her voice was shrill and incredulous. "You're old-fashioned, all right. Only a real guinea bastard from Italy with that respectful Signora horseshit would pull something like that. But I finished high school, I read Zola, and I have gone to the theater, so find some greenhorn girl off the boat you can impress and try to screw her. Because I know you for what you are: a four-flusher full of shit."

"Octavia, Octavia, stop," Lucia Santa shouted in horror. She turned to the young man to explain. "She is ill, she has a fever." But Mr. La Fortezza was flying through the door and down the stairs. He had left his brown parcel behind him. His face as he fled was the face of a man caught redhanded in the most shameful of sins and it was a face they never saw again. Two weeks later there was a new investigator, an American old man, who cut their relief down but told them the money in trust was not counted by welfare as assets of the family, since the magistrate could release the money only in some dire need for a particular child, and one child's money could not be used for the other two children or for the mother.

But the final scene with Mr. La Fortezza was one that Gino

and Vincent never forgot. They shook their heads at the girl's terrible cursing. They resolved with all their hearts that they would never marry a girl like their sister. But at least now it ended that atmosphere, that special treatment accorded to the sick, the strain of politeness toward a member of the family who returned from the hospital or from a long voyage. There was no question. This was the Octavia of old. She was well again. Even the mother could not remain angry at her daughter's behavior, though she never understood her indignation with Mr. La Fortezza. After all, everyone must pay to stay alive.

13

T HE DAY THE letter came from Ravenswood, Octavia did not read it to her mother until all the children were in bed. It was a very short, official communication saying that the father could be released to his family on a trial basis if his wife would sign papers. It made plain that he would need constant care and supervision. With the letter came a questionnaire to be filled out. It asked the ages of the children, the income of the whole family and of each of its members. With it all, the letter made clear that the father was still an invalid, even though he was fit to be released.

Lucia Santa sipped her coffee nervously. "But he is not really well, then, they just want to test him," she said.

Octavia wanted to be absolutely fair. "He is all right. He just can't work or do anything. He has to be taken care of like a sick person. Maybe after a while he can go back to work again. Do you want him back?" she asked. She cast her eyes downward and blushed, for she was thinking shameful things of her own mother.

Lucia Santa watched her daughter's blush with interest. "Why would I not?" she asked. "He is the father of three of my children. He earned our bread for ten years. If I owned a donkey or a horse who had worked so hard, I would treat him kindly when he was sick or in his old age. Why should I not want my husband back?"

"I won't make any trouble," Octavia said.

"There will be trouble enough," Lucia Santa said. "Who can tell, he may do the children harm. And who can live those years over again? We would all have to suffer, risk our lives to give him another chance. No, it's too much, too much."

Octavia said nothing. They sat together for hours, or what seemed like hours, Octavia holding pen and ink bottle and writing paper ready to send an answer to the sanitarium.

The mother brooded over her problem. She remembered stories of similar cases, of loved ones returning to their homes and committing murders and other crimes in their madness.

She thought of her daughter Octavia, who would suffer, be driven into leaving her home, to marrying early to get out of the house.

It could not be risked. In full knowledge of what her decision meant (in her mind she saw the image of an animal encaged in iron and brick for countless years), she consigned her husband, the father of her children, the sharer of that one summer of delight, to a human and earthly eternity of despair. Lucia Santa shook her head slowly and said, "No, I won't sign. Let him stay where he is."

Octavia was surprised and even a little shocked. The memory of her own father's death swept over her; she felt again that terrible sense of loss a little girl had felt. What if by some miracle he had been brought back to life, as now they could bring her stepfather back to life? She suddenly thought that she could never look Gino and Sal and little Aileen in the face if she did not bring their father home.

She said, "I think we should talk to Gino and Sal. After all, he's their father. Let's see how they feel. Maybe we should bring him home, Ma."

Lucia Santa gave her daughter a searching look which seemed to judge and find wanting. It was a look that always disconcerted Octavia because it was so impersonal. Then she said, "What can children know? Leave them alone, they will have enough woe later on. And we cannot afford to bring their father home."

Octavia said softly, bowing her head over her coffee, "Ma, let's give it a try, for the kids. They miss him."

When the mother answered her voice was surprisingly contemptuous. She shook her head and said, "No, my daughter, it's easy for you to be kind and generous. But think: when it all becomes so difficult and you regret your generosity, you will have to suffer. And how angry you will be that your generosity inconveniences you. This has happened to me before. Beware the goodhearted, tender people who give because they know not what their generosity will cost. And then later become angry, spurn you when you count on their humanity. How my neighbors flocked to help me when your father died, how I wept at their goodness. But alas, we cannot be eternally good, eternally generous; we are too poor, we cannot afford it. And even your aunt, who was rich, she rebelled. It is so good—it feels so wonderful to be generous for a short period of time. But as a steady thing, it goes against the grain, it's against human nature. You will get tired of your stepfather, there will be quarrels, shrieks, curses, and you will marry the first man you meet and disappear. And I will pay for your large, open heart." She paused. "He will be sick for the rest of our lives." With these words she condemned and sentenced her husband forever.

The women washed their coffee cups. The mother lingered in the kitchen to wipe off the table and sweep the floor; Octavia went to her room thinking of how she would talk to the children in the morning, realizing as she did so that she wanted to absolve herself from guilt.

In bed Octavia thought of the mother, her callousness, her cold decision. Then she remembered that she had left the letter in the kitchen. She rose and went down the hall in her slip. The light was still on.

Lucia Santa sat at the kitchen table with great bags of sugar, salt, and flour, filling the sugar bowl, the shakers, and copper flour jar. The letter, with its great black official seal and the printed government envelope, lay in front of her. She was staring down at it as if she could read, and seemed to be studying every word. She looked up at her daughter and said, "I'll hold the letter, you can answer it in the morning."

Gino, lying awake beside the sleeping Sal, heard everything through the open Judas window between the bedroom and the kitchen. He felt no resentment, no anger at his mother's decision, only a queasiness like a stomachache. A little later the light went out in the kitchen, he heard his mother go past his bed to her own room, and then he fell into sleep.

Lucia Santa did not sleep. She reached out in the darkness to touch Aileen and found the smooth skin and the bony shoulders, the little body huddled against the coolness of the plaster wall. In the touch of that innocent, vulnerable flesh she drew some strength. This was a life she touched, and in her keeping. She was the protector of them all, she held their fate in her hands. From her would come the good and the evil, the joy and the travail. It was for this she had cast her husband into the pit.

But this was not enough. She brought before her eyes the times he had struck her, cursed his stepchildren, raved through the night and frightened his own children; she remembered his erratic labor, his costly religiosity. But she rejected everything in one despairing inward cry—"Frank, Frank, why didn't you take care of yourself? Why did you let yourself become so ill?" She remembered his tearing up of his sweat-earned money, the look of hurt pride on his face, and his kindness when she had been a helpless widow. With a great sigh she accepted the truth. She was too weak in resources, too poor, to afford to show mercy to the man she loved. No, no mercy, she thought, no mercy, no mercy. She reached out again to touch the small sleeping body, the new satiny skin of the tiny human being beside her. Then she folded her arms, stared into the darkness, and waited patiently for sleep to come. She had condemned Frank Corbo never to see his children grown, never to share her bed, never to know a grandchild. In Italian, she murmured, "God, God, watch over me, *aiuta mi,*" as if she herself could never hope for the mercy she had refused.

After supper the next night, Octavia took Sal and Gino into the living room to speak to them. They were both a little apprehensive, because Octavia was so sweet, gentle, and schoolteacherish, but when she spoke Gino realized what was coming. He remembered what he had overheard the night before.

As Octavia explained why their father could not come home, Gino remembered the times his father had taken him for a haircut, and how they had watched each other, the little boy's eyes straight ahead seeing magically in the mirror before him his father sitting on a wire chair, a mirrored wall behind his head. And his father seeing his son's face in the mirror; though they were both facing the same way, one behind the other, yet they looked at each other without shyness, shielded by glass.

It had always seemed as if this mirror wall which brought them so magically face-to-face protected them enough so that they could study each other's eyes, recognize that each was a part of the other.

Between them the white-mustached barber snipped hair on the black-and-white-striped sheet and gossiped in Italian with the father. Gino was mesmerized by the snip of the scissors and the soft falling of hair on his shoulders, by the white tiled floor, the white marble counter with its green bottles of hair lotion, all reflected in the mirrors around them. His father would smile at him through the glass wall and try to make him smile, but, protected by the intervening glass, the child would refuse; his face would remain solemn. It was the only time he could remember his father continually smiling.

When Octavia had finished explaining everything, Gino and Sal were ready to go downstairs to play. Their father was sick, which meant he would come back someday, and time had no meaning at that age. Octavia watched them closely for signs of distress. She asked gently, "Do you want him to come home right now?" And little Sal said almost tearfully, "I don't want him to come home. He scares me." Octavia and Gino were surprised because Sal had loved the father more than any of the other children.

Gino was uncomfortable because he felt responsible for his father. How many times had his mother said, "You're just like your father," when he had refused to do chores, been disobedient, shirked his responsibilities? So he accepted the fact that the troubles of the family all came from his father and so from himself. He said in a low voice, "Whatever Mom wants to do is O.K." He paused and added, "I don't care."

Octavia let them go. She went to the window and saw them come tumbling out of the door below. She felt an overwhelming sadness—not specific, but general, as if her stepfather had suffered some fate common to humanity and that some judgment waited for her, too.

14

LARRY ANGELUZZI BEGAN to understand something of life when his second child was born and the railroad gave him only three days' work a week. He also got a look at himself in a human mirror.

One Sunday, on their way to visit a friend, Larry and Louisa stood at the corner of 34th Street and Tenth Avenue waiting for the trolley. Louisa had one child by the hand and he carried the baby. Suddenly Larry saw his kid brother Gino watching them from the other side of the Avenue. On that dark, tough, small boy's face was a look of bewildered, sad pity and some sort of disgust. He motioned to Gino to come over, and as the boy walked across the Avenue, Larry remembered when Gino had been just a little kid and leaned back to watch his big brother on the horse. He smiled gently at Gino and said, "See what happens when you get married, kid?" Jokingly, not knowing that his kid brother would never forget.

Louisa, her face already bony and dry, frowned at both of them and said roughly, "You don't like it?"

Larry laughed and said, "I'm only kidding." But Gino looked at her gravely, bewitched by them both, seeing beyond them into something else.

Gino, out of necessary loyal courtesy, kept them company until their trolley came. Larry thought, He's growing up; I was working at his age. He asked, "How you doing at high school, kid?" Gino shrugged. "O.K.," he said.

When Larry got onto the trolley with his family he saw Gino watch after them as they moved away.

Rolling on steel, moving almost magically off from his younger brother in the clear cold air of that Sunday morning, Larry felt a sense of loss; that his life was over. And it was this morning, this encounter, this moment of insight that led to his new way of life, quitting the railroad and his eight years' seniority and his surely lifetime steady job.

One morning the following week, Larry went down to the *panetteria* for some breakfast buns. He had not worked the night before, the railroad still slow. Guido, the baker's son, his upper lip hairy with a small mustache, greeted him with real pleasure. They chatted. Guido had quit school to help full time in the bakery. Feeling himself a man of affairs, he asked, "Larry, how'd you like a good job?"

Larry smiled. "Sure," he said with natural agreeableness, with no intention of leaving the railroad.

Guido said, "Come on." They went into the back room. There was the *Panettiere,* a glass of anisette before him, chatting with a man his own age, definitely Italian but dressed American, with no trace of the greenhorn; hair trimmed close, tie skinny and plain and solid-colored.

Guido said, "Larry, I want you to meet Zi' Pasquale, Mr. di Lucca, he grew up with my father in Italy. Zi' Pasquale, this is my friend, Larry, I told you about."

Larry flushed with pleasure at the knowledge that people had been talking about him. He wondered if the man was really Guido's uncle, or whether this was a courteous term of address to a close friend of the family. Larry gave them a big smile and shook hands firmly with the stranger. The *Panettiere* said, "Sit down," and poured him a glass of anisette. Larry laughed and said, "I don't drink, I could use a cup of coffee." He saw Mr. di Lucca looking him over with the frankly appraising stare an Italian father gives the courter of his daughter, eyes narrowed, wary, suspicious, weighing.

Guido served coffee and filled the stranger's anisette glass. He said casually, "Pa, Zi' Pasquale told you he was looking for a new man, right, Zi' Pasquale? I got just the guy, my friend Larry. Remember all I told you about him?"

Both of the older men gave him a tolerant, affectionate smile; the *Panettiere* raised his hands in a gesture of disavowal, and Zi' Pasquale shrugged as if to say, "No harm—youth." In Italy things were not done this way. Zi' Pasquale said in Italian to the *Panettiere,* "This one, he's a good boy?" The *Panettiere* said reluctantly, *"Un bravo."* They all smiled at one another. They drank leisurely, and the two older men lit up De Nobili cigars. Everyone could see that Mr. di Lucca was impressed.

Larry was used to it. He had come to know that there was something extremely pleasing in his smile and manner, something that made him instantly likeable to both men and women. He knew this in all modesty, enjoyed it, and was thankful for his gift, which made him even more likable.

"You think you like a job with me?" Mr. di Lucca asked.

Here Larry's more positive virtues came into play, his instinctive feeling for what was proper with these particular people. This was a personal question. Do you respect me as a man? Do you accept me as a tribal chief, as a second father, as an honorary godfather? If he dared now to ask what kind of a job, how much money, where, when, how, what guarantees, then all was finished. Everything would be over.

So even though he did not want the job, could not conceive of giving up his eight years' seniority in the railroad, yet out of sheer natural courtesy and meaningless agreeability, Larry said with great sincerity, "It would be a pleasure to work for you."

Pasquale di Lucca brought both hands together with a great thunderclap of flesh. His eyes flashed, his face took on a look of astonished pleasure. "Now by Christ in Heaven," he said. "Is it possible that Italians still grow young men like this in America?" Guido burst out laughing with delight, and the *Panettiere* beamed at them all. Larry kept a modest smile on his lips.

"Now I show you what a man I am," Pasquale di Lucca said. He took out a roll of bills and held out three twenties to Larry, saying, "This is your first week pay. You come to my office tomorrow morning and start work. You wear a suit and tie, neat, not flashy; like an American, like me. Here's my office." He took a small card out of the breast pocket of his jacket and gave it to Larry. Then he leaned back in his chair puffing on his cigar.

Larry accepted the money and the card. He was too stunned to say anything further except to murmur his thanks. This was twice the money he earned in the railroad, even full time.

Guido said proudly, "What did I tell you, Zi' Pasquale?" And Mr. di Lucca nodded his head in agreement.

They all had fresh drinks, and now Larry could ask about the work. Mr. di Lucca explained that Larry would be a collection agent for the bakery union, that he would have a very quiet, easy territory and, if he did well, a more lucrative one in a year or two. He explained that all the bakery owners also paid dues, not just the hired help, and on a higher scale. Larry would have to keep account books like an insurance man, he would have to show tact, be able to pass the time of day, keep on friendly terms with everyone, never drink while working, never get involved with any women in the bakeries. It would be hard work, he would earn his salary. Mr. di Lucca finished his glass of anisette, rose, shook hands with Larry, and said, "Ten o'clock tomorrow." Then he embraced the *Panettiere* with a manly hug, tapped Guido on the cheek and slipped him a folded bill, saying affectionately, "Work well for your father, eh? He's too easy, like an American, but if I hear stories—your Uncle Pasquale comes down and makes you into a good Italian son." Underneath the affection there was iron.

Guido gave him a playful push and said, "Don't worry about me, Zi' Pasquale." He linked arms with him and took him to the door, and they laughed at each other as they went out. Zi' Pasquale said, "Marry a good Italian girl to help in the store."

When Guido came back he danced all around Larry shouting, "You made it, you made it." When he quieted down, he said, "Larry, in two years you got your own house on Long Island. My Zi' Pasquale is no piker. Right, Pop?"

The *Panettiere* drank his anisette slowly, then sighed. "Ah, Lorenzo, Lorenzo, my brave one," he said. "Now you will learn what the world is and become a man."

Larry Angeluzzi had a good living. He slept late, had lunch at home, and then made the rounds of the bakeries in his territory. The Italian bakers were fine, they gave him coffee and cookies; the Polish bakers were sullen but soon warmed to his charm, even though he would not drink hard liquor with them. They delighted in his success with the young Polish girls who came for Coffee An, and stayed until Larry had to move on to his next stop. Sometimes he even used the back room of a bakery for a quick screw, knowing the baker would be delighted to have something on the girl and would himself take her back there regularly.

The Italians paid their dues without question, as befitted people who in the old country gave eggs to a priest for reading a letter and wine to a village clerk for telling them what the laws were. The Poles paid the money just for his company and charm. He had trouble only with the German bakers.

It was not so much that they did not want to pay, but he felt they did not want to pay an Italian. They rarely offered him coffee and buns or chatted to show their friendliness. They paid him as they paid their breadman or the milk guy. That was O.K., he drank too much coffee now anyway, but it made him feel like a gangster.

But maybe he felt this way because he had trouble with only one bakery and that was German. And what made him more uncomfortable for some reason was that this baker made the best bread, the most delicious and generous birthday cakes, the fanciest cookies. He did a tremendous business, and yet he refused to pay any dues. He was the only one Larry could not collect from. When he reported it to Mr. di Lucca, that man shrugged and said, "You make a good living? Earn it. Try a coupla months, then talk to me."

One day Larry was late on his rounds. On one stop, out of sheer nervousness, he had screwed an extremely ugly girl who then had the nerve to try and make a big deal out of it. It hadn't helped. He dreaded stopping at Hooperman's. The short, squat, squareheaded German now actually kidded him, treated him like a jerk, made jokes. It always ended with Larry buying some bread and cookies, not only to show good will, not only because they were the best in the city, but to give Hooperman a chance to say they were on the house and so to start some sort of friendly relationship.

Up to now the job had been great. Larry understood what it was all about but refused to face his own part in it, refused to face the fact that some day he would have to make Hooperman pay. Larry paid Hooperman's dues himself just to avoid trouble. This was O.K. until the day two other German bakers stiffed him. They told him with a sly grin to ask next week. Larry started thinking about getting back his old job in the railroad.

He walked past Hooperman's and around the corner. There was the precinct police station house. No wonder the bastard was so brave. Cops right around the corner. Larry kept walking and tried to think things out. If he didn't make Hooperman pay, it was back to the railroad and the lousy fifteen bucks a week. He would have to wait until Hooperman was alone and tell him that Mr. di Lucca was coming personally. Then he realized with a shock that it was Larry himself Mr. di Lucca would send. Soon he would try to scare the kraut, and if that didn't work, he would quit. A gangster! How Octavia would scream with laughter. His mother would probably get the *Tackeril* to give him a beating. Ah, hell, it was too damn bad just because of one lousy thickheaded guy.

After walking around an hour he passed the Hooperman bakery window and saw the store was empty. He went in. The girl behind the showcases nodded and he went into the back rooms of ovens and tray-laden tables. And there was Hooperman, guffawing with two guests, the bakers who had stiffed Larry earlier in the day. There was a large tin can of beer on the table and three heavy golden steins circled it.

Larry felt a shock of betrayal, then bitter resentment. The men saw him and they all burst out in unrestrained, delighted laughter. Its very lack of malice was insulting. Larry understood what they thought of him, that they knew him for what he was, that he would never make Hooperman pay, that he was just a kid trying to be a grown-up because he had a wife and two babies.

Mr. Hooperman turned a whoop of laughter into speech. "Oooh, here is the collector. How much I give you today, ten dollars, twenty dollars, fifty dollars? Look, I'm ready." He stood up and emptied his pockets of change and crumpled wads of green paper money.

Larry could not force a smile, or even his charm. He said as calmly as he could, "You don't have to pay me, Mr. Hooperman, I just came to tell you you're out of the union. That's all."

The other two men stopped laughing, but Hooperman got hysterical. "I never was in your union," he roared. "I shit on your union. I never pay dues and I never give free coffee and cake, so shit on your union."

Larry said, trying one last time to get in good, "I paid your dues, Mr. Hooperman. I didn't want you in trouble, a good baker like you."

This sobered the baker. He pointed a finger at Larry. "You loafer," he said with quiet anger. "You gangster. You try to frighten me, then you try the friend stuff. Why don't you work like me? Why do you come to steal my money, my bread? I work. I work twelve, fourteen hours, and I must give you money? You little shit you, get out. Get out of my store."

Larry was so stunned by this defiance that he turned away and walked out of the back room. Still dazed, but trying to compose himself and to show he had not been frightened, he stopped and asked the girl behind the counter for a loaf of corn bread and a cheesecake. The girl picked up the heavy tin of powdered sugar and sprinkled the cake. There was a roar from the back of the shop. "Don't sell that crook nodding," and Hooperman came charging out to stand behind the counter. He snatched the can of sugar from the girl and said to Larry with real hatred, "Out. Out of here. Out." Larry stared at him, frozen with surprise and shock. The baker reached over and flicked his arm. Larry felt the powdered sugar spray his face and smelled the sweet scent in his nostrils. With absolutely no mental order, his left hand went out and fastened onto the baker's right arm. Then Larry took his right fist and drove it into the short, blunt face. The head actually bounced away on its neck like a ball on a tight string and then bounced back again into his fist. He let go.

The face was ruined. The nose was smashed flat and flooded the sugared marble counter with blood. The lips were mashed into a red blob of flesh and on the left side the teeth had caved in. The baker looked down on the blood and then ran drunkenly around the counter to stand between Larry and the door. He called out thickly, "The police, get the police."

The girl ran through the back room and out of the store. The two other bakers followed her. Hooperman stood barring the front door, arms outstretched, a wild maniacal glare looking out over his ruined face. Larry started around the corner to get out the back exit. He felt Hooperman rush at him, hang on him, not trying to punish, as if he did not dare, but dragging on him. Larry flung the baker away. Because he could not hit the man again, and because he realized now that he had disgraced the family and would go to prison, he swung his foot through the great shining glass front of the show counter. Broken glass flew around him and then he kicked the exposed long trays of cookies. The baker let out a howl of anguish and dragged him to the floor, and so the police found them, rolling over a glass- and cookie-covered floor in an embrace stronger than love.

In the police station two huge detectives took Larry to a back room. One of them said, "O.K., what happened, kid?"

Larry said, "I wanted to buy a cake and he threw sugar in my face. Ask the girl."

"You shaking him down?"

Larry said no.

Another detective stuck his head through the doorway. "Hey, the kraut says this kid collects for di Lucca." The detective who had been questioning Larry got up and left the room. In five minutes he came back and lit a cigarette. He didn't ask Larry any more questions. They all waited.

Larry was overwhelmed. He could only think of his name in the papers, his mother in disgrace, himself a criminal and in prison, everyone despising him. And now he had spoiled everything for Mr. di Lucca.

The detective looked at his watch, left the room, and came back in a few minutes. He jerked a thumb toward the door and said, "O.K., kid, scram. You're all squared away."

Larry didn't understand, and couldn't believe what he heard. "Your boss is waiting outside," the detective said.

One detective held the door open for Larry, and, as he walked out, he saw Mr. di Lucca standing at the bottom of the steps outside the precinct house.

Mr. di Lucca said, "Thanks, thanks," and shook hands clumsily with the detective. Then he grabbed Larry by the arm and walked him down the street to a waiting car. The driver was a kid Larry had gone to school with and never seen since. He and Mr. di Lucca got into the back seat.

Then came the second surprise. Mr. di Lucca grabbed him by the arm and said in Italian, "*Bravo,* what a beautiful fellow you are. I saw his face, that animal, you did a lovely job. That bastard. Oh, you're a beautiful fellow, Lorenzo. When they told me you hit him because he wouldn't sell you bread, I was in heaven. Ah, if you were only my son."

THEY WERE ON Tenth Avenue going downtown. Larry stared out the window at the railroad yard. It was almost as if he were changing second by second, each drop of blood, each bit of flesh, into someone else. He would never go back to work in the railroad yards, he would never be afraid as he had been in that station house. The whole majesty of law had crumbled before his eyes with that handshake between Mr. di Lucca and the detective; his swift rescue and the admiration that marked his freedom. He thought of the baker's blood, of the baker's arms outstretched to bar his escape, of the mad staring eyes above that smashed pulpy face, and he felt a little sick.

Larry had to speak the truth. He said, "Mr. di Lucca, I can't go around beating guys up for the money. I don't mind collecting, but I'm not a gangster."

Mr. di Lucca patted him soothingly on the shoulder. "No, no; who does these things for pleasure? Am I a gangster? Don't I have children and grandchildren? Am I not godfather to the children of my friends? But do you know what it is to be born in Italy? You are a dog and you scratch in the earth like a dog to find a dirty bone for supper. You give eggs to the priest to save your soul, you slip the town clerk a bottle of wine merely to bandy words. When the *padrone,* the landowner, comes to spend the summer at his estate, all the village girls go to clean his house and fill it with fresh flowers. He pays them with a smile, and ungloves his knuckles for a kiss. And then a miracle. America. It was enough to make one believe in Jesus Christ.

"In Italy they were stronger than me. If I took an olive from the *padrone,* a carrot, or, God forbid, a loaf of bread, I must flee, hide in Africa to escape his vengeance. But here, this is democracy and the *padrone* is not so strong. Here it is possible to escape your fate. But you must pay.

"Who is this German, this baker, that he can earn his living, bake his bread without paying? The world is a dangerous place. By what right does he bake bread on that corner, in that street? The law? Poor people cannot live by all the laws. There would not be one alive. Only the *padroni* would be left.

"Now this man, this German, you feel sorry for him. Don't. You see how nice the police treat you? Sure, you're my friend, but this baker, right around the corner from the police, he doesn't even send coffee and buns over to make friends. How do you like that? The man on the beat, the baker makes him pay for his Coffee An. What kind of a person is this?"

Mr. di Lucca paused, and on his face came a look of almost unbelieving, finicky disgust.

"This is a man who thinks because he works hard, is honest, never breaks the law, nothing can happen to him. He is a fool. Now listen to me."

Mr. di Lucca paused again. In a quiet, sympathetic voice, he went on, "Think of yourself. You worked hard, you were honest, you never broke the law. Worked hard? Look at your arms, like a gorilla from hard work.

"But there is no work. Nobody comes and gives you a pay envelope because you are honest. You don't break no law and they don't put you in jail. That's something, but will it feed your wife and children? So what do people like ourselves do? We say, *Good*. There is no work. We have no pay. We cannot break the law, and we cannot steal because we are honest; so we will all starve, me, my children, and my wife. Right?" He waited for Larry to laugh.

Larry kept his eyes on Mr. di Lucca, expecting something more. Mr. di Lucca noticed this and said gravely, "It will not always be like this, living by a strong arm. Enough. Do you still work for me? One hundred dollars a week and a better territory. Agreed?"

Larry said quietly, "Thanks, Mr. di Lucca, it's O.K. with me."

Mr. di Lucca raised a finger paternally. "Don't pay no more dues for nobody."

Larry smiled. "I won't," he said.

When Mr. di Lucca dropped him off on Tenth Avenue, Larry walked along the railroad yards for a while. He realized that you couldn't always be nice to people and expect them to do what you wanted, not with money, anyway. You had to be mean. What puzzled him was the admiration people had for a man who did something cruel. He remembered the kraut's face all smashed and wondered at Mr. di Lucca's exultation over it. Because of this he would make money, his wife and child would live like people who owned a business, he would help his mother and brothers and sisters. And honestly, he didn't hit the kraut because of the money. Hadn't he paid the guy's dues all the time?

15

LUCIA SANTA MAKES the family organism stand strong against the blows of time: the growth of children, the death of parents, and all changes of worldly circumstance. She lives through five years in an instant, and behind her trail the great shadowy memories that are life's real substance and the spirit's strength.

In five years the outer world had thinned away. The black circles of gossiping women had shrunk, the children shouting and playing in the dark summer night seemed not so thickly clustered. Across the Avenue the clanging locomotives used an overhead roadway, and so the dummy boys with their peaked, buttoned caps, their sneaker spurs, and their red lanterns had vanished forever. The footbridge over Tenth Avenue, no longer needed, had been torn down.

In a few years the western wall of the city would disappear and the people who inhabited it would be scattered like ashes—they whose fathers in Italy had lived in the same village street for a thousand years, whose grandfathers had died in the same rooms in which they were born.

Lucia Santa stood guard against more immediate dangers, dangers she had conquered over the last five years: death, marriage, puberty, poverty, and that lack of a sense of duty which flourishes in children brought up in America. She did not know she defended against an eternal attack and must grow weaker, since she stood against fate itself.

But she had made a world, she had been its monolith. Her children, wavering sleepily from warm beds, found her toasting bread by early morning light, their school clothes hanging over chairs by the kerosene stove. Home from school, they found her ironing, sewing, tending great brown pots on the kitchen stove. She moved in clouds of steam like a humble god, disappearing and reappearing, with smells of warm cotton, garlic, tomato sauce, and stewing meats and greens. Betraying her mortality, the old cathedral-shaped radio poured out olive-oil songs by Carlo Buti, the Italian Bing Crosby and darling of Italian matrons, whose face, thin, suffering, and crowned with its greenhornish white fedora, leaned against salamis in every grocery store window on Tenth Avenue.

The door was never locked against any child returning from school or play. Neither birth nor death could keep smoking dishes from appearing on the supper table. And at night Lucia Santa waited until her house was quiet and at rest before she sought her own sleep. Her children had never seen her eyes closed and defenseless against the world.

There were days in her life or months or seasons that were like cameos. One winter existed only because Gino had come home from school and found his mother completely alone, and they had spent a happy afternoon together without even speaking.

Gino studied his mother ironing clothes by the cold gray of falling twilight. He ran his nose over the stove, lifting pot covers to sniff, and he was not pleased. He didn't care for the green spinach slick with olive oil. The pot with the boiled potatoes annoyed him further, so he slammed down the cover and said angrily, "Ah, Ma, ain't you got anything good to eat?" Then he leaned over the radio to switch it to an American station. His mother made one threatening gesture and he jumped away. He really liked to listen to the Italian station, especially the *romanze* like the one his mother had on now. They always sounded as if they were killing each other, and he understood enough to follow it. It was nothing like the American soap operas. Here blows were struck; parents were not understanding, but firm and intolerant; men killed the lovers of their wives on purpose, and not by accident. Wives actually poisoned their husbands, usually with something that caused horrible pain, and there were screams to go with it. Their torture was a comfort to the living.

Gino got his library books and read at the kitchen table. On the other side his mother ironed clothes and the warm steam heated the room. It was very quiet in the apartment; everyone out of the house, Sal and Lena down in the street playing, Vinnie working. It grew darker, until suddenly Gino could not see to read. He raised his head and saw his mother watching him, motionless, a strange look on her face. There was the smell of the garlic and hot olive oil and floury potatoes, the sizzling of the pot of water on the kerosene stove. Then his mother reached her hand upward to turn on the light.

Gino smiled at her and his head went down to his book. Lucia Santa finished her ironing, folded the board away. She watched Gino at his reading. He rarely smiled; he had become a very stern-looking young boy, very quiet. How children changed. But he was still headstrong, still stubborn, sometimes as crazy as his father before him. She took the clothes into the bedroom and laid them away in the bureau. Then she returned to the kitchen and very quietly peeled some fresh potatoes, sliced them thin, made room on the stove for her great round black frying pan. A spoonful of brown homemade lard melted quickly. She fried the potatoes to a golden brown then splashed two eggs over the crusts. She heaped up a platter and, without saying a word, thrust it over Gino's book and under his nose.

Gino let out a yelp of pure delight. Lucia Santa said, "Hurry up and eat before the others come and see, or no one will eat that good spinach." He gobbled up the potatoes and helped her set the table for the others.

Another winter lived, belonged to her life, because of the death of Zia Louche. She had wept for the old woman more tears than she would shed for her own mother. The poor crone had died alone, in the cold of winter, in the bare two rooms that for the last twenty years had been her solitary nest. She had died like a beetle, her scaly skin stiff with cold, her stick-like legs twisted together, her veins iced blue by death. Her only comforter the black kerosene stove topped by a white enamel water pot.

Zia Louche, Zia Louche, where were your loved ones to care for your body? Where were the children to weep over your grave? And to think that she had envied that proud old woman's lack of responsibilities, her life without worldly care. Lucia Santa knew her own good fortune then. She had created a world that would not end. It would never cast her out and she would never die alone and be buried in the earth like some forgotten insect.

But what a miracle she had brought them all so far, a miracle not possible without the formidable Zia Teresina Coccalitti, who, in the same winter that Zia Louche died, became an intimate of Lucia Santa and an ally of the Angeluzzi-Corbo family.

Teresina Coccalitti was the most feared and respected woman on Tenth Avenue. Tall, rawboned, dressed always in the black she wore for her husband twenty years dead, she terrorized fruit peddlers, grocers, and butchers; landlords never dared scold her for late rent, home relief investigators allowed her to sign necessary papers and never asked a single embarrassing question.

1111

Her tongue was venomously foul, the tight bones of her face were pointed to the very devil's mask of cunning. Yet when it suited her purpose she could show a fawning charm dangerous as a snake.

Four sons working, she collected home relief. When she bought a dozen fruit she reached out after paying and took an extra piece. She browbeat the butcher for the left-over scraps of veal, for the fat from a cut roast. Her hand was against the world.

It was Zia Coccalitti who taught Lucia Santa how to stretch a dollar. Eggs were bought from a fine young fellow who stole crates out of the backs of poultry trucks and sometimes even had fresh chickens. Suits and bananas came from those bold longshoremen who unloaded ships, though what suits were doing on a ship who could know. Dress material, good silks, genuine wool were sold door-to-door by polite and eloquent hijackers, neighborhood youths who kidnaped them by the trailerful. And all of these people dealt more honestly with you than the shopkeepers from Northern Italy who roosted on Ninth Avenue like Roman vultures.

Who lived otherwise? No one in their world.

And so the years passed. Only five? Seeming more, yet so quickly gone. Only death could mark off time.

The *Panettiere* one day found his wife dead like the dragon she was, talons buried deep in a pail of heavy silver, on her face the peaceful look of one who had found the true Jesus. Then what a change came over the *Panettiere*. That horse of work left everything to his son, Guido, who grew thin over the hot ovens. He closed the bakery early, no longer made lemon ice or kept the glass-walled stand clean for pizza. Day and night he roistered with his old cronies in the back of the barber shop, losing those buckets of silver and copper his dragon-wife had so faithfully guarded. And he took the air regularly, strolling along Tenth Avenue like a duke, fat American cigars smoking in his mouth.

And so it was the *Panettiere* who first spied Octavia towing her future husband around the corner of 31st Street onto Tenth Avenue. He watched them with interest and compassion as they approached Lucia Santa, who was seated innocently on her backless chair before the tenement. One look at the young man was enough. The Angeluzzi-Corbo family was about to suffer another misfortune.

This macaroni carried a stack of books—a grown man— and with high pompadour black hair, his horn-rimmed spectacles, thin sliced features curved like a bow, proclaimed himself a Jew. Not only a Jew, but a Jew not in the best of health.

At once it became known that Octavia Angeluzzi was to marry a heathen. A scandal. Not because the man was a Jew, but because he was not an Italian. Worse than that was the girl's sheer contrariness. Where did she find a Jew, in Christ's name? For blocks uptown and downtown, east side and on the western wall of Tenth Avenue, there were only Catholic Irish, Polish, and Italians. But then, what could be expected of an Italian girl who wore business suits to cover her breasts?

There was no prejudice or ill-feeling. The old crones, uncles, aunts, and godparents were happy that a relative had found a breadwinner so late in life. She must be at least twenty-five years of age, ripe for trouble.

Now, thanks to the good Jesus, she would be married, know life: in short, she would open wide her legs. She would never have to bear that tactful deference given to old maids, the crippled, and the deformed. They rejoiced that Octavia would not go rotten like uneaten fruit. And remember—Jews were moneymakers of the finest feather. Octavia Angeluzzi would lack for nothing, and, good Italian daughter that she was, she would not let her mother, little brothers, and sister go free of luxury. So said the neighbors, the *Panettiere,* Zia Coccalitti, and the mad jealous barber, who eyed the Jew's high pompadour with an inflamed covetous eye.

Lucia Santa did not share these optimistic views. True, this young man was handsome, fair, slender of build, and gentle as a girl. As for his being a Jew, it was not that she had no prejudice, it was merely that her distrust was so great that it included Christians, Irish, Turks, and Jews alike. But this particular fellow carried a stigma. Wherever he went, there was a book under his arm or open in his hands.

It is easy to laugh at the prejudices of the poor, their reasoning springs from a special experience. How irritating to hear some thieving Sicilian rascal say, "If you seek justice, put a gift in the scale." How insulting to a noble profession when the sly Teresina Coccaliti whispered, "When you say lawyer, you say thief." Lucia Santa had a saying of her own. "They who read books will let their families starve."

Had she not seen with her own eyes how Octavia devoured books long into the night (she had never dared say it, but could not this be the reason for her daughter's illness and visit to the sanitarium?) when she could have been sewing dresses for the budding daughters of the Santini, the *Panettiere,* and that maniac barber, earning God knows what sums of dollars? Her sons, too—Vinnie, Gino, and now even little Sal—went to the library for books of nonsense, insensible to the outside world and its duties. And for what? To numb their brains with stories that were not true, to enter worlds in which they could never live. What foolishness.

Illiterate, she was safe from corruption and could have no idea of the magic of books. Still, she sensed their power and rarely protested. But she had seen too many people, finding life painful, evade battle duty. As a poor man should not waste time and money on drink and cards, as a woman should not waste her strength and will on dreams of happiness, so youth, with a great struggle ahead, should not poison its will with fairy tales and dreams that enchanted them from paper pages they turned and turned and turned into the night.

If Lucia Santa had known how right she would prove to be, she would have chased Norman Bergeron out of her tenement with the *Tackeril.* A true renegade, he refused to battle for his bread against his fellow man. Foolishly, innocently kind, he wasted his college degree to become a social worker; but he was not capable of that stern force of character so necessary to those who administer charity. He was like a butcher who faints at the sight of blood. An uncle gave him a minor clerical post in his garment business, and it was there he met Octavia.

Like all weak men, Norman Bergeron had a secret vice. He was a poet. Not only in English, but—much more terrible—in Yiddish. Worse, he knew only one thing thoroughly: Yiddish literature—a talent he himself said was less in demand than any other on earth.

But all this was yet to be known. And despite her many misgivings, Lucia Santa seemed (to Octavia's amazement) to take some pleasure in her daughter's not marrying an Italian.

Now it was true that Lucia Santa wanted each of her sons to marry a good Italian girl who knew from the cradle that man ruled, must be waited on like a duke, fed good food that took hours to prepare; who cared for the children and the house without whining for help. Yes, yes, all her sons should marry good Italian girls. Her son Lorenzo had found his fortune with Louisa, and that was the proof.

On the other hand, what mother who had suffered under the masculine tyranny could wish on her tender daughter those guinea tyrants, those despotic greenhorns, who locked up their wives at home, never took them out except to a wedding or funeral; who made an uproar fit for wild goats if spaghetti was not steaming on the table at the precise moment their baronial boots crossed the doorsill; who never raised a finger to help their pregnant wives, and sat calmly smoking stinking De Nobili cigars while their big-bellied women stood on window sills, so top-heavy as they washed dirty glass that they were in danger of tumbling like balloons to the pavement of Tenth Avenue.

Thank God Octavia was marrying a man who was not an

Italian and therefore might show mercy to womankind. Only once did Lucia Santa make an insulting remark about her daughter's choice, and that was years later. One day, in the course of gossip, cursing her children one by one for their ingratitude and pigheadedness and finding no fit crime for Octavia, she said with withering scorn, "And she, my most intelligent child, picked for a husband the only Jew who does not know how to make money."

But all in all this marriage was the fitting crown to five years of good fortune. Lucia Santa insisted on a big wedding, properly in church. There was no trouble with Norman Bergeron. His reading of books was a virtue here. He made no objection to being married as a Christian or to bringing up his children as Christians. There were no objections from his family. He explained to Lucia Santa that they had declared him dead and outcast because of his marriage. Lucia Santa was pleased to hear this good news. It would simplify everything. Octavia and Norman would belong to her.

16

LUCIA SANTA SPARED no expense. The wedding party in the tenement was done in the finest style. Great purple jugs of wine from the *Panettiere*'s cellar lined the outside hall of the apartment, mountains of succulent prosciutto and logs of the strongest cheeses covered the table and waited on linen-sheeted beds, brightly colored wedding cookies and long candy-covered almonds filled borrowed silver trays. In the kitchen there were tiers of soda boxes—orange, cream, and strawberry—stacked to the ceiling.

Everyone on Tenth Avenue came to pay respects, and even those proud relatives who owned their own homes on Long Island to gossip and lord it over the poor peasants they had left so far behind. For who could resist such a wedding and what for some was the first intimate sight of a heathen bridegroom?

The young people danced in the front room amidst colored streamers and to the music of a gramophone borrowed from the mad barber. In the dining room and kitchen at the other end of the flat, the old Italians gossiped on rows of borrowed chairs that stood against the blue-painted plaster walls. Octavia gave the great ceremonial silken pouch for presents of money envelopes to Lucia Santa, who clutched it lovingly against her hip. With dignity, she pulled at its silvery strings to open its jaws and let it gulp proffered treasure.

For Lucia Santa it was a day of glory. But there is no day so fine that it does not hold some displeasure.

An old schoolmate of Octavia's high school days, an Italian girl whose family lived in their own house with a telephone, by name of Angelina Lambecora, dropped in for a short time to wish Octavia well and bring an expensive, patronizing present. But this slut proceeded to turn the heads of all the young men and even some of the old. Her beautifully planed face was made up as by a professional, rouge, even eye-shadow and some delicate lipstick that hid the sluttishness of her wide mouth and made it as inviting as those deep red grapes of Italy. She was dressed in the fashion of who-knows-what—half-suit, half-dress, with the top half of her pushed-up breasts plumped high for the eyes to feast on. Every man danced with her. Larry deserted his wife for her, until poor Louisa wept. He trailed the hussy, thrusting himself before those painted eyes, giving off clouds of his dazzling charm, showing those white square teeth in his most disarming and flattering smile. Angelina flirted with them all, waggled her tail in dance as the *Panettiere,* his son Guido, the narrow-eyed barber, and the white-haired Angelo of seventy-five years, whose life was his candy store, all deserted the gossip and the wine to stand like dogs, tongues hanging, knees bent to relieve pressure on the groin, eating her up with their hot glances. Until Angelina, feeling her mascara melting in the stuffy apartment, announced she must leave and catch her train to Long Island. Octavia kissed her quickly to speed her on her way, for even Norman Bergeron, shorn of his books this one night, had fixed Angelina with his horn-rimmed poet's eye.

All very well. The world was never made without its proper

number of sluts. One day she too would have children, grow fat and old, and gossip in the kitchen as others took her place. But this finicky morsel, coolly rejecting the flower of Tenth Avenue, old and new, went into the kitchen to say good-bye to Lucia Santa, cooing in the best American style, as if she were an equal because she was young and beautiful. Lucia Santa smiled as coolly and distantly as any baroness and accepted the honeyed words with pleasure, thinking meanwhile that if little Lena grew up like this one in that house they would buy on Long Island, little Lena would be a young American lady whose strapped ass matched the colors on her face.

Angelina turned to take her leave and then the misfortune fell. Her eyes lighted on Gino, barely sixteen, but tall and dark and strong, handsome in the new gray suit bought from the hijacking longshoreman just for this occasion.

Gino had made himself useful opening bottles of soda and jugs of wine to serve the Italians in the kitchen. He was quiet and distant, he moved with a quick fluidity that had a strange attractiveness. All this made him seem respectful, in the old Italian tradition, a servant to his elders. Only Lucia Santa knew it meant the people here in this room were completely meaningless to him. He did not see their faces, he did not hear their speech, he did not care if they thought well or ill of him, and he did not care if they lived or died. He moved in a world that did not exist but in which he had been trapped and jailed for this one night. He served them to make time pass.

But since the relatives had no way of knowing all this, they were impressed—especially a distant cousin from Tuckahoe, Piero Santini, dark-bearded, thin as a rail from work, who owned four trucks. He had a fat and foolish wife, bedecked with false jewels, at present gobbling cookies by the ton, and a shy daughter of seventeen, who sat between her father and mother and could not take her eyes off Gino.

Piero Santini noticed his daughter's heated glance, which was no surprise since he guarded her like a dragon. At first he was displeased, then reflected. His little Caterina had been brought up very strictly, in the old Italian style. Never mind "boy friends this" and "go on dates that" or dance outside the family circle. "Ha, ha, ha! Damma the dance," Piero Santini would say as he did an obscene little jig.

He drummed into Caterina's noodle what men wanted: to stick something between her legs and blow her belly up, then off, leaving her to shame, misery and the suicide of her parents. But she was ripe. How long could this go on? His wife was a numbskull and he himself was ready to buy two more trucks. He would be busy far into the night counting his money and spying on his help so that they did not steal the very balls from between his legs.

So Piero Santini, with that adaptability which had proven his success in business, switching his trucks from hauling produce to hauling garbage, sometimes even to carrying whisky when the price was right, turned his thoughts another way. Perhaps the time had come. He watched Gino and was impressed. What a quiet boy, and not lazy by any means. The way he moved showed a strong quick body; no doubt he could load a truck in half the time it took two lazy helpers and driver. He would be worth his weight in gold. (How Lucia Santa and all her friends and neighbors would have laughed at his thinking so of Gino—the champion job-loser on Tenth Avenue, an absolutely hopeless case.) Santini kept watching Gino. When his wife moved nearer a fresh pile of cookies and Gino served him a glass of wine, he patted the empty chair beside him and said in Italian, "Come sit here a minute, let me talk to you."

This mark of favor drew the attention of everyone. Piero Santini, the rich cousin from Tuckahoe, so charming to this starving, poverty-stricken youth? All eyes devoured them. Teresina Coccalitti nudged Lucia Santa, who, despite her lack of cunning, understood what was afoot.

For like a magnet all glances must shift from the two males to the young maiden. Caterina Santini was a legend, a myth, an Italian flower who bloomed in the evil American soil without being corrupted. A credit to her parents, and at a tender age, skilled in all the secrets of cookery, she prepared for her father at the Sunday feast handmade macaroni; she did not use paint, did not wear high heels to weaken her pelvic bones.

But now her day had come, as it comes even to saints. Sin and desire were stamped on her face. Flushed red, her breast rising and falling, she was bursting out of her skin. You could feel the heat coming off her, and her eyes, demurely cast down to her twitching lap, fooled no one.

What a stroke for Lucia Santa, and for her son with the ugliest face, though true, he was a magnificent young animal, as why shouldn't he be, playing in the sun all day instead of working after school? What a blessing to the nuptial feast. Lucia Santa, eager as a wolf scenting blood, leaned forward to catch what the sly Santini spoke to her son, but the cursed music from the front room drowned those words she lusted to hear.

And now this saturnine Piero in oily Italian inquired after Gino, "So, young man, what do you do, what do you plan for your life, eh, still at school?" But strangely enough this young man regarded him with grave eyes as if he did not understand good Italian. Then he gave a little smile, and Piero understood: the lad was overcome by this attention from majesty and too shy to answer. To put him at his ease and get nearer the subject, Piero clapped Gino on the shoulder and said, "My dear daughter is dying of thirst. Bring her a glass of cream soda like a good chap. Caterina, isn't it true, you're dying of thirst?"

Caterina did not raise her eyes. She was terrified at what was happening to her. She nodded her head.

Gino caught the word "soda" and the girl's nod. He rose to serve her. He understood nothing of what was happening, and how could he, since these people did not exist. When he brought the soda, he turned away quickly and did not see Piero Santini pat the chair again. Piero Santini, astounded at this insult, grimaced and shrugged his shoulders for all to see, as if to ask, "With such ill-mannered starving wretches, what use to show a kindly courtesy?" Everyone snickered at the humiliation of the proud close-fisted rich Santini and sighed for his poor daughter, who dipped her red unpowdered nose into a fizzing cream soda, mortified. And it was like a play to see the look of rage on Lucia Santa's face at the behavior of her son Gino, who everyone knew was as mad as his father and would end up in the same fashion, and wasn't this the proof?

It was at the end of this comedy that the beautiful Angelina appeared and made her farewells; and, to the astonishment of all, Gino made his second conquest. The second was more logical than the first. For one thing, Gino was the only male who did not see Angelina when he looked at her, and this immediately demanded her interest. Then, too, she sensed the general disapproval of the role she played, and in defiance she played it to the hilt. She caught hold of Gino, swayed toward him, and said to Lucia Santa, "What handsome sons you have." And Gino was shocked awake; he smelled her perfume, felt the warmth of her arm, saw those wide, perfectly painted lips pouted up at him. He didn't know what was happening, but he was perfectly willing to stay still and find out. When Angelina asked for her coat, all the men volunteered and, what's more, like gallant cavaliers, offered to walk her to the subway, but she said very prettily, "Gino will take me to the station—he's too young to be wicked."

Since all the beds were laden with platters of food awaiting their turn for table, Larry and Louisa's apartment below was used as a coat room. Angelina said, "I'll go down with him." She took Gino by the arm and they both left. The wedding party went on. Lucia Santa thought of sending Vincenzo down to Larry's apartment on some excuse, to make sure nothing happened, and then thought better of it. Her son was old enough and grown enough to taste a woman, and here was a fine opportunity with no danger to him. *Manga franca.* He would not have to pay in any fashion. Let it be.

Dr. Barbato came to drink his glass of wine, eat the icy-looking pastries, and dance with the bride. He observed Lucia Santa, surrounded like a queen, and went to put his little envelope in her great satin bag. He was greeted with regal coolness. He became angry; he had expected to be fussed over after all he had done for this mangy family. But what had his father said, "Never expect gratitude from a donkey or a peasant." However, a glass of good wine mellowed Dr. Barbato, and the second glass mellowed him even further. Without wanting to, without affection, he understood these people. How could a person like Lucia Santa show gratitude to everyone who had helped her? She would be constantly on her knees. To her such help was merely fate. As she blamed no living man for her misfortunes, so she gave no one credit for little strokes of luck, which included the stray charity of Dr. Barbato.

Dr. Barbato touched his mustache, straightened his vest. He had attended many of these Italians, and some of them had been children with his father in Italy, but they showed him a coolness, as if he were a usurer, a *padrone,* or even an undertaker. Oh, he knew very well how they felt behind the respectful, honeyed *Signore Dottore this* and *Signore Dottore that.* He fed on their misfortunes; their pain was his profit; he came in their dire need and fear of death, demanding monies to succor them. In some primitive way they felt the art of healing to be magic, divine, not to be bought and sold. But who then should pay for the colleges, the schools, the long hours of study and nerve-racking toil while they, the ignorant clods and louts, drank their wine and bet their sweaty silver on the turn of a dirty playing card? Let them hate me, he thought; let them go to the free clinics, let them wait for hours before some intern bastard looks them over like a bull or cow. They could croak in Bellevue and he would work on Long Island, where people would fight to pay his bills and know what they were getting. Dr. Barbato, to show that such poor greenhorns could in no way affect him, gave his best farewell smile and said his goodbyes in his best university Italian, which made him almost unintelligible, and then, to the relief of everyone, he took his leave.

As the festivities went on above them, Angelina and Gino tried to find her coat among the heaped-up garments in Larry's apartment. Lucia Santa's fears were groundless. Angelina was not the reckless girl she appeared, and Gino was still too innocent to take advantage of her weakness. Before he walked her to the subway, she gave him a long kiss, the warmth of her heavy mouth coated with a layer of lipstick. Her body pressed against his so fleetingly that Gino could only use it in his dreams.

YES, THE WEDDING was a success, one of the best on the Avenue, a credit to the family of Angeluzzi-Corbo, and a feather in the cap of Lucia Santa. Who did not rest on her glory, but invited the family of Piero Santini for Sunday dinner so that Gino could perhaps show Caterina the sights of the city she had missed from living up there in the distant woods of Tuckahoe.

SUCH A MAN as Piero Santini does not amass four trucks and contracts to haul city garbage by being sensitive to humiliation. The Santinis came to dinner the very next Sunday.

Lucia Santa outdid herself. On Sunday morning she broke a wooden spoon over Gino's head, parting enough skin to let in common sense, and convincing him it was wise not to go out in the street to play stickball. She then made sauce fit for a king of Naples and rolled out wide macaroni from homemade dough. For the green salad she opened the bottle of almost sacred oil sent from Italy by her poor peasant sister—oil impossible to buy, first blood of the olive.

Gino, in his new gray suit from the long shore, Caterina in her red silk dress, were trapped side by side. Vincenzo, the favorite of old ladies, amused the enormous Signora Santini by telling her fortune with cards. Salvatore and Lena cleared the table and washed the dishes, industrious and grimly efficient as elves. Finally Gino, as coached by his mother, asked Caterina if she would like to go to the movies, and she, always dutiful, looked toward her father for permission.

For Piero Santini the moment was terrible. It was like those few times he let his trucks be used to haul whisky and did not see them for days at a time, did not know where they were, what was happening to them. He suffered now almost as much. But it could not be helped; this was America. He nod-ded assent, but said, "Don't be back too late, eh, tomorrow is work."

Lucia Santa beamed as the young couple left. Victorious, she cracked walnuts and fed the working Salvatore and Lena greasy, knotty morsels. She filled Piero Santini's wineglass, placed a platter of iced cream puffs next to the elbow of Sig-nora Santini. Larry and his wife, Louisa, came up to join them for a coffee that was steaming black and oily with anisette. Piero Santini and Lucia Santa exchanged sly, satisfied glances, gossiped with the newborn familiarity of those about to be-come relatives. But not an hour had passed when there was the clatter of heels on the stairway, and in came Caterina, alone, wild-eyed, with a tear-stained face, to seat herself at the table without a word.

Consternation. Santini swore, Lucia Santa clasped her hands in prayer. What had happened? Had that *animale* of a Gino raped her in the streets, or in the movie house itself? Had he brought her up to the roof? What! In God's name! At first, Caterina did not answer but finally she whispered that she had left Gino in the movies; he was watching a picture she did not want to see. Nothing had happened.

Who believed her? No one. Gone was the cozy friendliness, the good cheer. Air and speech turned cold. But what in the sa-cred name of Jesus Christ could possibly have happened? Ah, the clever young, what evils they perpetrated, no matter how unfavorable the circumstances. But no coaxing of Caterina would make her reveal the mystery, and finally, bewildered, the Santinis took their leave.

The family of Angeluzzi-Corbo—Lucia Santa, Vinnie, Larry and Louisa, the stern-faced Sal and Lena—waited, grouped around the table like judges, for the appearance of the criminal. At last Gino, hungry as a wolf from his four hours in the movies, leaped up the stairs, dashed through the door, and almost skidded to a halt when the force of all those accusing eyes struck him.

Lucia Santa rose but wavered; she was raging, yet helpless. Of what was he guilty? She began on safe ground. "*Animale, bestia,* what did you do to that poor girl in the movies?"

Gino, wide-eyed with surprise, said, "Nothing."

His innocence was so plain that Lucia Santa assumed he was crazy, that he did not know right from wrong.

She controlled herself. She asked patiently, quietly, "Why did Caterina leave you there alone?"

Gino shrugged. "She said she was going to the ladies' room. She took her coat. When she didn't come back I figured she didn't like me, so I figured the hell with it, and I saw the movie. Ma, if she didn't like me, what's the sense of you and her father making her go with me? She acted funny all the time—wouldn't even talk."

Larry shook his head pityingly at the whole affair. He said to his mother jokingly, "See, Ma, if it was me, we would have a truck in the family by now." Louisa sniffed and Vinnie said to Gino kindly, "You dope, she's supposed to be stuck on you."

Now to most of the family it was a joke. But Lucia Santa, the only one who saw to the core of the matter, became truly angry. She seriously considered opening up Gino's head a little more with the *Tackeril,* for surely he was as mad as his father.

How like an idiot saint he had said the girl didn't like him;

without a flicker of rancor, not a bit of hurt masculine pride. What was Caterina, then, to this proud son of hers? Shit? The daughter of a wealthy man who could assure his future and his bread; comely, with strong legs and breasts, far above this wastrel, this good-for-nothing, this fodder for the electric chair; and he didn't care? It was beneath his notice, if you please, that a jewel of an Italian girl didn't like him. Who did he think he was, the king of Italy? What a fool if he could not see how the eyes of poor Caterina devoured him. Oh, but he was hopeless, hopeless, his father all over again, and on the road to some terrible misfortune. She grabbed the *Tackeril* to beat him, unjustly, for her pleasure and the alleviation of her bile, but her son, Gino, with the instinct of true criminals who flee even when innocent, whirled and flew down the stairs. So was shattered another dream for Lucia Santa, and foolish and comical though it was, it planted the first seed of hatred in her breast.

17

FOR SEVEN YEARS Frank Corbo had left his family in peace. Now he was to trouble them again. Far out on Long Island, in the Pilgrim State Hospital for the Insane, he decided to make his final escape. And so one dark night he hid in his caged bed and secretly sent his brain spinning against the bones of his skull. Slowly, divinely, he called up the great wave of cerebral blood that hurled his body onto the tiled floor of the ward and freed forever that tiny spark that was the remainder of his soul.

WHEN THE TELEGRAM came, Lucia Santa was drinking her mid-morning coffee with the formidable Teresina Coccalitti. And that terrible woman, to show her great friendship, revealed one of her secrets. She could read English. This astounded Lucia Santa more than the news in the telegram. How armed this woman was against the world. And how coolly she now regarded Lucia Santa. There could be no false grief before those cunning eyes.

It is most terrible to know that another human being who

las put his life in trust to you can no longer move you to pity for his fate. To herself Lucia Santa was completely honest: Frank Corbo's death brought a sense of relief, a freedom from hidden, nagging fear that someday she must again condemn him to his cage. She dreaded him; she feared for her children; she begrudged the sacrifices his living would demand.

Go further. Trust in the forgiveness of God: the death of her husband lifted a terrible burden from her spirit. On her rare visits, seeing him caged behind barred windows, her faith in life drained away, she had lost her strength for days afterward.

Lucia Santa felt no grief; only an enormous relief from tension. The man who fathered three of her children had died gradually in her heart during those years he was hidden away in the asylum. She could not keep before her eyes his living flesh.

Now Teresina Coccalitti showed the iron mind that was the legend of Tenth Avenue. She put Lucia Santa on the right path. Why bring her husband's body all the way to New York, pay an undertaker, make a big fuss, remind everyone that her husband died insane? Why not take the whole family out to the hospital and have the funeral there? Frank Corbo had no family in this country to take offense or to pay their respects. Hundreds of dollars would be saved, gossip cut off.

A queen could not have reasoned more coldly.

Lucia Santa prepared a huge supper, too heavy really for the warm summer weather, and the Angeluzzi-Corbo family ate together that night. No one was grief-stricken by the death of the father. Lucia Santa was shocked when Gino took the news very coolly, looking into her eyes and shrugging. Salvatore and Aileen could not be expected to remember him, but Gino was eleven when his father was sent away.

As they ate, they made plans. Larry had already called the hospital long distance and arranged for the funeral to be held at noon and for a headstone to be put up in the hospital cemetery. He had borrowed his chief's limousine—Mr. di Lucca had insisted—to drive them all up there. They would start at seven sharp in the morning; it would be a long drive. They would be home by evening. Only one day of work would be missed. Octavia and her husband would sleep in Lucia Santa's house, in Octavia's old room. Lena could sleep again with her mother this one night. It was comfortably arranged.

Gino ate hurriedly and then put on a clean shirt and trousers. As he went out the door, Lucia Santa called after him anxiously, "Gino, be home early tonight. We leave at seven in the morning."

"O.K., Ma," he said and ran down the steps.

Larry was annoyed. "Doesn't he know he should stay home tonight?" he asked his mother.

Lucia Santa shrugged. "Every night he goes to his Hudson Guild. He is the duke of his club of snotnoses."

Larry said righteously, "That's no way to show respect for his father. I go past the Guild when it's dark, and him and his friends are loving up the girls. You shouldn't let him do that tonight."

There was a shout of laughter from Octavia. Larry being moral always made her giggle. "You should talk," she said. "Remember the stuff you pulled when you were that age?"

Larry grinned, gave his wife a swift glance. She was busy with the infant. "Aw, come on, Sis," he began, and then, as if nothing had happened, the family history and adventures began to be retold as Sal and Lena cleared away the table. Norman Bergeron opened a book of poetry. Vinnie leaned his sallow face on his hand and listened intently. Lucia Santa brought out bowls of walnuts, a jug of wine, and bottles of cream soda. Teresina Coccalitti dropped in, and with her as a new audience they told all the old stories about Frank Corbo. Octavia began with the familiar line, "When he called Vinnie an angel I knew he was crazy. . . ." They would go on until bedtime.

The next morning Lucia Santa found that Gino had not

come home that night to sleep. He often stayed away during the hot summer months, bumming around with his friends, doing God knows what. But on this day of all days, when he might make them late for the funeral? She was truly angry.

Everyone finished breakfast, and still Gino did not come. His good suit was laid out on his bed with a fresh white shirt and a tie. Lucia Santa sent Vinnie and Larry out to look for him. They cruised in their car past the Hudson Guild Settlement House on 27th Street and then went to the candy store on Ninth Avenue, where the boys sometimes gambled all night at cards. The bleary-eyed owner said yes, Gino had been there until just an hour ago and had left with some friends to see the morning show at the Paramount movie house or the Capitol or the Roxy, he wasn't sure which.

When they returned and told Lucia Santa the news, she seemed dazed. All she said was, "Well, then, he can't come."

As they were all getting into the car, Teresina Coccalitti came around the corner of 31st Street to wish them a good voyage. In her usual black, with her dark sallow face and raven hair, she looked like a snip of the night that had refused to disappear. Now that there was an empty place in the car, Lucia Santa asked her to come along. Teresina was honored—a day in the country would be a real treat. She did not hesitate for a moment but pushed in and took Vinnie's seat next to the window. And so it was that she could tell the whole story to her friends on Tenth Avenue of how the Angeluzzi-Corbo family drove out to Long Island to bury Frank Corbo, how his eldest son disappeared and did not look upon his natural father's face before it disappeared into the earth. And how only Lucia Santa wept—but tears so full of gall that they could only have sprung from a well of anger, not grief. "There will be a day of reckoning," the Coccalitti woman said, shaking her black hawk's head. "He is a serpent in the heart of his mother."

18

LUCIA SANTA ANGELUZZI-Corbo rested, her shadow thick in twilight. Sitting at the round kitchen table, she awaited the strength to go down on Tenth Avenue and take the cool evening breeze.

During the day, for no reason, she had suffered, in some mysterious way, a blow to the spirit which for this one night had weakened her hold on life. She hid in the empty dark kitchen, out of reach, deaf and sightless to everything she loved and held dear. She yearned to sink into untroubled sleep, where there would not be a single ghost of dreams.

But who can leave the world unguarded? Lena and Sal played in the street below, Gino roamed the city like a wild beast in the jungle, Vincenzo slept defenseless in the back room that had been Octavia's, waiting to be roused and fed for his four-to-midnight shift on the railroad. Her grandchildren, the children of Lorenzo, waited for her to put them to bed. Lorenzo's wife, sick and bitter, must be cheered over a cup of hot coffee and restored to some faith in life, must be taught that her dreams of happiness were only fairy tales of girlhood every woman must lose.

Lucia Santa did not know her head was drooping over the great round table. For a moment the cool oilcloth against her cheek comforted her before she fell into that profound slumber in which everything rests except the mind. Her thoughts and cares raced up and up like little waves until they completely possessed her body and made it tremble in sleep. She suffered as she had never suffered when awake. She cried out soundlessly for mercy.

America, America, what different bones and flesh and blood grow in your name? My children do not understand me when I speak, and I do not understand them when they weep. Why should Vincenzo weep, that foolish boy, tears running down cheeks blue with the beard of manhood. She had sat on his bed and stroked his face as if he were still a child, terribly frightened. He had work, he earned his bread, he had a family and a home and a bed to rest his head, yet he wept and said, "I have no friends." But what did that mean?

Poor Vincenzo, what do you wish from life? Isn't it enough to stay alive? *Miserabile, miserabile,* your father died before you were born and his ghost shadows your life forever. Live for your small brothers and sister, and then for your wife and children, and time will pass and you will grow old and it will all be just a dream as I am dreaming now.

But never tell him fate is a demon. Vincenzo and Octavia, her best children, and both unhappy. How could this be, when Lorenzo and Gino, those two villains, smiled falsely at her and, holding joy in their teeth, ran through life their own way? Where were God and justice? Oh, but they would suffer too—they were not invincible; the evil are subject to fate. Still, they were her children, and those spermless bitches who whispered that Lorenzo was a thief and murderer were false as God.

No. Lorenzo would never be a real man as the peasant fathers on Tenth Avenue were real men, as her father in Italy was a real man: husbands, protectors of children, makers of bread, creators of their own world, accepters of life and fate who let themselves be turned into stones to provide the rock on which their family stood. This her children would never be. But she was finished with Lorenzo; she had done her duty and he was no longer a real part of her life.

Deep down inside her dream stirred a secret monster. Lucia Santa tried to wake herself up before she could see its shape. She knew she was sitting in her dark kitchen, but thought only a moment had gone by and that now she was about to pick up her backless chair and go down the stairs to the Avenue. Her head fell forward again on the cool oilcloth. The monster rose and took shape.

"You are like your father." Thus had she always met rebellion in her most dearly beloved son. Gino's stricken eyes would stay with her as he walked out of the house. But he never held a grudge. The next day he would behave as if nothing had happened.

It was a true curse. He had the same blue eyes, startling in a dark, Mediterranean face; he had the same withdrawn air and reluctance to speak, the same disregard for the concerns of those nearest to him in blood. He was her enemy, as his father before him, and she dreamed vengefully on his crimes: he treated her as a stranger, he never respected her commands. He injured her and the family name. But he would learn, this son of hers; she would help life be his teacher. Who was he to frolic in the streets at night and run in the park all day while his brother Vincenzo earned his bread? He was nearly eighteen; he must learn he could not be a child forever. Ah, if that could only be.

In her sleep Lucia Santa heard the rising monster begin to laugh. What were these petty crimes? Even in Italy there were sons who found pleasure in selfish sloth and dishonor. But now judge the crime for which she had never reproached him and for which he had never suffered, for which there could be no pardon. He had refused to look upon the face of his dead father before it disappeared forever into the earth. And so now in the dream she began to scream and curse him down eternally to the bottomless pit of hell.

Light flooded the kitchen and Lucia Santa really heard steps coming to her door, knew she would awake before she uttered those irrevocable words of damnation. Gratefully she raised her head to see her daughter Octavia standing over her. She had never said those terrible words about Gino; she had not cast her most beloved son into the pit.

Octavia smiled. "Ma, you were groaning so much I heard you all the way down to the second floor."

Lucia Santa sighed and said, "Make some coffee, let me stay in my own house tonight."

How many thousands of nights had the two of them sat in the kitchen together?

Through the Judas window opening onto the row of bedrooms they had always listened for the steady breathing of the young children. Gino had been a troublemaker long ago, hiding under the round table surrounded by its huge clawed legs. To Octavia everything here was known. The ironing board, upright and ready in the window corner; the huge radio, shaped like a cathedral; the small bureau, with drawers for tableware, dish towels, buttons, and patching cloth.

It was a room to live in and to work in and to eat in. Octavia missed it. Her immaculate Bronx apartment had a table of porcelain with chromium chairs. The sink glistened white as a wall. Here was the debris of life. After a meal the kitchen looked like a battlefield with scorched pots, greasy bowls slippery with olive oil and spaghetti sauce and enough smeary dishes to fill a bathtub.

Lucia Santa sat motionless, her face, every line of her squat body, showed a terrible weariness of spirit. It was a look that had frightened Octavia as a child, but now she knew that it would pass, that in the morning her mother would rise mysteriously renewed.

Merely to show her sympathy, Octavia said softly, "Ma, don't you feel good? Should I get Dr. Barbato?"

With deliberate, theatrical bitterness, Lucia Santa said, "I'm sick of my children, I'm sick of my life." But saying the words cheered her up. Color flooded into her face.

Octavia smiled. "You know, I miss that most—you cursing me all the time."

Lucia Santa sighed. "I never cursed you. You were the best of my children. Ah, if only the rest of these beasts could behave like you."

The sentimentality alarmed Octavia. She said, "Ma, you always talk as if they were so bad. Larry gives you money every week. Vinnie hands over the pay envelope without even opening it. Gino and the kids stay out of trouble. What the hell do you want anyway, for Chrissakes?"

Lucia Santa's body straightened, and her weariness flowed away almost visibly. Her voice grew vibrant as she prepared herself for a quarrel that was really passionate conversation, the pleasure of her life. She sneered in Italian, that language lovely for sneering, "Lorenzo, my oldest son. He gives me ten dollars every week—me, his mother, to feed his poor little fatherless brothers and sisters. But the little whores he runs with, they take the fortune he earns at the union. That poor wife will murder him in his bed. And I, I won't say a word against her at the trial."

Octavia laughed happily. "Your darling Lorenzo? Ah, Ma, you're such a phony. Tonight he comes with his ten-dollar bill and his bullshit and you'll treat him like a king. Just like those young chippies that fall for his crap."

Lucia Santa said absently in Italian, "With a husband I thought your mouth would get cleaner as the other got dirty." Octavia flushed deep red. Lucia Santa was pleased. Her daughter's surface vulgarity, American, was no match for her own, bred in the Italian bone.

They heard footsteps coming through the rooms and then Vinnie entered the kitchen, his face dazed with sleep. He was wearing only slacks and an undershirt.

He had grown into a short young man with a husky frame on which there was not a single ounce of extra flesh, so that he appeared rawboned and awkward. His face was dark and unhealthy-looking, and he had a heavy shadow of beard. He should have looked fierce and tough with his craggy features, his thick mouth and heavy nose, but the dark wide eyes were peculiarly defenseless and timid and he rarely smiled. Worst of all for Octavia, his personality had changed. He had always had something engagingly sweet and obliging about him; he had always been kind and thoughtful in a completely natural way. But now, though he was obedient to his mother and put himself out for other people, he followed his courtesies with a sort of bitter, mocking complaint. Octavia would much rather he just told everybody to screw off. She worried about him, but he irritated her, too. He was a disappointment. She smiled grimly at the thought. Aren't we all? She reflected on her husband alone in the Bronx apartment, reading, writing, waiting for her.

Vinnie growled with sleepy irritation. His voice was deeply masculine, yet childish and petulant. "Ma, why the hell didn't you wake me up? I told you I gotta go out. If I hadda go to work you woulda woke me up on time."

Octavia said sharply, "She fell asleep. It's no picnic taking care of you bastards."

Lucia Santa turned on Octavia. "Why do you pick on him? He works hard all week. He sees his sister, when? And she curses him. Come sit down, Vincenzo, have some coffee and something to eat. Come, my son, and maybe your sister can find a pleasant word for you."

Octavia said angrily, "Ma, you're such a phony." Then she saw something in Vinnie's face that made her stop. At first, when his mother reproached Octavia, Vinnie looked smugly satisfied, pathetic with gratitude at her sticking up for him, but when Octavia laughed, he had suddenly realized that he was being softsoaped by his mother. He smiled sourly to think that he could be so easily consoled, and then he laughed with Octavia at himself and his mother. They drank coffee and chatted together with that deep familiarity a close family feels, which keeps them from boring each other, no matter how dull the talk.

Octavia saw Vinnie's sullen face lighten into tranquillity, and she remembered the gentle sweetness. He smiled and even laughed at Octavia's stories about being a forelady in the dress shop. He made jokes about his job in the railroad. And Octavia realized how much her brother missed her, how her marriage had broken the pattern of the family—and for what? Oh, she knew what it was now; she heeded its call and her body rose and fell in consummating passion and she could not spurn it now as once she had, but still she was not happy.

No, she was not as happy with her husband as she was at this instant, happy that she had lightened the look of suffering and loneliness on her young brother's face, caught so naked and fresh from sleep. She had wanted to do so much for him, and had done nothing—and for what? The desire for flesh had been too strong for her and she had found a gentle husband who overcame her fears. There would be no children, and thanks to this and other elementary precautions against fate, she and her husband would rise out of poverty to a better life. She would be happy someday.

When Vinnie was dressed, Lucia Santa and Octavia regarded him with the special fondness women of a family have for their young males. They both imagined Vinnie walking down the street and beating girls off with a stick. They assumed he would have a night of pleasant, conquering adventure, among friends who could not fail to admire and love and cherish him for the prince that they, his mother and sister, knew him to be.

Vinnie put on his blue serge suit and his sleazy silk tie with its great swirling patterns of red and blue. He slicked his hair with water, framing his craggy, sensitive face in neatly combed, symmetrical blocks of heavy black hair.

Octavia teased, "Who's the girl, Vinnie? Why don't you bring her home?" And the mother said, not sternly, American enough to make a joke, "I hope you picked a good Italian girl, not an Irish tramp from Ninth Avenue."

Vinnie found himself smiling a pompous, satisfied smile, as if he had a dozen girls at his feet. But, knotting his tie and seeing his face and his phony smile in the mirror, he became depressed and scowled.

He was used to family flattery, to remarks like "Ah, he is the quiet one, the one you never know anything about; that's the one you have to watch out for; God knows how many girls he has hidden away in another neighborhood." He couldn't help looking fatuous under their praise, but how the hell could they believe such things?

For Chrissakes, he worked from four in the afternoon until midnight, Tuesdays through Sundays. Where the hell was he supposed to meet girls? He didn't even know any guys his own age, only the men he had worked with the last four years at the freight office. Quickly and gruffly he took his leave.

Lucia Santa sighed heavily. "Where does he go late at night?" she asked. "What kind of people go with him? What do they do? They will take advantage of him, he's so innocent."

Octavia settled comfortably in her chair. She longed for a book in front of her and wished that her bed waited just down the hall. But far away, in the quiet, antiseptic apartment in the Bronx, her husband would not sleep until she returned. He would read and write in the draped and lamp-shaded living room with its carpeted floor, and he would welcome her with the fond yet pitying smile and say, "Did you have a good time with your family?" And then he would kiss her with a gentle sadness that made them alien to each other.

Lucia Santa said, "Don't stay too late. I don't want you on the subway when all the murderers ride up and down."

"I have time," Octavia said. "I'm worried about you. Maybe I should stay a couple of nights and give you a rest, take care of the kids."

Lucia Santa shrugged. "Take care of your husband, or you will be a widow and know what your mother has suffered."

Octavia said gaily, "Then I'll just move right back in with you." But, to her surprise, Lucia Santa looked at her grimly, searchingly, as if it were not a joke. She flushed.

The mother saw that her daughter's feelings were hurt and said, "You woke me at a bad time. In my dream I was about to curse my devil of a son as I should curse him awake."

Octavia said quietly, "Ma, just forget it."

"No, I will never forget it." Lucia Santa put her hand to her eyes. "And if there is a God, he will suffer for it." She bowed her head and the look of utter weariness spread over her face and body. "His father was covered with earth and there were no tears from his oldest son." Her voice was truly anguished. "Then Frank Corbo was nothing on this earth, he suffered for nothing and he burns in hell. And you made me let Gino back into the house without a beating, without a word. He never cared what we felt. I thought some terrible thing had happened to him, that he had gone mad like his father. And then he calmly returns, refuses to speak. I swallowed my bile, I choked on it, and it chokes me now. What kind of beast, what kind of monster? He brings the contempt of the world on his dead father and on himself, and then returns and eats and drinks and sleeps without shame. He is my son, but in my dreams I curse him and see him dead in his father's coffin."

Octavia yelled at her mother, "Shit! Shit! Shit!" Her face was contorted with anger. "I went to his funeral and I hated him. So what? You went to his funeral and you didn't let go one goddamn tear. You didn't visit him once in the asylum the year before he died."

That quieted both women. They sipped their coffee. Octavia said, "Gino will be all right, he has a good brain. Maybe he'll be something."

Lucia Santa laughed with contempt. "Oh, yes, a bum, a criminal, a murderer. But one thing he will never be. A man who brings home his pay envelope by honest labor."

"See, that's why you're mad, really—because Gino won't work after school. Because he's the only one you can't boss around."

"Who should be his boss if not his mother?" Lucia Santa asked. "Or do you think he will never have a boss? That's what he thinks. He will eat free the rest of his life, isn't that it? But it isn't so. What will happen to him when he finds out what life is, how hard it is? He expects too much, he enjoys life too much. I was like him at his age and I suffered for it. I want him to learn from me what life is, not from strangers."

"Ma, you can't." Octavia hesitated. "Look at your darling Larry, all the trouble you took over him, and now he's next thing to a gangster, collecting money for that phony union."

"What are you talking about?" Lucia Santa gestured with contempt. "I couldn't even get him to beat his little brothers for me, he was so chicken-hearted."

Octavia shook her head and said slowly, wonderingly, "Ma, sometimes you're so smart. How can you be so stupid?"

Lucia Santa absently sipped her coffee. "Ah, well, he's out of my life." She did not see Octavia turn her face away, and she went on. "Gino is the one who hurts my brains. Listen to this now. That nice job at the drugstore, he stayed two days. Two days. Other people keep jobs for fifty years, my son two days."

Octavia laughed. "Did he quit or get fired?"

"Oh, you find it laughable?" Lucia Santa inquired in her politest Italian, betraying her complete exasperation. "They threw him out. After school one day he stopped to play football, then went to work. He thought surely they would close the store until he got there, no harm done. Little did he think the *padrone*, not wishing to kiss his trade away, would stay on himself. No, our dear Gino did not finish out his first week."

"I'd better talk to him," Octavia said. "What time does he come home?"

Lucia Santa shrugged. "Who knows? A king comes and goes when he pleases. But tell me this. What do these snotnoses have to talk about until three in the morning? I look out the window and see him sitting on the steps and talk and talk worse than the old women."

Octavia sighed. "Hell, I don't know." She made ready to leave. Lucia Santa cleared away the coffee cups. There was no gesture of affection, no farewell kiss. It was as if she were going away to visit and would be back. Her mother went to the front-room window to guard her daughter with her eyes until she turned off Tenth Avenue toward the subway.

19

MONDAY NIGHT WAS Vinnie Angeluzzi's night off from the railroad. It was the night he rewarded his flesh for the poverty of his life.

His mother and sister's teasing had embarrassed him because he was going out to pay his five dollars and get laid, simply and efficiently. He was ashamed of this because it was another mark of failure. He remembered the pride hidden in his mother's voice when she reproached Larry for taking advantage of young girls. She and Octavia would be disgusted if they knew what he was going to do now.

Vinnie had worked the four-to-midnight shift in the railroad since he quit high school. He had never gone to a party, never kissed a girl, never talked to a girl in the quiet of a summer night. His one day off was Monday, and there was nothing to do on that night of the week. His shyness made it worse.

So Vinnie went for his poor but honest fare, to a respectable whore house recommended by the chief clerk of the freight office who didn't want his men hanging around bars to pick up clapped-up chippies or worse. Sometimes the chief clerk himself came along.

For this diversion all the clerks dressed in respectable fashion, as if they were going out to look for a job. They wore suits and ties and hats and topcoats, uniforms for the day of leisure, the seventh day to rest and celebrate the soul. Vinnie in his black fedora was always kidded about looking like a gangster, though he was the youngest of them all. They met in the Diamond Jim bar, which had a grill of hot dogs and hot roast beef sandwiches and cold cuts almost as gray as the skin on the chief clerk. Ceremoniously they would order whisky, and one of the clerks would say commandingly, "This is my round," and lay his money on the bar. When each had carefully paid for a round of drinks, they stepped out into 42nd Street, into the raging neon fire of the movie houses that stretched stone to stone along both sides of the street. By this time there were so many wandering human beings that they took great care to keep together, as though if one of them became separated he would float away, helpless to rejoin the others. As they walked along 42nd Street, they passed the great, painted cardboard women soliciting in upright wooden frames, their nudity etched in electric reds and purples.

It was a sedate, four-story hotel, demurely invisible in that fire of cold, burning flesh. When they marched through the entrance they went directly to the elevator. They did not have to pass through the lobby since this particular entrance was used only by people like themselves. The elevator operator winked, a serious, business-like wink, by no means a frivolous comment on the job at hand, and took them up to the top floor. The elevator operator led them down a carpeted hall, left his iron cage open and unguarded to knock on the appropriate door and whisper the secret password, then studied them closely as they filed into the room.

It was the living room of a two-bedroom suite with too many small leather chairs. Usually there was a man reading a magazine, waiting his turn. There was a woman barely visible in the kitchen alcove, drinking coffee and directing traffic. In her cupboard were bottles of whisky and glasses. Anyone who wanted a drink could step into the alcove and put down a dollar bill, but usually things moved so fast there was not time. This woman had very little to do with the customers and seemed more like a guardian of this world.

It was this woman's face that Vinnie remembered always—never the girls who worked in bedrooms. She was short and her hair was heavy and very black and though there was no way of telling her age, she was too old for the trade. But it was her face and voice that made her inhuman.

The voice was the horrible hoarse voice that some whores have, as if torrents of diseased semen flooding the body had rotted the vocal cords. She spoke only with some great effort of will. Her voice was more frightening than any visible scar. Her features were to Vinnie's young eyes the very mask of evil. The mouth was thick and formless and pressed firmly over teeth that thrust out the flesh. The cheeks and jowls were heavy, pendulous, dowager-like, but the nose was bold and thickened by something more mysterious than nature, the eyes black and soulless as two pieces of coal. Beyond all this there was something in her every word and gesture which showed, not that she hated or despised the world, but that she no longer felt any fleshly emotion for anyone or anything in it. She was sexless. When she passed near you her head tilted sideways, sharklike. Once she glided by and Vinnie shrank back as if she would rend flesh from his body. As a man came out of a bedroom she pointed to the next customer but only after opening a bedroom door to croak inside, "O.K., honey?" Hearing that voice Vinnie's blood would run cold.

But he was young. When he entered the bedroom, his blood ran hot again. He would just vaguely see the painted face of the woman, always the same. Usually blonde, she moved in the golden circle of a heavily shaded lamp so that the colors on her face seemed to refract the light, the painted red mouth, the long pale nose glistening through its powdery white bone, the deathly, ghostlike cheeks, and black-smudged green-looking eyeholes.

What happened next always embarrassed Vinnie. The woman would lead him to a low table in the corner of a room, where there was a basin filled with hot water. He would take off his shoes, socks, and trousers, and she would wash his private parts, taking a good, clinical look.

Then she would lead him to the bed against the far wall, he still wearing his shirt and tie (once, presumptuous with passion, he had started to remove even these and the woman said, "No, for Christ's sake, I ain't got all night") and, slipping out of her robe, stand nude before him in the dim light of the fringed bedside lamp.

The painted red nipples, the rounded belly with roll of fat, the neat black triangle and two long columns of heavily powdered thighs all served the purpose. When the whore threw off her robe and presented that body, the blood rushed to Vinnie's brain with such force that he had a headache for the rest of the evening.

The embrace was formal, an earnest pantomime, the woman sinking back on the coverleted bed, Vinnie drawn over her, falling to one knee, braking his body down into the vise of scissoring limbs.

He was lost. Flesh; flesh hot soft against his own; melting wax; warm, yielding, sticky clinging meat without blood or stringy nerves. His body, separate tissue, chambered, soaked up what that meat distilled. His stretched taut frame impressed itself upon that wax which depressed with the shape of his own bones and in one blinding moment he was free, reprieved from loneliness.

That was all. His fellow clerks waited and they all went out for a Chinese dinner, and then a movie at the Paramount or bowling, topped off with late coffee in the Automat. As the clerks found steady girls or became engaged, they would not stop coming to the hotel, but they cut the evening short afterward to visit their girl friends. Defanged.

For Vinnie it was like the food he ate, the bed he slept in, the money he earned, part of the necessary routine of life to stay alive. But as time went on he felt himself becoming separate from the world around him and its inhabitants.

20

WHERE WERE THOSE wretches who cursed America and its dream? And who could doubt it now? With the war in Europe, English, French, Germans and even Mussolini lavishing millions for murder, every Italian along the western wall of the city had his pockets full. The terrible Depression was over, a man no longer needed to beg for his bread, home relief investigators could be cursed down the stairs. Plans were made to buy houses on Long Island.

True, it was money earned to help people kill each other. The war in Europe made all the jobs. So grumbled those with a fresh head begging for troubles. But in what other country could even the poor get rich on the world's misfortune?

Natives of the south, Sicily, Naples, the Abruzzi, these Italians on Tenth Avenue did not concern themselves about Mussolini's winning the war. They had never loved their country of birth; it meant nothing to them. For centuries its government had been the most bitter enemy of their fathers and fathers' fathers before them. The rich had spat on the poor. Pimps of

Rome and the north had sucked their blood. What good fortune to be safe here in America.

Only Teresina Coccalitti was displeased. She could no longer declare her sons not working in these good times, and she had been kicked off the home relief. Now she went about secretly, buying great bags of sugar and tins of fat and endless bolts of cloth. She said mysteriously to Lucia Santa, "There will come a day—ah, there will come a day . . ." but then she zipped up her mouth with her fingers and would not say another word. What did she mean? True, there was a military draft, but only one boy from Tenth Avenue had been called. Nothing grave.

Lucia Santa was too busy to let the Coccalitti's words buzz in her head. Floods of gold were washing over the tenements. Children were working after school. Sal and Lena had part-time jobs in the new drug factory on Ninth Avenue. Vinnie worked seven days a week. Let the people in Europe kill each other to their hearts' content if that was their pleasure. The village of Lucia Santa's parents was so small, the land so worthless, that none of her relatives could be in danger.

Only that scoundrel Gino did not work. But this was his last summer of idleness. He would graduate high school in January and there would be no more excuses. There was no profit in asking friends to find him jobs. Lucia Santa had tried, and Gino always got himself fired.

But there was one thing that *mascalzone* could do. Vinnie had forgotten his lunch bag again; Gino could take it to him. Lucia Santa blocked Gino's way as, baseball bat under his arm, that midwife's glove on his hand, he sought to get past her bulky form. Like a duke with cane and hat. "Bring this to your brother on the job," she said, holding out the greasy brown bag, and she could have laughed to see his finicky disgust. How proud he was, all people are who do not have to sweat for bread. How tender.

"I'm late, Ma," Gino said, ignoring the bag.

"Late for what?" Lucia Santa asked impatiently. "Late to get married? Late to put all the money you earned this week in the bank? Late to see a friend about some honest work?"

Gino sighed. "Ma, Vinnie can get something to eat in the diner."

It was too much. Lucia Santa said bitterly, "Your brother is giving his life away for you—he never plays or runs in the park. You never even ask him to go out with you, and he is so lonely. But you can't even bring him his bread? You are a disgrace. Go play your baseball and bum around with your friends. I'll bring it myself."

Shamed, Gino took the lunch bag. He saw the light of victory in his mother's eyes, but he didn't care. He really wanted to do something for Vinnie.

He trotted easily along Tenth Avenue up toward 37th Street and then down to Eleventh Avenue. He loved the full freeness of his body moving through the heavy summer air. When he was smaller he had taken giant leaps to see if he could fly as it seemed he might, but he was too old now. Just before he reached the freight building, he threw the brown paper bag high in the air in front of him, then put on a dazzling burst of speed to catch it before it hit the ground.

He rose slowly through the old rat-smelling building in an iron-grilled elevator. The operator, in a gray dirty uniform with wormy yellow insignia on the lapels, opened the metal doors with that mysterious contempt some adults have for the young, and Gino stepped out into a loft office that stretched away to the far end of the building.

It was like a nightmare in which a man sees a prison that he knows he will someday come to live in. There were long rows of desks with billing machine typewriters spewing forth rolls of multiple lading accounts. The men who operated these machines were all in vests and white shirts and loose, dangling ties. They were older than Vinnie, and they were very quick. The machines clattered blindly. Each desk had its own yellow lamp; the rest of the office was in darkness except for a long counter heaped with printed bills. At this counter a long thin bent man with the grayest face that Gino had ever seen was sorting out bills under a huge spotlight. There was no sound of voices. There was no hint of daylight outside. It was as if these people were all entombed above the rumbling of the coupling freight trains that moved below in the pit of the building. Gino looked, and at last he spotted Vinnie.

Vinnie was the only man without a vest, and he wore a colored shirt so he could use it two or three days without changing. His curly black hair looked damp under the yellow steel-armed lamp. Gino saw that Vinnie was slower than the others and that his face was screwed up with intense concentration to his task. The others had the blank expressions of sleepwalkers.

Suddenly Vinnie looked up. He stared at Gino without expression. He lit a cigarette. With surprise, Gino realized that Vinnie couldn't see him, nor could any of the others. He was standing in darkness outside their world. He walked past the first line of desks into the living yellow square. As if he had blocked out the sun, heads snapped up. Vinnie raised his eyes.

There was a heartbreaking gladness on Vinnie's face. His smile was sweet, as it had been in their childhood. Gino raised the lunch bag and threw it. Vinnie caught it expertly and Gino went to stand awkwardly by his desk.

"Thanks, kid," Vinnie said. The men on either side of him stopped typing, and he said to them, "This is my kid brother, Gino."

Gino was embarrassed at the pride in Vinnie's voice. The two men said "Hiya, kid," and gave him cold, appraising looks. He became conscious of his blue dungarees and white wool sweatshirt and felt foolish, as if he had come to some grave assembly frivolously attired. The gray-faced man called out, "Bill freight, you guys, we're running behind." Then he shambled over to Vinnie and gave him a sheaf of bills. He looked like a lean old rat. "You're behind your count now, Vinnie," he said.

Vinnie said nervously to the retreating back, "I won't take my break later." Gino turned to leave. Vinnie got up and walked him out of the circle of light to the elevator. They waited, listening to the grind of iron cables and the growl of the ascending cage.

"Take a short cut through the railroad yard," Vinnie said. "But watch your ass when those engines come down." He rested his hand on Gino's shoulder. "Thanks for bringing my lunch. You got a game Saturday?"

"Yeah," Gino said. The elevator was taking a long time. He wanted to get out. He saw Vinnie glance nervously toward the clattering machines in the circle of light and flinch as the gray rat face turned, blindly seeking them in the darkness.

"If I get up in time I'll come watch," Vinnie said. Then the elevator was there, its two iron doors sliding back, and Gino stepped in and began the slow descent. The smell of decay, of rats, and of old shit made him sick. When he stepped out of the building he lifted his head to the warm, lemon, September sunlight. He stood still in almost joyful relief and freedom.

He didn't give Vinnie another thought. He started to run slowly through the railroad yard, a great field of gleaming white steel that alternately fanned out and converged mysteriously in the sun. He cradled his right arm as if he were carrying a football and sped over the wooden ties, slipping around the steel rails that came together to trap his flying feet. Black locomotives came toward him and he slipped away easily to the left and right, picking up speed. A locomotive came up behind him, its engineer seated at the window on Gino's side. Gino raced it, going full speed across the wooden ties alongside the engine, flying ahead, until the engineer gave him a casual glance and then the black engine chugged louder and clacked past him. When it swerved off into a maze of stationary brown and yellow freight cars, Gino stopped, exhausted.

He felt a little sweat beneath his white woolen jersey and he was ravenously hungry, thirsty—and then suddenly he found himself strong and fresh again. He swung into a long, loping run to Chelsea Park. There he saw his friends tossing a baseball and waiting for him.

21

ONE MORNING A week later Lucia Santa woke up sensing that something was wrong. Sal and Lena were still in bed. Sometime in the early morning hours Lucia Santa had heard Gino come home; she knew his careless, noisy undressing. But Vinnie she had not heard. Then she remembered that Monday was his night off, and on those nights he sometimes came home even later than Gino.

Though she knew it was impossible for anyone to enter the house without her waking, she checked Vinnie's bed. He now used Octavia's old room, the only private one in the apartment. The bed had not been slept in, but Lucia Santa was not seriously alarmed. Later, when she had sent the children off to school, she leaned on the pillowed window sill and watched for him to appear on the Avenue. Time went by; she saw the early shift of trackwalkers come across the Avenue for lunch and knew it must be nearly noon. For the first time she became worried. She put on a heavy knit wool jacket and went downstairs to see Lorenzo.

She knew her oldest son was always at his worst in the morning, but she was too nervous to wait. She found Larry at his morning coffee, rumpled undershirt draped over with black wiry chest hair. He sipped his coffee and said with real impatience, "Ma, he's not a baby, for Chrissakes. Whatever he's doing, he got through too late to come home. When he wakes up he'll go to work."

"But what if something happened to him?" Lucia Santa asked anxiously. "How would we know?"

Larry said drily, "Don't worry, the cops got their nose in everything."

Louisa poured coffee for the mother. Her beautiful heavy face, usually placid, was also worried. She was fond of Vinnie—she knew him better than anyone except his mother, and she felt the absence strange. "Larry, please go and look," she said.

This was so unusual for her that Larry gave up. He patted his mother on the shoulder. "I'll go up to Vinnie's office, O.K., Ma? Now let me finish my coffee." And so Lucia Santa had to go back upstairs and wait.

At three o'clock Gino and the children came home from school, and still Larry had not returned. The mother tried to make Gino stay with her, but he seemed not to understand. He fled without even answering, stopping only to grab his football. Sal and Lena did their homework on the round kitchen table and she fixed bread with olive oil and vinegar for them. Finally, at five o'clock, Larry came to tell her that Vinnie was not at work and that nobody had heard from him. She could see that Larry was worried, too, and she began wringing her hands and calling on God in Italian.

LOUISA CAME UPSTAIRS with her children and tried to quiet the mother. In the turmoil no one heard the other footsteps coming up behind her. Suddenly there was the black uniform of a railroad Bull in the doorway, beside him the gray face of the *Panettiere*. The *Panettiere* stepped in front of the Bull, as if to stop Lucia Santa from seeing and hearing him, unconsciously holding both his hands up, palms toward her, in a gesture of such unutterable pity that Lucia Santa was struck dumb. It was Louisa who suddenly wailed in terror.

GINO WAS SITTING quietly on the Hudson Guild stoop with his frends when Joey Bianco came by and said to him, "You better go home, Gino, there's a lot of trouble at your house."

Gino rarely saw Joey Bianco anymore. They had grown out of their comradeship, as children do, and now they felt embarrassed by each other. So Gino did not try to stop Joey as he kept walking, or ask him what had happened. He almost didn't even bother to go home, but then decided to see what it was all about.

He short-cutted diagonally across Chelsea Park and ran easily along Tenth Avenue until he reached the corner of 30th Street. Then he saw a crowd in front of his tenement and started walking very slowly.

There was no one from the family in the crowd. Gino ran up the stairs and into the apartment.

It was thronged with neighbors. In the corner by the window Gino saw Sal and Lena standing stiff and alone, faces blank with fright. Part of the crowd eddied away, and he could see his mother seated in a chair. Dr. Barbato was holding a needle in the air. Larry was gripping his mother with all his strength to keep her from bucking up and down in convulsions.

She looked horrible, as if the muscles connecting each feature of her face to the other had been smashed. Her mouth was twisted oddly and she seemed to be trying to speak. Her eyes had the peculiar direct stare of the blind. The lower part of her body was jerking up out of her chair and then Dr. Barbato's arm flashed as he stabbed the needle into her arm. Then he stood over her and watched.

Slowly, Lucia Santa's features flowed together in some sort of peace. Her eyelids closed down and the tension went out of her body.

"Put her to bed," Dr. Barbato said. "She'll sleep now for an hour. Call me when she wakes up."

Larry and some of the women carried Lucia Santa into the bedroom. Gino saw he was standing next to Teresina Coccalitti. Very low, the first time he had ever spoken to her, he asked, "What happened to my mother?"

Zia Teresina was glad to tell him. It was her pleasure this black day to set one thing right. "Oh, nothing happened to your mother," she said, measuring her words. "It is your brother Vincenzo. They found him in the railroad yards run over by an engine. As for your mother, that's what happens to parents when they grieve for their children. Show a little pity for her now."

Gino remembered always the look of hatred on her black hawk's face; he remembered always how little grief he felt at his brother's death and how shocked he was that anyone, his mother or anyone, could be so destroyed by sorrow.

WHEN LARRY CAME out of the bedroom he motioned for Gino to follow him. They ran down the stairs together and into Larry's car. It was growing dark. They drove up to 36th Street and Ninth Avenue and stopped in front of a brownstone tenement. Larry spoke for the first time. "Go up to the third floor and tell Lefty Fay to come downstairs. I wanta talk to him." But at that moment he saw someone come down the stoop and lowered his window, and called out, "Hey, Lefty." Then said to Gino, "Let him in your place, go in the back."

Lefty Fay was a tall, big-shouldered Irishman and Gino remembered he had grown up with Larry—in fact had been the only one on the block who could lick Larry in a fist fight. As both men lit cigarettes, Gino huddled in the back seat. Zia Teresina's brutal message was still just so many words. He did not feel Vinnie was really dead.

Larry's voice was calm in the darkness. Weary. "Christ, what a lousy day for everybody."

"Yeah," Lefty Fay said. His voice was rough by nature, but now held a note of real sadness. "I was just going out for a drink. I couldn't even eat supper."

"How come you didn't know it was my brother after your engine hit him?" There was no accusation in Larry's voice, but Lefty Fay said angrily, "Christ, Larry, you ain't blaming me? It was deep in the yard near 42nd Street." When Larry didn't answer he went on more calmly, "I only saw him as a kid when you and me used to hang out together. He changed a lot since then. And he didn't have any identification."

"I don't blame you," Larry said. His voice was very tired. "But the Bull says you wrote in your report that my brother jumped in front of the engine. How come?"

In the darkness Gino waited for Fay to answer. There was a long silence. Then the rough voice, curiously muted, said, "Larry, I swear to Christ that's the way it seemed to me. If I'd known it was your brother, I'd never put it in the report, but that's the way it seemed to me."

Gino could feel Larry forcing some strength back into his voice. "C'mon, Lefty," he said. "You know my brother Vinnie wouldn't do something like that. He was always afraid of his own shadow even when he was a kid. Maybe he was drunk or just got confused. You can change the report."

Fay said quickly, "Larry, I can't, you know I can't. The cops'll be all over me. Then I lose my job."

Larry's voice, decisive, said, "I guarantee you a job."

There was no answer. Larry went on. "Lefty, I know you're wrong. But if you stick with the report, you know what happens to my mother? She'll go off her nut. You used to eat at my house when we were kids. You gonna do that to her?"

Fay's voice wavered. "I gotta think of my wife and kids." Larry didn't answer. "If I change the report, the railroad may have to give your mother compensation. That means they'll go after my ass, sure as hell. I just can't do it, Larry. Don't ask me."

"You get half the dough," Larry said, "and I'm asking you."

Fay laughed with nervous anger. "Just because you work for di Lucca you gonna strong-arm me, Larry?" It was almost a challenge, a reminder of the days when they were kids and Lefty had beat Larry down into the sidewalk.

Suddenly a voice spoke that Gino did not recognize and that made his blood chill with animal fear. It was a voice deliberately saturated with all the venom and cruelty and hate that a human creature can summon from the depths of his being. The voice was Larry's. "I'll crucify you," he said. It was beyond a threat. It was a deadly promise, and it was inhuman.

The fear that filled the car made Gino feel physically ill. He swung the door open and got out into the fresh air. He wanted to walk away, but he was afraid that if he did so Larry might do something to Fay. But then he saw Fay get out of the car and Larry reaching out the open window to hand over some folded bills. When Fay walked away Gino got into the front seat. He couldn't look at his brother. As they drove home, Larry said in a tired voice, "Don't believe that guy's crap, Gino. Every time there's an accident, everybody lies. Nobody wants to get blamed. And the Bull told me Vinnie was drunk— he smelled the booze. It was his fault, all right, but he never jumped in front of no engine." He paused, and then, as if he had to explain, he said, "I worry about the old lady, Christ, I worry about the old lady." Neither one of them could speak of Vinnie.

22

EVEN DEATH BRINGS labor and toil: coffee to be made for intimate mourners, wine served, gratitude and affection shown for the dutifully presented sorrow of relatives and friends.

Without fail, everyone must be notified officially by the closest blood relative of the deceased. There were the godparents who lived in New Jersey, the prickly cousins in their castles on Long Island, the old friends in Tuckahoe; and all these must be treated this one day like dukes, for the bereaved are in the public eye, and their manners must be faultless.

Then, too, since only greenhorns mourned in their own homes, the wake must be held in a funeral parlor and a member of the family must always be on hand to greet the mourners. The body of poor Vincenzo must never be left alone on this earth. He would have more companions in death than he ever had in life.

Early on the first evening of Vincenzo's wake, the Angeluzzi-Corbo family gathered in the kitchen on Tenth Avenue. The room was cold. Since no one would be back until very late, the kerosene stove had been put out.

Lucia Santa sat at the table, straight, heavy, and squat in black, her eyes thick-lidded and narrowed. She drank coffee, not looking at anyone, her sallow face almost yellow. Octavia sat beside her, half-turned toward her, ready to touch her and ready to do her bidding in any way. The mother's strange immobility frightened her daughter.

Lucia Santa looked around the room as if seeing them all for the first time. Finally she said, "Give Salvatore and Lena something to eat."

"I'll do it," Gino said instantly. He was in a black suit, with a black silk band on his left arm. He had been standing behind his mother, out of her sight, leaning against the window sill. Now he moved quickly through the door to the icebox in the hall. He was glad to be out of the room even for a moment.

All that day he had stayed in the house to help his mother. He had served coffee, washed dishes, greeted visitors, taken care of the kids. All that day his mother had not spoken one word to him. Once he had asked her if she wished something to eat. She had given him a long, cool look and turned away from him without speaking. He had not spoken to her again, and had tried to stay out of her sight.

"Anybody else want something?" he asked nervously. His mother looked up, directly into his eyes, two spots flushing mysteriously high on her cheeks.

"Give Mamma some more coffee," Octavia said. She spoke softly, as they all did, almost in a whisper.

Gino got the coffee pot and poured his mother's cup full. Doing so, he touched her body and she leaned away from him, looking up at him in such a way that he froze, stupidly holding the great brown pot high over the table.

Larry said, "We'd better get started." He looked startlingly handsome in his black suit and black tie and snow white shirt.

254 • MARIO PUZO

The mourning band on his arm was flapping loose. Lucia Santa leaned over to pin it shut.

Octavia asked, "What about Zia Coccalitti?"

"I'll come back for her later," Larry said. "Her and the *Panettiere* and Louisa's mother and father."

Octavia said nervously, "I hope there aren't too many little kids running around the funeral parlor. I hope they have enough sense to leave the kids home."

No one answered. They were all waiting for Lucia Santa to make the first move. Gino leaned back against the window sill, slouched, head down, not looking at anyone, out of his mother's sight.

Finally Octavia could wait no longer. She got up and put on her coat. Then she fastened black silk mourning bands on Sal and Lena. Louisa got up and put on her coat. Larry waited impatiently at the door. Still Lucia Santa did not move. They were all a little frightened by her calm. Octavia said, "Gino, get Mom's coat." Gino went to the bedroom, put on his own and then came back to stand beside his mother's chair. He held her coat wide open so that she could rise easily into it. His mother took no notice of him. "Come on, Ma," he said softly, and in his voice for the first time was all the pity he felt for her.

It was only then she turned in her chair, looked up at him with a face so merciless and cold that Gino stepped back. Finally she said, quite calmly, "Oh, you're going to this funeral, are you?"

For a moment they were all stunned, unbelieving, not understanding what she had said out of sheer disbelief in its cruelty, until they saw Gino's face go white and stricken. He held the coat between himself and his mother as if to shield himself. His eyes had a sick fascination.

The mother continued to look at him with a terrible, merciless stare. She spoke again quite calmly. "But why the honor? You never went to see your father in his coffin. And while your brother was alive, you never helped him, you never had time to spare from your precious friends to comfort your own flesh and blood. You never had any pity for him, you never gave him anything." She paused to let an insulting forgiving contempt enter her voice. "You want to show how sorry you are now? You pour coffee, you hold my coat. Then maybe you're not an animal, after all. Then even you must know how your brother loved you, how good he was." She waited, as if for a reply, then said quite simply, "Go away. I don't want to see your face."

Everything she had said, he had known she was going to say. Without knowing he did so, he looked around the room for someone to help him, but on their faces he saw the sick horror of people watching some terribly mangled victim of an accident. Then it was as if he had gone blind and he could see nothing. He let the coat drop to the floor and stepped back, until he touched the window sill.

He never knew whether he closed his eyes or simply refused to see his mother's face as she began to shout at him, "I don't want you to go. Take off your coat. Stay home and hide again like the animal that you are." And then Octavia's voice rose against hers, angry yet pleading. "Ma, are you crazy? Shut up, for Chrissake." He could hear Lena begin to whimper with terror. And then finally there were sounds of people leaving the room and going down the stairs. Gino recognized a strange laugh as his mother's, mingled with the rustle of stiff new clothes. Then he heard Octavia's voice whisper, "Don't pay any attention to Mom. Wait a while, then come to the funeral parlor. She wants you to come." There was a pause, then she said, "Gino, are you all right?" He nodded his head toward her voice.

It was very still. Slowly he could see again. The electric bulb threw a dirty yellow circle of light, and floating in it was the great round table littered with coffee cups and little spills of muddy liquid caught in the folds of scarred oilcloth. Since he had to wait before going to the funeral parlor he cleaned up the kitchen and washed the dishes. Then he put on his jacket with the black arm band and went out of the house. He locked the door with the big brass key and put the key under the icebox. When he went out the tenement door downstairs, he brushed against the tailed funeral wreath nailed to it. The flowers were black with night.

Gino walked downtown on Tenth Avenue, past where the bridge used to be, following the elevated track until it was swallowed up by an enormous building. Suddenly he saw a street sign that said St. John's Park, but there were no trees. He remembered his brother Larry had always said he rode the dummy horse from St. John's Park, and as a kid Gino had thought it was a real park, a grove of trees with grass and flowers.

The funeral parlor was on Mulberry Street and he knew he must walk east. Going crosstown, he dropped into a lunch counter to buy some cigarettes.

The men sitting at the counter were all night workers, even the clerks dressed in rough clothes. There was a terrible loneliness in the smoky air, as if nothing could bring these people together. Gino left.

Outside, the streets were dark, except for small circles of light cast by the street lamps. Far down the block he saw a small neon cross. Suddenly Gino felt a strange trembling weakness in his legs and he sat on a stoop to smoke a cigarette. For the first time he realized that he would see Vinnie's dead face. He remembered himself and Vinnie late at night alone in the house sit-sleeping on the childhood window sill, counting the stars above the Jersey shore.

He put his hands over his face, surprised by tears. A band of little children came swirling down the street through circles of yellow light. They stopped and watched him, laughing. They were fearless. Finally he got up and quickly walked away.

There was a long black awning from the door of the funeral parlor to the gutter, a veil for mourners against the sky. Gino went through the door into a little anteroom, from which an archway opened into an enormous cathedral-like hall filled with people.

Even those he knew seemed like strangers. There was the *Panettiere,* lumpy as coal in his old black suit; his son, Guido, sinisterly dark of jowl. The barber himself, that solitary maniac, sat quietly on a chair, his inspecting eyes gentled by death.

The women from Tenth Avenue sat lined against the walls in formal rows, and the billing clerks from Vinnie's night shift stood around in clusters. There was Piero Santini from Tuckahoe and his daughter Caterina, married now, and her belly swelling, face rosy, and eyes cool and confident with known and satisfied desire. Louisa, her beautiful face peculiarly grief-stricken, sat with her children in a corner and watched her husband.

Larry stood with a group of men from the railroad. Gino was shocked to see them acting quite normally, smiling, gossiping about overtime on the job, buying a house on Long Island. Larry was talking about the bakery business, and his genial smile was setting them all at ease. They could have been sitting over Coffee An in the bakery.

Larry saw Gino and motioned him to come over. He introduced Gino to the men, who shook his hand with solemn firmness to show their respectful sympathy. Then Larry took Gino aside and whispered, "Go in and see Vinnie and talk to your mother." For a moment Gino was bewildered by his saying "go in and see Vinnie," as if his brother were alive. Larry led him deep to the far end of the room, where there was another, smaller, archway almost hidden by a group of men gathered in front of it.

Two little boys skittered past Gino on the polished black floor, and an outraged shouted whisper followed from their mother. A young girl not more than fourteen chased after them, cuffed them soundly, and dragged them back to their chairs against the wall. Gino finally made his way through the second archway into another small room. Against the far wall was the coffin.

Vinnie lay on white satin. His bones, his brows, his high, thin nose swelled like hills around his closed, hollowed eyes. The face was remembered, but this was not his brother. Vinnie wasn't there in any way. It was all gone—the awkward posture of his body, the shielded, hurt eyes, the awareness of defeat, and the gentle, vulnerable kindness. What Gino saw was a soulless, invincible statue, without interest.

And yet he was offended by the women in this small room. They sat against the wall at right angles to the coffin, talking in soft voices but in a general way. His mother spoke little, but in a quite natural tone. To please her, Gino walked to the coffin and stood directly over his brother, looking more at the satin coverlet and feeling nothing because it wasn't really Vinnie—only some general proof of death.

He turned to go out the archway but Octavia rose and took his arm and led him to his mother. Lucia Santa said to the woman sitting next to her, "This is my son Gino, the oldest after Vincenzo." It was her way of telling them he was the child of her second husband.

One of the women, face wrinkled like a walnut, said almost angrily, "*Eh, giovanetto,* see how mothers suffer for their sons. Take care you don't bring grief to her." She was a blood relative, and could speak with impunity, though Octavia bit her lip with anger.

Gino bowed his head and Lucia Santa said, "Did you eat anything?" Gino nodded. He couldn't speak, couldn't look at her. He felt a physical fear that she would strike out at him in front of everyone. But her voice was completely normal. His mother dismissed him. "Go help Lorenzo talk to people, do what he tells you." And then Gino was amazed to hear her saying to the women around her, in a voice heavy with satisfaction, "There are so many people, Vincenzo had so many friends." It sickened him. None of these people knew Vinnie or cared about him.

His mother saw that look and understood it. The callow, arrogant contempt the young have for sham because they are ignorant of the terrible need for shields against the blows of fate. She let him go. He would learn.

Time became a shadow in that dark hall. Gino greeted newcomers and led them across the mirror-black floor to where his mother sat and Vinnie waited in his coffin. He saw Lucia Santa draw solace from the people who meant nothing to her or his dead brother. Zia Louche would have truly mourned her godson, but Zia Louche was dead. Even Octavia didn't seem to care as much as he thought she would.

As if in a dream, Gino showed all these strangers where to sign the registry, where to put their contributions in the box on the wall. Then he turned them loose like pigeons to home their way across the black polished floor to relatives they had not seen since the last funeral.

For the first time in his life he played the role of a member of the family. He ushered people in and then ushered them out. He chatted, inquired after families, shook his head politely at their horror over the accident that had brought this tragedy, identifying himself, yes, he was the oldest son of the second husband, watching them classify him as the *disgrazia*. The Santinis could not hide their relief that they had not become allied to this family and this tragedy. Dr. Barbato came only for a few minutes, patted Gino on the shoulder with unexpected kindness, and for once did not look guilty or aloof. The *Panettiere*, more intimate than the others, almost one of the family (after all, he had been for a time the employer of the deceased), said to Gino, "Eh, was it an accident then? The poor boy, he was always so sad." Gino didn't answer.

Zia Teresina Coccalitti, that shark in human form, never said a word to anyone. She sat by Lucia Santa paralyzed with fright—as if death, being so close, must jealously discover the existence of her and her four sons, their cheating the home relief, their house packed with the sugar and flour and fats she was so sure would make her fortune some day.

Guido, the *Panettiere*'s son, was there in his Army uniform. He was one of the first soldiers picked in the peacetime draft, and home on his first leave. He seemed a true mourner. There were tears in his eyes when he bowed his head to kiss Lucia Santa's cheek. Don Pasquale di Lucca came, out of consideration for Larry, to pay his respects, and no doubt the hundred-dollar bill in the contribution box was his, though like a true gentleman he put it in an envelope without a note. The enormous hall was now filled with people, the little children had fallen asleep in their chairs along the wall.

Near eleven o'clock, when people had stopped coming in, Larry took Gino by the arm and said, "Let's go out for Coffee An. I told Guido to take over."

They went out in just their jackets, down the street to a small luncheonette. Over the coffee, Larry said to Gino kindly, "Don't worry about the old lady screamin'. She'll forget it tomorrow. And listen, kid, me and Octavia are gonna help you carry the load. I'm givin' fifty a month and she's gonna give fifty."

For a moment Gino didn't know what in hell Larry was talking about. Then he saw that his world had turned around. His mother and sister and brother depended on him now. All the years had been spun away to bring him finally to what had always been waiting for him. He would go to work, sleep, there would be no shield between himself and his mother. He would be drawn into the family and its destiny. He could never run away again. And he was surprised by the acceptance, near relief, he felt, now that he understood. It was almost good news.

"I gotta get a job," he said to Larry.

Larry nodded. "I set it up. You take Vinnie's place in the railroad. You gonna keep going to school?"

Gino grinned. "Sure."

Larry reached over and touched his arm. "You were always a good kid, Gino. But now you gotta straighten out a little, you know what I mean?"

Gino knew what he meant. That he had to think of the family. That he had to stop doing whatever he felt like doing. That he must please his mother more. That he must stop being a kid. He nodded. In a low voice he asked, "You think Vinnie really walked into that engine?"

The change in Larry's face was frightening. Still heavily handsome, the flesh in his face had become the color and weight of bronze, and now that bronze seemed to smoke over with some poisonous rage.

"That's a lot of shit. Now I straightened that engineer and fireman out. If you hear anybody, anybody, being smart, just let me know and I'll straighten them out." He waited a moment. "And don't you tell anybody what happened when I talked to Lefty Fay." The rage faded from his face; his skin became lighter. "If the old lady ever asks anything, swear on the cross it was an accident."

Gino nodded.

They started walking back to the funeral parlor. Larry held Gino's arm and said, "Don't worry too much, kid. In a couple of years I'll be in the big money, what with the war and all, and then I'll bail the family out and you can do what you want." He smiled. "I was like you once."

Under the black awning they found Octavia waiting for them, shivering with cold. She asked shrilly, "Where did you two go? Mom is terribly nervous—she thinks Gino left."

"Oh, Christ," Larry said. "I'll talk to Ma. You stay in the parlor, Gino."

Gino felt the now-familiar physical fear and realized he must have looked frightened. Larry was protecting him. He was bewildered by the terror that swept over him.

In a few minutes Larry came back smiling and said, "Octavia just making a big deal out of nothing, like she always does. The old lady wants to make sure we're here when they close up."

People were filtering out. The undertaker appeared and, as

a blood relative of death, he helped Larry and Gino speed the mourners on their way, until finally only those closest to the family remained. The huge funeral parlor empty, Gino could hear the chairs behind the small archway being scraped back as his mother and her friends prepared to leave the coffin. The long night was over. There was a strange silence in the other room, and Gino thought about walking home ahead of the others to avoid his mother. This one day he feared her as he had never feared anything in his life.

THE TERRIFYING SHRIEK caught Gino completely by surprise, freezing him with horror. It was followed by another scream that broke into a wail of anguish and his mother's voice crying out, "Vincenzo, Vincenzo," with such pitiful grief that Gino wanted to fly out the door and away where he could never hear her. The undertaker, perfectly calm, as if he had been waiting for just this, and as if he understood Gino's thoughts, put a restraining hand on his shoulder.

Suddenly the archway was filled with black—four women coiling and twining around each other like snakes. Octavia, Louisa and Zia Teresina were trying to drag Lucia Santa through the archway, the struggle in terrible earnest.

They had tried words and caresses beside the coffin, but to no avail. They had tried to recall Lucia Santa to her duties as the mother of five other children, and she had dug her nails into her dead son's coffin. Now the three women had no pity on her. They would not let her stay. They would not let her drive herself mad with grief. They were merciless. Octavia had one arm and shoulder. Louisa dragged on the other arm but with less force, so that Lucia Santa's heavy body slewed around to one side. Zia Teresina clutched Lucia Santa cruelly by the neck and breasts and was dragging her forward along the mirror-black floor.

But the mother, like some stubborn animal, huddled up her heavy body in one resistant heap and could not be budged further. She did not protest. She did not wail again. Her black hat and veil fell sideways, raffishly, on her head. Her face was swollen, obstinate, and inhuman with almost bestial anguish. And yet she had never been more terrible, unconquerable, as if this world of death must smash into bits and vanish before her imperious grief.

The three women stood away from her. Louisa burst into tears. Octavia covered her face with her hands, then called out in a muted voice, "Larry, Gino, help us."

They crossed the floor and stood with the women around the mother. Gino did not dare touch her. Lucia Santa raised her head. She spoke to Gino: "Don't leave your brother alone," she said. "Don't let him stay by himself tonight. He was never brave. He was too good to be brave."

Gino bowed his head in assent.

"You never obey me," she said.

Gino said very low, "I'll stay all night. I promise." He forced himself to reach out and straighten her hat, very quickly, the first time in his life he had done such a thing for her. His mother reached up slowly to touch her veiled hat and took it off. She carried it in her hand as she walked to the door, as if she could not bear to shield her face, as if now, her head uncovered, she could face life again, its unreversible injustice, its inevitable defeat.

The undertaker offered to bring Gino a cot and apologized for having to lock the street door, showing Gino a bell he could ring in the registry if he wanted to get out. He himself slept in a room directly above. Gino kept nodding his head to show he understood until the man disappeared through an interior doorway.

Alone in the dark funeral parlor, knowing his dead brother's coffined body hid just behind the small archway, Gino felt safe as he had not felt since before his brother died. He arranged wooden folding chairs in a row to serve as a couch and rolled up his coat for a pillow. Lying so, smoking, one arm against the cool wall, he tried to think of how his world had changed.

He thought of the things he had learned. Larry was really a gangster and people were afraid he would kill them. How dopey that was. Larry had never even punched his kid brothers. And Lefty Fay was a jerk saying Vinnie had walked into the engine—Vinnie was so timid he had stopped sitting on the window sill. And his mother crying and hollering and making all that trouble. Drowsily he let his mind tell what he truly felt, that her grief was excessive, that she made a ceremony of death. And then he remembered his own tears on the stoop. But he had been weeping for Vinnie as a small boy, when they had played together and sat on the star-bright window sill at night. Gradually it came to him that there was so little pity for the dead in grief. That it was a wailing for something lost, by only a very few, and so ceremony must be made of death, to hide what all must know to be true: that the death of a human being means so very little.

Poor Vinnie? Who grieved for him? He had become a whining, unhappy young man whom no one wanted to be with. Even his mother was sometimes impatient with him. She had wept for the many different little Vincents that had come before. As I did, Gino thought. I never cared for him after. Larry didn't. Even Octavia didn't really care. But Larry's wife had cared, for some reason Louisa had cared. And old Zia Louche would have wept. Just before he fell asleep, Gino wanted to go through the archway and look at his brother's dead face, to force himself to feel more pain, but he was too tired. His cigarette dropped to the glittering black floor, its tiny red ember like a coal in hell. Sleeping, he huddled on his row of chairs, cold against the paneled wall. He tried to struggle away from sleep, not knowing he had let out a cry that woke the undertaker in the room above.

It was not true. He had never killed his brother. He held his mother's coat before her face, but his arms were so terribly tired. Her accusing eyes bore him back, and seeking some sort of mercy, he whispered, "I cried on the stoop down the street, see my face is still wet." But his mother only sneered and said, "It's just another one of your tricks. *Animale—animale—animale—*"

And she was smiling at him. The dazzling smile of a young woman. Gino almost fell into the trap that would have destroyed them both. He almost spoke about the day he had stood in front of the tenement, waiting for her to bring his father home. But slyly, cunningly, he bowed his head. As she had not accused him in life, he would not accuse her in his dreams. Trembling, he promised to become another Vinnie, work in the railroad, marry, live in the tenements along the Avenue, wait at trolley stops with a child in his arms, chain himself in the known, lightless world he had been born in.

23

T HE OLD WOMEN of Tenth Avenue circled in the summer night and incanted the woes of the family Angeluzzi-
Corbo.

At first they all cried out in sympathy, "Ah, what a terrible
life! Poor Lucia Santa—her first husband dead, the second destroyed for life, and now a grown son, already a breadwinner,
struck down. What tragedy, what misfortunes. Maledictions
on God, His world, and all His mysterious saints and fates."

Their heads wagged in agreement. But another woman—
no stranger to misfortune, respected for her hard life—nodded
a gray head and then said, True, true, and yet she has a grown
daughter, a forelady—intelligent, married to a sober man. She
has masculine children who would do credit to any mother.
Lorenzo, married, giver of grandchildren, making his fortune
in the bakery union; Gino, now a good dutiful boy, a head of
the family that made you think of Italy with his hard work on
the railroad and never in trouble with the police. Salvatore,
who won medals in school and would surely be a professor.

Lena, an Italian daughter of the old school, a worker in the home, ever obedient, ever dutiful. Look how they all respected Lucia Santa. The two married ones still gave money; Gino brought his pay envelope home unopened.

Five good children. True, no husband, but considering some husbands on Tenth Avenue, this might not be a real misfortune. At least Lucia Santa had now only a small family. Even poor Vincenzo, dead, had never brought *disgrazia* to his family. He had been ill and fallen beneath a railroad engine. It was an accident. And he had been buried in holy ground. Poor Vincenzo, born under an unlucky star, had met a destiny prepared for him at the beginning of time.

So the balance was struck. Many women had suffered as much or more. Husbands had been killed on the job, infants born misshapen, children had died from harmless colds, small injuries. There was not a woman in the circle who had not buried at least one child.

And look at those misfortunes Lucia Santa had escaped. Daughters pregnant without a husband in sight for miles around; sons who became jailbirds of the finest feather or found a way to rest their disobedient legs in the electric chair. Drunken, gambling, whoremastering husbands.

No, no. Lucia Santa had been fortunate to escape for so long a period of time that measure of sorrow due her station in life. All her children were strong, healthy, handsome, the world was before them. Soon she would reap the rewards of all her travail. So, courage. America was not Italy. In America you could escape your destiny. Sons grew tall and worked in an office with collars and ties, away from the wind and earth. Daughters learned to read and write, and wore shoes and silk stockings, instead of slaughtering the bloody pig and carrying wood on their backs to save the strength of valuable donkeys.

Had not misfortune entered once even into heaven? Who could escape sorrow? Who could pass through life without weeping? Only the dead do not suffer. Ah, the happy, happy dead. The old women clasped their hands to give thanksgiving for the day they would leave this earth, this unhappy vale of tears. Yes, yes, the happy dead who suffered no more.

Their eyes flashed fire; energy and power radiated from their black-clad, lumpy bodies. They devoured everything that happened on the Avenue as they spoke. They hurled curses like thunderbolts at children headed for mischief. They sucked greedily on ridged paper cups of chilling lemon ice and took great bites of smoking hot pizzas, dipping brown invincible teeth deep into the lava of hot tomato sauce and running rivers of cheese to the hidden yeasty dough. Ready to murder anyone who stood in the way of so much as a crust of bread for themselves or their children, implacable enemies of death. They were alive. The stones of the city, steel and glass, the blue-slate sidewalks, the cobblestoned streets, would all turn to dust and they would be alive.

24

CAN A DEVIL turn into an angel? The *Panettiere,* the mad barber, Dr. Barbato, and even the cunning Zia Teresina Coccalitti marveled at the change in Gino Corbo. It was true: disaster made a boy into a man, for now Gino slaved like a peasant in the railroad, gobbling up overtime and bringing his envelope home unopened to his mother.

Lucia Santa was so pleased that she gave Gino twice the spending money she had given Vinnie, swearing to Octavia that it was only just because Vinnie had always stolen his overtime. "See," the mother said to Octavia on her Friday night visits, "Gino was always a good boy." And Octavia had to agree, because despite his working at night and even overtime on Sunday, Gino was finishing his last term of high school and would graduate in January. He was even making the honor roll for the first time. This especially delighted Lucia Santa. "Wasn't I right?" she asked Octavia. "It is the playing in the street that tires a child's brain, not honest work."

Octavia, still shaken by Vinnie's death, was amazed and

puzzled at how quickly her mother seemed to recover. She was quieter, more permissive with Sal and Lena but otherwise the same. Only once did she betray emotion. One night, when they were talking of Vinnie as a little boy, Lucia Santa said with bitter self-reproach, "If I had left him with Filomena in Jersey, he would be alive." Relinquishing one of her proudest memories, and yet she still lived each day with the eager trust of a believer in good fortune.

And why not? Never had the world treated the family of Angeluzzi-Corbo so well. Gino made a fortune in the railroad. Sal was brilliant in high school and would surely go to college. Lena was equally brilliant and would be a schoolteacher. Both worked now in the *panetteria* selling bread after school, earning good wages, which made Lucia Santa gloat with Octavia over the bank books on Friday nights. Lucia Santa could only control her dangerous optimism by reminding herself that in a few short months, right before Christmas, the *Panettiere*'s son, Guido, would finish his year of Army service and take Sal and Lena's place in the bakery. She could not count on this flood forever.

Even Octavia's husband was working. Poor Norman Bergeron was miserable writing pamphlets for some Government agency—Civil Service, security, and good money. Octavia knew he was unhappy, but she thought it was just too bad about him. He could always write poetry when the people in Europe stopped killing each other and there was another Depression.

But best of all for Lucia Santa was Gino becoming a man, part of the real world. She would not have to quarrel with him anymore, she had almost forgiven him all the injuries he had made her suffer. He had even become more serious. Could it be that her struggles were at an end? Lucia Santa did not believe it for a moment, but she would never let it be said that she was one of those pitiful rags who refused to enjoy good fortune when it came.

Each night Gino went to work it was with the same feeling of unbelief. Ascending in the elevator of the freight building, then stepping into the circle of light with clattering billing machines, seemed just the beginning of a dream. But gradually he believed.

The railroad put him on the midnight-to-eight-in-the-morning shift, and during these hours the dusty office was spooky with filing cabinets, dead black typewriters, and the almost invisible wire mesh of the cashier's cage. Surrounded by these Gino typed the night away. He was very good at the job—his athletic coordination and his sharp eyesight helped. The quota was 350 bills a night, and he easily surpassed it. Sometimes he had an hour free to read while he waited for new bills to come up from the loading platform.

He never talked to the men he worked with, or joined in their general conversation. The night boss gave him the toughest bills to do, but he never protested. It didn't matter. He hated it so much that nothing mattered. He hated the building and the rat-smelling office. He hated the dirty metal touch of the typewriter keys. He hated walking into that yellow circle of light that held the six billers and the boss rate clerk.

It was a pure hatred, physical; sometimes his body actually chilled, his hair bristled, and his blood turned so sour in his mouth that he could not help walking away from the light to the darkened windows to stare down at those imprisoned streets sentineled by yellow lamp posts. When the boss rate clerk, a young man named Charlie Lambert, called out, "Let's bill freight, Gino," in that voice men use to debase other men, he never answered, never went back to his machine right away. Even after he knew he was being singled out, he couldn't hate Charlie Lambert. He felt such a cold contempt for the man that he could not think of him as something human or react to him with emotion.

To labor merely to exist, to spin away your life just to stay alive, was something he had never known. But his mother had known, Octavia had known, his father had surely known. Vinnie must have stood at this dark window a thousand nights while he himself roamed the streets of the city with his friends or slept trustfully in his bed.

But as the months went on, he found it easier to endure. What he could not think about was that it would never end. He understood that it might never end.

AS BEFITTED THE mother of a family in such goodly circumstances, Lucia Santa now ran her household like a real signora. The apartment was always warm, no matter what the price of coal and kerosene. There was always enough spaghetti in the pot for friends and neighbors who dropped in after mealtime. The children could hardly ever remember leaving the table without there being still enough meatballs and sausage soaking in a platter of sauce for one last foray. There were new forks and spoons for use at the Sunday feast, which everyone in the family, married or not, must attend—though no command was ever heeded more willingly.

On this first Sunday of December there was to be a special *peranze*. Larry's oldest child was receiving his First Communion, and Lucia Santa was making ravioli. She had started the dough early, and now she and Octavia were building a fortress of the flour on the large square mixing board. They broke a dozen eggs into it, and another dozen, and another, until the four white powdery walls crumbled into a sea of white with floating yellow yolks. They mixed it all together into great crumbly balls of dough as bright as gold. Octavia and Lucia Santa grunted with labor as they rolled the balls out into thin sheets. Sal and Lena stirred a deep bowl full of ricotta cheese, and into the white creamy mass they beat pepper, salt and eggs that made it a filling fit for heaven.

While the ravioli boiled and the rich tomato sauce simmered, Lucia Santa put platters of prosciutto and cheese on the table. Then came platters of rolled beef stuffed with boiled eggs and onions, a huge piece of pork—dark brown, so tender from simmering in the sauce that it shed its flesh tenderly from the bone with just the touch of a fork.

At dinner, Octavia gossiped with Larry as she seldom did, laughing at his jokes and stories. Norman quietly sipped his glass of wine and chatted with Gino about books. When they finished, Sal and Lena cleared the table and started washing the mountain of dishes.

It was a beautiful Sunday for December, and visitors came—the *Panettiere* and Guido, finally out of the Army after his year's service, the jealous barber, looking through the glass curtain of red wine, inspected all heads present for scars of a strange scissors. The *Panettiere* quickly took a plate of warm ravioli; he was mad about them, a dish his dragon of a wife had always been too busy counting money to prepare.

Even Zia Teresina Coccalitti, who had made her whole life a secret merely for advantage, who for so many years had made her fortune on home relief, with four strapping sons working—no one knew how; even she ventured to drink more than one glass of wine, munch a bread full of sausage, and chat with Lucia Santa about the happy days when they were girls in Italy shoveling manure from their backyards. Though usually Zia Coccalitti zippered her mouth with warty fingers when anyone asked her a personal question, today she smiled when twitted by the *Panettiere* about her swindling of the home relief. Made rash and generous by two glasses of wine, she told them all, free of charge, to take everything the Government gave, since in the long run you would pay the cursed State ten times over whether you took it or not.

Gino, bored by the talk, went to sit on the floor next to the cathedral-shaped radio and turned it on. He wanted to listen to the Giant football game. Lucia Santa frowned at this rudeness, though the radio was so low no one could hear it. Then she paid no more attention to him.

It was Norman Bergeron who first noticed something odd

about Gino. His head was bent close to the radio, but he was watching everyone in the room. Then Norman saw that he was watching his mother very intently. There was a smile on his face. It was a smile that was in some way cruel. Octavia, seeing her husband watching Gino, turned toward the radio.

She couldn't hear, but there was something so brilliantly alive in Gino's eyes that she called out, "Gino, what is it?"

Gino turned his back to hide his face. "The Japs just attacked the United States," he said. He turned up the radio and drowned out all the voices in the room.

GINO WAITED UNTIL after Christmas. Then directly from work one morning he enlisted in the Army. That afternoon he called Octavia's husband at his office and asked him to tell Lucia Santa where he was. Sent to a training camp in California, he wrote regularly and sent money home. In the first letter he explained that he had volunteered to save Sal from the draft later on, but he never mentioned this again.

25

"A IUTA MI! AIUTA mi!" Screaming for help against the ghosts of her three dead sons, Teresina Coccalitti ran along the edge of the sidewalk, her body tilted strangely, her black clothes flapping in the morning breeze. When she reached the corner she turned and ran back again, crying out, "Aiuto! Aiuto!" but on that first familiar cry for help, windows had slammed shut above Tenth Avenue.

Now the woman stood in the gutter, legs apart. She raised her head to the sky and accused them all. She spoke in the vulgar Italian of her native village, and on that thin hawk's face all native cunning, greed and vicious slyness had been eaten away by suffering. "Oh, I know you all," she shouted up to the closed windows. "You wanted to fuck me, you whores and daughters of whores. You wanted to put it up my ass, every one of you, but I was too clever." She tore at her face with claw-like nails until it was a mass of bloody strips. Then she raised her arms to the sky and screamed, "Only God. Only God." She started running along the curb, her black hat bobbing up and down, as her only remaining son came around the corner of 31st Street to catch her and drag her home.

It had happened many times before. At first Lucia Santa used to rush into the street to help her old friend, but now she watched from her window like everyone else. Who would have thought that fate would dare to strike such a blow against Teresina Coccalitti? Kill three of her sons in one year of war, and she such a cunning sly person, always secretive and capable of any treachery for her own advantage. Did nothing help then? Was there no escape for anyone? For if evil cannot prevail against fate, what hope is there for the good?

26

WHILE THE WAR raged over the world, the Italians living along the western wall of the city finally grasped the American dream in their calloused hands. Money rolled over the tenements like a flood. Men worked overtime and double-time in the railroad, and those whose sons had died or been wounded worked harder than all the rest, knowing grief would not endure as long as poverty.

For the clan of Angeluzzi-Corbo the magic time had come. The house on Long Island was bought, for cold cash, from people mysteriously ruined by the war. A two-family house, so that Larry and Louisa and their children could live in one apartment under the watchful eye of Lucia Santa. There would be separate, doored bedrooms for everyone, even Gino when he came home from the war.

On the last day Lucia Santa could not bear to help her children strip the apartment, fill the huge barrels and wooden boxes. That night, lying all alone in her bed, she could not sleep. The wind whistled softly through the window cracks that had always been shielded by drapes. Lighter patches of wall that had held pictures gleamed in the darkness. There were strange sounds in the apartment, in the empty cupboards and closets, as if all the ghosts of forty years had been set free.

Staring up at the ceiling Lucia Santa finally became drowsy. She put out her arm to trap a child against the wall. Falling into dreams she listened for Gino and Vincenzo to go to bed and for Frank Corbo to come through the hallway door. And where had Lorenzo gone again? Never fear, she told little Octavia, no harm can come to my children while I live, and then, trembling, she stood before her own father and begged linen for her bridal bed. And then she was weeping and her father would not comfort her and she was alone forever.

She had never meant to be a pilgrim. To sail a fearful ocean.

The apartment turned cold and Lucia Santa awoke. She got up and dressed in the dark, then put a pillow on the window sill. Leaning out over Tenth Avenue, she waited for light and for the first time in years really heard the railroad engines and freight cars grinding against each other in the yards across the street. Sparks flew through the darkness and there was the clear ringing of steel clashing on steel. Far away on the Jersey shore there were no lights because of war, only stars caught on the shade of night.

In the morning there was a long wait for the moving vans. Lucia Santa greeted neighbors who came to wish the family good luck. But none of the old friends came, none were left on Tenth Avenue. The *Panettiere* had sold his bakery when his son, Guido, came home wounded too badly for work. He had moved far out on Long Island, as far out as Babylon or West Islip. The mad barber with his houseful of daughters had retired; with so few male heads to cut because of the war, he too had moved out to Long Island to a town called Massapequa, near enough the *Panettiere* for a game of cards on Sundays. And others too had left for all those strange towns dreamed of for so many years.

Dr. Barbato, to everyone's surprise, had volunteered for the Army and in Africa had become a hero of some sort, with his pictures in the magazines and a story of his exploits so terrifying that his father suffered a stroke from sheer exasperation at his son's foolishness. Poor Teresina Coccalitti never moved out of her apartment, fiercely guarding the countless tins of olive oil and fat that would some day ransom her sons from death. Gino's childhood friend, Joey Bianco, had in some clever fashion escaped the Army, no one knew how, had become rich, and bought a palace for his mother and father in New Jersey. So now it was really time for the Angeluzzi-Corbo family to leave.

FINALLY PIERO SANTINI came with his trucks from Tuckahoe. The war made such services dear to arrange, but Santini came as a favor to a native of his very own village in Italy. And because, mellowed now, it gladdened his heart to help the happy end to this story.

Lucia Santa had shrewdly left out a pot and some scarred cups. She gave Santini coffee and they drank it while looking down on Tenth Avenue, balancing their drinks on the window sill. Octavia and Sal and Lena carried light packages down to the waiting vans while two old muscular Italians, grunting like donkeys, let their backs be saddled with enormous bureaus and beds.

After a time the only thing left in the apartment was the backless kitchen chair deemed too worthless for the fine house on Long Island. Louisa and her three little children came up the stairs then to wait with them, the little villains wading through a sea of discarded clothing and the litter of stripped cupboards and left-over newspaper.

And then the final moment had come. Mr. di Lucca's limousine, now Larry's, was waiting in front of the tenement. Octavia and Louisa swept the little children down the row of dirty, deserted bedrooms and out the door. Then Octavia said to Lucia Santa, "Come on, Ma, let's get out of this dump."

To everyone's surprise a dazed look came over Lucia Santa's face, as if she had never really believed she must leave this house forever. Then instead of going toward the door, she sat on the backless kitchen chair and began to weep.

Octavia shooed Louisa and her children down the stairs before turning on her mother. Her voice was shrill, exasperated. "Ma, what the hell's the matter now? Come on, you can cry in the car. Everybody's waiting." But Lucia Santa bowed her head into her hands. She could not stop her tears.

Then the mother heard Lena's angry voice say, "Leave her alone"; and Sal, who never spoke, said, "We'll bring her down, you go ahead."

Octavia went down the stairs and the mother raised her head. Her two youngest children guarded her on each side. She had not realized they were so grown. Lena was very pretty, very dark, with her father's blue eyes, but her face was like Gino's. Then she felt Salvatore's hand on her shoulder. He had the eyes of a man who could never get angry. In that moment the mother remembered how Sal and Lena, silent in their corner, had watched and surely judged them all. She could not know that to them their mother had been a heroine in some frightening play. They had watched her suffer the blows of fate, their father's fury, her hopeless struggles with Larry and Gino and the terrible grief of Vinnie's death. But as she reached out to touch their bodies she knew that they had judged her and found her innocent.

THEN WHY DOES Lucia Santa weep in these empty rooms? Who is better than her?

She goes to live in the house on Long Island, her grandchildren beneath her feet. Salvatore and Lena will become doctors or schoolteachers. Her daughter Octavia is a forelady in the dress shops, and her son Lorenzo is the president of a union, giving out jobs as grandly as a duke in Italy. Her son Gino is still alive while millions die. There will always be enough food and money for an old age surrounded by respectful and loving children. Who is better than her?

In Italy forty years ago her wildest dream had not gone so far. And now a million secret voices called out, "Lucia Santa, Lucia Santa, you found your fortune in America," and Lucia Santa weeping on her backless kitchen chair raised her head to cry out against them, "I wanted all this without suffering. I wanted all this without weeping for two lost husbands and a beloved child. I wanted all this without the hatred of that son conceived in true love. I wanted all this without guilt, without sorrow, without fear of death and the terror of a judgment day. In innocence."

AMERICA, AMERICA, BLASPHEMOUS dream. Giving so much, why could it not give everything? Lucia Santa wept for the inevitable crimes she had committed against those she loved. In her world, as a child, the wildest dream had been to escape the fear of hunger, sickness and the force of nature. The dream was to stay alive. No one dreamed further. But in America wilder dreams were possible, and she had never known of their existence. Bread and shelter were not enough.

Octavia had wanted to be a teacher. What had Vinnie wanted? Something she would never know. And Gino—what dreams he must have had, surely the wildest of them all. But even now through the tears, through the anguish, a terrible hatred rose, and she thought, Most of all he wanted his own pleasure. He had wanted to live like a rich man's son. Then she remembered how she had broken her own father's heart to win linen for her marriage bed.

With terrible clarity she knew Gino would never come home after the war. That he hated her as she had hated her father. That he would become a pilgrim and search for strange Americas in his dreams. And now for the first time Lucia Santa begged for mercy. *Let me hear his footsteps at the door and I will live those forty years again. I will make my father weep and become a pilgrim to sail the fearful ocean. I will let my husband die and stand outside that house in Jersey to scream curses at Filomena with Vincenzo in my arms and then I will weep beside his coffin. And then I will do it once again.*

But having said this, it was all too much. Lucia Santa raised her head and saw that Salvatore and Lena were watching her anxiously. Their grave faces made her smile. Strength surged back into her body, and she thought how handsome her last two children were. They looked so American, too, and this amused her for some reason, as if they had escaped her and the rest of the family.

Salvatore held her coat open so that she could rise easily into it. Lena murmured, "I'll write Gino the new address as soon as we get there." Lucia Santa glanced at her sharply, sure she herself had said nothing aloud. But the young girl's face, so like Gino's, made her want to weep again. She took one last look at the naked walls and then left her home of forty years forever.

Out on Tenth Avenue three women clad in black waited for her with folded arms. She knew them well. One raised her withered hand to salute her, called out, "Lucia Santa, *buona fortuna.*" Truly meant, without malice, yet on a warning note, as if to say, "Beware, there are years to come, life is not over." Lucia Santa bowed her head in thanks.

Larry tapped the steering wheel with impatience as they all scrambled into the limousine. Then he moved it forward slowly so that the two moving vans could follow, moving east toward the Queensborough Bridge. At first, because of the mother's tears, there was a heavy silence, then the three little children squirmed and began fighting. Louisa shouted and slapped them quiet. The tension relaxed and they all talked about the house. Larry said it would take an hour to get there. Every two minutes the children asked, "Are we in Long Island yet?" and Sal or Lena would say, "No, not yet."

Lucia Santa rolled down the window to enjoy the fresh air.

She took one of the little boys on her lap, and Larry smiled at her and said, "It'll be great living together, huh, Ma?" Lucia Santa caught Lena's eye, but that innocent was like Gino, too simple to understand her mother's grin. Octavia smiled. They had always seen through Larry. They both understood. Larry was delighted that Louisa and the children would have company, while he, animal that he was, chased young girls starved by the war.

Then they were ascending the slope of Queensborough Bridge, running through the slanted, flashing shadows of suspended cables. The children stood up to see the slate-gray water below, but in just a few moments they were off the bridge and rolling down a wide, tree-lined boulevard. The children began to shriek, and Lucia Santa told them, yes, now they were on Long Island.

© Carol Gino

ABOUT THE AUTHOR

Mario Puzo was born in New York and, following military service in World War II, attended New York's New School for Social Research. His best-known novel, *The Godfather,* was preceded by two critically acclaimed novels published in the early sixties, *The Dark Arena* and *The Fortunate Pilgrim;* in 1978 he published *Fools Die,* in 1984 *The Sicilian,* and in 1992 *The Fourth K.* His latest novel is *The Last Don* (1996). Mario Puzo is also the author of nine screenplays, including *Superman* and *Superman II,* as well as the screen adaptations of all *Godfather* movies, for which he received two Academy Awards.